36.35

The Concise Guide to
BRITISH POTTERY
AND PORCELAIN
Geoffrey A. Godden

OTHER REFERENCE BOOKS BY GEOFFREY GODDEN

Victorian Porcelain
Encyclopaedia of British Pottery and Porcelain Marks
An Illustrated Encyclopaedia of British Pottery & Porcelain
The Handbook of British Pottery and Porcelain Marks
Minton Pottery and Porcelain of the First Period
Caughley and Worcester Porcelain, 1775–1800
Coalport and Coalbrookdale Porcelains
The Illustrated Guide to Lowestoft Porcelains
The Illustrated Guide to Ridgway Porcelains
Jewitt's Ceramic Art of Great Britain, 1800–1900
British Porcelain: An Illustrated Guide
British Pottery: An Illustrated Guide
Godden's Guide to English Porcelain
Oriental Export Market Porcelain and its Influence on European Wares
Godden's Guide to Mason's China and the Ironstone Wares
Chamberlain-Worcester Porcelain, 1788–1852
Staffordshire Porcelain
English China
Lowestoft Porcelain
Ridgway Porcelain
*Eighteenth-century English Porcelain – a selection from the Godden
Reference Collection*
Encyclopaedia of British Porcelain Manufacturers
Davenport China, Earthenware and Glass (with Terence A. Lockett)

The Concise Guide to
BRITISH POTTERY
AND PORCELAIN
Geoffrey A. Godden

BEING
AN ENLARGED, UP-DATED AND REILLUSTRATED
VERSION OF
MARY AND GEOFFREY PAYTON'S
**THE OBSERVER'S BOOK OF
POTTERY AND PORCELAIN**
Published by Frederick Warne & Co. Ltd in 1973

BARRIE & JENKINS
LONDON

First published in Great Britain in 1990 by
Barrie & Jenkins Ltd
20 Vauxhall Bridge Road, London SW1V 2SA

British Library Cataloguing in Publication Data
Godden, Geoffrey A. (Geoffrey Arthur) *1929-*
    The concise guide to British pottery and porcelain.
    1. British pottery & porcelain
    I. Title
    738.2'0941

    ISBN 0-7126-3600-5

Designed by Carol McCleeve

Typeset by SX Composing Ltd, Rayleigh, Essex
Printed by Scotprint Limited, Musselburgh, Scotland

Contents

Appendices

To 'The Girls of Yarcombe'

About the Authors

Mrs Mary Payton (Mrs Essex) runs a charming small antiques shop in the centre of Chagford in Devon. She, with her late husband Geoffrey Payton (the author of *Payton's Proper Names*), wrote the popular *Observer's Book of Pottery and Porcelain* from which this enlarged, reillustrated, and revised book has arisen.

The present work has been revised and enlarged by Geoffrey Godden, the well-known dealer, lecturer, and author of over twenty-five reference books. Having joined the family antiques business some forty-five years ago, Mr Godden has now semi-retired – to give more time to research and writing! Although by no means the largest of Mr Godden's internationally famous standard reference books, this inexpensive work should reach an audience of new collectors who will be able to share some of his wide knowledge and benefit from his advice.

About the Book

This book has primarily been written to guide the amateur collector, rather than the expert collector, auctioneer, or dealer. It is not claimed to be a comprehensive Encyclopaedia, but we do hope that it will give help and encouragement to thousands of new or would-be collectors.

It has two popular and helpful parents. Firstly, it is based on Mary and Geoffrey Payton's 1973 small work *The Observer's Book of Pottery and Porcelain*, then published by Frederick Warne & Co. Ltd but which is now out of print. The second parent is Geoffrey Godden's very popular *The Handbook of British Pottery & Porcelain Marks*, originally published by Herbert Jenkins Ltd in 1968 and produced in a revised edition by the present publisher in 1972. The present book complements this by giving a text and an instructive range of illustrations.

The new text gives basic facts on our main British pottery and porcelain manufacturers. It also contains helpful information on a host of collectable subjects or articles. Many later, non-antique, types are featured as these are not only the antiques of the future but are both decorative and interesting today and, more importantly, they are more readily found than some of the eighteenth-century rarities. Geoffrey Godden has been at pains to give, where appropriate, references to specialist books, magazine articles and learned papers so that the interested reader can dig deeper into the subject if he so desires.

The helpful appendices include useful dates, listings of Museum collections, reference books, collectors' magazines, and societies, as well as a section on general guidelines on the dating of old pottery and porcelain.

This is a helpful book to have handy in the car or bag as you browse around antique shops, Stately Homes, Museums, Antique Fairs, or auction sales.

Preface to the First (Payton) Edition
of 1973

This book is primarily for the amateur collector, but those who enjoy just browsing among the unattainable in museums, country-house collections, and salerooms have not been forgotten. The widespread and still growing interest in pottery and porcelain has been reflected in the number of requests our publishers have had in recent years for just such a book.

As we draw nearer to the end of the twentieth century most eighteenth-century pottery and porcelain has passed beyond the reach of the average collector – though there are exceptions, e.g. the smaller items of First Period blue-and-white Worcester, and the earliest New Hall. Thus the attention of dealers and their customers alike has of necessity become increasingly focused on the nineteenth and even the twentieth century. Many of us would very much like to possess a Chelsea Red Anchor figure – but its price would now run to many hundreds of pounds.

For these reasons fine eighteenth-century porcelains and the fascinating field of early English pottery have been treated as of historical rather than practical interest to the active collector today, and relatively greater space has been given to later and less expensive items, e.g. Staffordshire figures, that offer wider scope and variety to those whose urge to collect is restrained by the harsh facts of budgetary considerations.

For browser and collector alike, an introductory chapter outlines the development of ceramics from the earliest times, while the main part of the book deals, in alphabetical order, with the various potteries and the main types of collectable items with, where possible, aids to recognition and warnings of pitfalls. In addition there are appendices listing useful dates, guides to dating, useful books, and an index to facilitate quick reference.

South Zeal

Mary Payton
Geoffrey Payton

Preface to the Revised Edition

In the sixteen years since Mr and Mrs Payton published their charming and helpful little book under the title *The Observer's Book of Pottery and Porcelain* and the period when I turned my attention to revising, enlarging, and reillustrating the original book there have been very many developments.

Firstly, and on a personal note, Mary Payton's husband Geoffrey has died so we have only one of the original authors still with us. Secondly, the original publishers Frederick Warne & Co. Ltd have, like so many others, been taken over and the excellent series of Observer Books has been greatly curtailed. Mrs Payton, who still deals from her delightfully situated small shop in the middle of Chagford in South Devon, rightly wished for this popular book to remain in print and consulted me as to the best way of achieving this aim. I too shared her desire, but in many respects the original work had become out of date and needed, in my opinion, complete revision and enlarging. Fortunately my publishers, Barrie & Jenkins, were prepared to take under their wing such a revamped work and to publish it in the present style.

I have greatly enjoyed this editing and revision and believe that I have in so doing both kept the feeling and spirit of the Payton writing and added much helpful information. In particular I have endeavoured to lead the reader on to specialist books or other sources of information, for in such a general work as this one can only précis the various subjects. I have endeavoured to bring the reader up to date on recent developments in ceramic research and have included such newly rediscovered factories as Vauxhall in London.

The changes in the collecting world since the early 1970s have been great. In the second paragraph of the original Preface it was remarked that 'the smaller items of First Period blue-and-white Worcester and the earliest New Hall' were still within the reach of the average collector. Today this is not true. The earliest New Hall can be extremely expensive, if it can be found at all, and as a general rule the smaller the size of Worcester blue and white the greater the price. This is not to say that all eighteenth or early nineteenth-century ceramics are out of reach, but the rising prices have resulted in a growing interest in some later wares. Doulton is a good example, with a growing library of specialist books and price guides being devoted to the products of this one continuing firm. Strangely it is already true that some Doulton can be more costly than an average Chelsea, Bow, or Worcester specimen. Other makes and styles have also come into fashion, for example the Clarice Cliff designed earthenwares or the fine quality Shelley porcelains. These and a host of others are mentioned in the main, alphabetical section of this book.

The majority of the illustrations featured are of objects formerly in the commercial stock of Messrs Godden of Worthing Ltd or of Geoffrey Godden, chinaman (at 19A, Crescent Road, Worthing, West Sussex, BN11 1RL) although since the photographs were taken the objects will most probably have changed hands and be residing in new homes.

Credit has been given where the illustrations have been supplied by other dealers, by auction houses, or by museum authorities. My thanks are gladly given to all those who have so generously helped with photographs or in other ways. The uncredited illustrations are the author's.

I have purposely retained the basic format of Mr and Mrs Payton's child because I think for its low price and scope this arrangement cannot be bettered. The various appendices, like the main text, have been enlarged and the result is, I believe, a new book that the late Geoffrey Payton might have been proud of and one which will achieve the original authors' intention: an unpretentious, helpful guide for the amateur or would-be collector. A book that would see them safely through the first steps of collecting and lead them on to a lifetime of pleasure.

Worthing, 1990   *Geoffrey A. Godden*

INTRODUCTION

Ceramics, a word derived from the Greek, is the only satisfactory term that covers both porcelain and pottery; 'china' no longer has a precise meaning and is best avoided unless qualified (as in 'bone china'). It should be remembered, however, that the word china relates, or originally related, to the country of origin of porcelain. The term in the seventeenth and eighteenth century used to describe such imports was 'China Ware', meaning ware from China. The relatively small imports of Japanese porcelain were likewise termed 'Japan Ware' but it was the Chinese designation which has stayed with us. These oriental imports were the main inspiration of all our early porcelain manufacturers who, to a very large degree, sought to copy the Chinese wares. The interesting story of the trade to and from China is told in Geoffrey Godden's book Oriental Export Market Porcelain and its Influence on European Wares *(Granada, 1979).*

Porcelain is a fine variety that you can see through (usually) if you hold it up to the light. Pottery is of much coarser texture, and (normally) opaque; the two main types are earthenware, which is porous, and stoneware, which is not. The differences between these forms arise from the materials used, the temperature at which they are fired in the kiln, and the proportion of vitreous (i.e. glassy) elements in them.

POTTERY

As every gardener knows, clay is sticky (and thus easily moulded or plastic) when wet, bone hard when dried by the sun. That was how the first pottery was made, perhaps 8000 years ago, with shaped pots being left to bake under the Mesopotamian sun. For it was in this region, it is thought, that man first turned from a roving life of hunting and food gathering to the settled life of the farmer, a change known as the Neolithic Revolution. Since those days successive generations of potters have learnt how to solve many problems: how to generate enough heat to bake the clay harder (from sun-heat to today's 1400°C is a long step); how to make the finished product less easily breakable, less porous, smoother in texture and surface, more attractive to look at, lighter in weight.

The first step forward was to 'fire' the clay over an open wood fire. Porosity, before the discovery of glazing, was dealt with by covering the pot with a gum and resin varnish. The urge to decorate came surprisingly early (a child of a very tender age will naturally make patterns in sand or mud), first as dots and lines scratched with a stick developing into chevrons and geometrical patterns. Colour decoration also came early; a polychrome plate found in Iraq has been dated to 4500 BC; while from Susa, a future Persian capital, came a painted terracotta cup and vase, made a thousand years later, and a beaker with finely executed geometrical design. An early example of glazing, also from Susa, occurs on a vase decorated with rosettes, c.2500 BC.

Meanwhile the Neolithic Revolution had seeped east and west, to reach both China and Western Europe by, at the latest, 2000 BC, the probable date of pottery well decorated with coloured clays found in Kansu, an early centre for Chinese pottery. Not much later the Egyptians were making their finest glazed vitreous earthenware, and the Bronze Age Beaker Folk in England were leaving a legacy of beakers finely decorated with herring-bone and cross-hatched designs.

The potter's wheel may have reached England not long before the Romans, who brought with them the craft of making glossy red earthenware ('samian'). However, much of this was imported and even after the Romans left, Anglo-Saxon and English medieval ware, though widespread in use, was generally of poor quality. There are examples of coloured lead glaze, e.g. on a jug splendidly decorated in low relief with a stag-hunting scene (c.1300); a rich dark-brown glaze is also found on redware from the great Cistercian houses such as Fountains Abbey. No doubt much undecorated domestic earthenware was produced but little of it has survived. At the time it was broken in use or superseded as new styles came into favour or the owners acquired some wealth. It was not collected. Examples found today tend to be damaged pieces found on kiln sites or discarded in wells etc. and excavated by later researchers. Rare as such early English earthenwares may be, there are specialist books on the subject including **Medieval Pottery from Excavations** *(John Baker, 1974) and the late Bernard Rackham's* **Medieval English Pottery** *(Faber & Faber, 1948, revised edition 1973). Many museums will feature local finds of such wares showing that earthenware vessels were widely used and were made over a large area, not necessarily in the centres which we associate with pottery production today.*

The sixteenth century saw the introduction to England from the Netherlands of tin-enamelled earthenware later called Delftware. Today we do not like this old term but as it will most probably continue in use we would merely point out that in referring to English tin-glazed earthenware one uses a small 'd', 'delftware', the capital D being reserved for the Dutch wares. The chief centres of its manufacture in the seventeenth century were London, Liverpool, and Bristol. However, there were several smaller centres and much research has been carried out on these decorative and interesting wares in recent years. In general the production of tin-glazed earthenware had been superseded by creamware by about 1780.

Another standard type of pottery produced in the sixteenth and seventeenth centuries was slipware. Here the clay body was not coated with a white (tin-glazed) surface, but partly decorated in slight relief with trailed clay of one or more different colours. The basic technique is simple and similar to icing a cake! Simple as the process may be, genuine old examples especially inscribed or dated examples may be extremely costly, running into thousands of pounds for even damaged specimens. For further information see under Slipware.

By this time a new factor was arising to spur on pottery development: the rapid spread of the vogue for the new exotic hot drinks, coffee, chocolate, and tea. The first London 'Cophee House' opened in 1652; in 1660 Pepys could record: 'I did send for a cup of tea (a China drink) of which I never had drank before'. But a century later imports of the light-weight tea-leaf exceeded five million lbs a year. At first it was usually served from the red stoneware tea-pots imported from China by the Dutch and English East India Companies, or in the mysterious and expensive blue and white porcelain which, noted Sir Thomas Browne c.1650, 'according to common belief is made of Earth'. Tea and ceramics are closely linked in that most of the standard products of our porcelain manufacturers comprised tea wares.

While Continental potters tried to make porcelain, in England the challenge was met by an Oxford MA, John Dwight of Fulham, who in 1684 took out a patent for fine stoneware (which he called porcelain), and by the Elers brothers (see Elers Ware) who, at Fulham from c.1690 and thereafter in Staffordshire produced similar wares, including fine redware. Elers ware was unglazed but, since it was fired at high temperature (1200°C), was not porous and, unlike delftware, not so vulnerable to being chipped. Dwight also developed a white saltglaze stoneware, which was nearer to Chinese porcelain in colour. It was in this material that Staffordshire and other potters first made the little figurines of horsemen etc. in a style which was also adapted to earthenware by Astbury and Whieldon (q.v.).

Various factors contributed to a steady improvement in stoneware which made it very different from the coarse grey stonewares of sixteenth-century Germany and Flanders. The addition of calcined flints to the clay (variously attributed to Dwight, Astbury, or Heath) gave stability in the kiln, durability, and whiteness. The important discovery was made that Cornwall yielded a particularly pure china clay, used ever since in Britain and exported all over the world, as the 'slag-heaps' that disfigure the neighbourhood of St Austell and elsewhere testify. Ball clay, a fine white pipeclay imported in ball form from Devon and Dorset, was added to give greater plasticity and strength; and felspar later was added as a flux. The remaining problem was surface texture. Unglazed stoneware (except for the Dwight-type redware) was too rough; impure lead glaze detracted from appearance; saltglaze was better, but nevertheless had a characteristic dimpled surface which has been likened to the skin of an orange. The saltglaze is extremely hard and durable and the slight surface rippling is not a defect.

In the 1720s some genius discovered that the stoneware ingredients, if fired at the much lower temperature of 750°C, produced a useful cream-coloured earthenware. Whieldon used this with tortoiseshell and mottled colour glazes. A clear lead glaze was then evolved which, applied to this ware as a liquid dip and replacing to some degree saltglaze, produced an ideal body that, under the name of creamware, came to displace saltglaze and other wares not only in Britain but on the Continent and in America for a century. Its further development was mainly due to Josiah Wedgwood who used the term 'Queen's Ware' for his refined well-potted creamwares. By about 1765 there was hardly a pottery in the country that was not producing creamware as its staple product. This sold well without any decoration but the smooth surface enabled it also to have printed or hand-painted decoration added. The creamware, when well potted, was light yet strong and of a pleasing tint.

Between 1767 and 1785 Wedgwood also took the lead in developing new forms of stoneware, notably Black Basalt, Jasper Ware, and Caneware. The black basalt was also known as 'Egyptian Black' and all these unglazed so-called dry bodies were extremely popular and were produced by many different firms over a long period into the nineteenth century, and even up to the present time. The different types of body are listed separately in the main part of this book.

Staffordshire figures had also come to the fore; these might be regarded as the poor man's Chelsea. Some of the best of these were made by the Wood family, led by Ralph Wood, the first (from c.1754). The three Ralph Woods made many other things, e.g. Toby jugs, but a line of potters working on a small scale specialized in figures only, notably the bocage-backed figures of the Walton School (c.1806–46), and the less cosy products of Obadiah Sherratt. These Staffordshire figures, the small animals, etc. were often referred to as 'Toys' and particularly in the nineteenth century very many potters, or 'Toy makers', were engaged in producing such pieces from moulds. Several specialist books cater for the great interest in these wares, see Appendix C.

The main nineteenth-century developments in British earthenwares were the excellence of the blue printed wares which were made, not only for the home market, but also for our expanding export market. Many patterns were introduced especially for the North American and other markets. Other patterns such as the ever popular Willow sold well on a world-wide basis. Later developments were made in printing in other colours and this gave rise to the introduction, in the 1840s, of multicolour printing. Such colourful designs, often on the covers of meat (or fish) paste pots, are generally called 'Prattware' (q.v.), but several other firms specialized in this technique and in producing, for the meat paste and other manufacturers, low cost pottery pots, the first essay in colourful ceramic packaging! The customer chose the product by its package for its decorative merits. These are, of course, still widely collected (and much copied) and rare subjects may command vast sums.

Later developments include the introduction of the so-called Majolica body, introduced at Mintons c.1850 and taken up by a host of other firms. Decorative stonewares were popularized by Doultons of Lambeth in the 1870s and were again much copied by other firms well into the present century. Notable makers of hand-crafted stonewares in London were the Martin brothers (q.v.) and today the tradition is continued by hundreds, if not thousands, of Studio Potters.

In such an exercise as this introduction one tends to single out the few landmarks and to mention relatively few of the leading firms, but it must be remembered that for every large firm there were a hundred or more smaller potteries and that the bulk of the output was restricted to domestic table-ware, not to one-off decorative articles. Most of the potters were concerned with producing inexpensive earthenwares that would find a buyer because of their low cost. It follows therefore that the mass market was for inexpensive low cost articles that are not works of art. However, much of this is quite collectable today and one can specialize in given shapes or articles, egg-cups, amusing teapots, cheese dishes, etc., or collect the work of one little-known firm. A good selection of such nineteenth and present century items is featured in Geoffrey Godden's book British Pottery. An Illustrated Guide *(Barrie & Jenkins, 1974) including a range of 'Cheap Lines', not all of which are necessarily inexpensive today!*

PORCELAIN

True or hard-paste porcelain was first made in China in the ninth century AD (T'ang Dynasty); it was produced by mixing china-clay (kaolin, *a pure white clay formed by the decay of felspar, the chief constituent of granite) with china-stone* (petuntse, *less fully decomposed felspar). These were fused together by firing in a kiln, first at about 900°C, then dipped in glaze and refired at about 1300°C; this resulted in a translucent body under a tight-fitting glaze (it is also believed that some if not most Chinese porcelains were subject to only one firing). The china-stone bound the clay particles together and imparted translucency; the high temperature vitrified the whole body. The Chinese porcelains vary greatly from delicately-potted thin tea-bowls to massive thickly-potted vases.*

China exported its porcelain wares (especially blue and white) to Europe in ever increasing quantity from the mid sixteenth century, mainly through the English and Dutch East India Companies; by 1700 there was a vast trade in them, and earlier wares of the Ming Dynasty (1386–1644) were particularly prized. As they were very expensive and scarce, Europeans tried hard to discover the secret of hard-paste manufacture, but it was not until 1710 that the Duke of Saxony's captive alchemist Böttger found out how to make it, using local materials.

The Meissen factory (just outside Dresden, the Saxon capital) was set up to make this. Although the duke tried to keep the formula secret, it was soon leaked to Vienna (an early example of industrial espionage) and later elsewhere. In England William Cookworthy later discovered the requisite ingredients in Cornwall, thus enabling true hard-paste porcelain to be made by a formula which passed successively from Plymouth (Cookworthy, 1768) to Bristol (Champion, 1774). Subsequently, in the early 1780s, the Patent Rights to produce porcelain from the Cornish raw materials were sold to a group of potters in Staffordshire. This led to the establishment of the New Hall company (q.v.). Other potters and firms were slightly later to produce a rather soft but still dense porcelain body which we now call hybrid hard-paste. This was almost standard English porcelain from the 1790s to about 1810. Early Coalport, Miles Mason, Chamberlain-Worcester porcelains are of this type. For further information the reader is referred to Chapter 6 of Geoffrey Godden's Guide to English Porcelain *(Granada, 1978).*

Artificial or soft-paste porcelain had been produced in Europe as early as c.1575; this was the Medici porcelain made, for a few years only, in Florence. A fine creamy variety had also been evolved in France, at Rouen (1673) and St Cloud (near Paris). In the post-Meissen period French soft-paste wares were made at Chantilly, Mennecy, and (1756–1804) Sèvres; Italian at Capodimonte (Naples) from 1745; in England at Chelsea (1745), Derby, Longton Hall, Vauxhall, or at Liverpool and, in modified form, Bow and Lowestoft, was produced what we term soft-paste porcelain. These porcelains are not, of course, soft and malleable, indeed the word 'soft' really applies to the firing temperature, a soft fire rather than a hard one.

The essential difference between hard and soft-paste porcelain lies in the ingredients used. In soft-paste porcelain a glassy mixture of sand or calcined flint with potash or lead was used instead of the china-stone, and various locally available white clays for the Chinese type of china-clay; the result was a slightly creamy or ivory porcelain. The glassy mixture is technically known as a frit (from the Italian for 'fried'), i.e. a fusion of materials, finely ground, which gives stability to the body paste; a glassy frit is also the basis of glazes, giving them their waterproofing quality. In contrast to hard-paste, soft-paste porcelain was first fired at a high temperature (about 1100°C) to produce a translucent biscuit stage (i.e. fired but unglazed); the biscuit was then dipped in glaze and refired at about 900°C. In contrast, true or hard-paste porcelain had a low initial firing.

Both hard and soft-paste porcelains had their disadvantages, tending to distort or collapse in the kiln; a high proportion of such 'wasters' (spoilt unsaleable pieces) naturally increased the price of the products. Early soft-paste wares were also liable to crack under a sudden change of temperature as would happen when boiling water was poured into a cold teapot. Chinese teapots had a good reputation for withstanding this thermal shock – they were fit for their purpose!

The substitution of soapstone (steatite or hydrated magnesium silicate) for china-clay produced a soft-paste body better able to survive the rigours of the kiln and changes in temperature; it was denser, harder, much heavier, and it vitrified at a lower kiln temperature. Soapstone, found in Cornwall, was first used at Lund's Bristol factory (1749), Worcester (1751–1820s), Vauxhall (1753–64), Caughley (1775–99), and at some of the Liverpool factories. These soapstone-bodied porcelains tend to have a greenish translucency when held to the light.

Still more rewarding was the discovery that bone-ash, from calcined bones, also reduced kiln collapses. Added to soft-paste ingredients, it produced a whiter, more plastic body. Bow was the first to use Thomas Frye's patent for this (1749), followed by Lowestoft (1757), Chelsea (gold anchor, 1758), Chelsea-Derby, and some Liverpool factories. Calcined bones had been added to various other mixes, Neale porcelains for example, and to some types of earthenware.

The qualities of the calcined bones to strengthen and whiten the body led to the perfection of English bone china in about 1800. The exact date is not now known, although several of the old authorities opt for a date in the 1790s. It is now considered that Josiah Spode successfully marketed the perfected bone china in about 1800. He, however, used the name 'Stoke China' and it should be noted that the term bone china is a relatively modern one.

Essentially bone china is hard-paste porcelain plus bone-ash. All manufacturers had their own receipts for the mix but the approximate proportions were one part china-clay, one part china-stone and two parts bone-ash, for the better class porcelains. Others reduced the amount of bone or added cheaper raw materials, resulting in a body prone to discoloration or to the break-up of the covering glaze. It should be mentioned that even in one factory several different mixes of bone china might be employed. One would be produced for objects that had to be turned on the potter's wheel, another for wares that had to be cast in moulds, to mention only the two very basic different types.

At its best English bone china is a quite beautiful white, hard (but not too hard) body. It had few defects in the firing processes and served as a wonderful ground for the added painting and gilding. From about 1800 to the present day English bone china has set the highest standards and is unmatched. For further details the reader is referred to Staffordshire Porcelain *(edited by Geoffrey Godden, Granada, 1983) and in particular to chapter 7, the late Reginald G. Haggar's contribution.*

Perhaps even more beautiful than the standard bone china was the rather more glossy Felspar China. This was introduced by John Rose of Coalport in 1820 and was soon taken up by Spode and other manufacturers. The felspar was discovered by Thomas Ryan in 1818 at Middleton Hill on the borders of Shropshire and Wales. Seemingly the new mix was expensive and in general felspar was only used in porcelain for ten or fifteen years. Those firms that did use such a mix often employed special marks to distinguish the wares and, one presumes, to help sell the rather more expensive articles.

Several fancy names for various earthenware mixes incorrectly used the word 'china' or even 'porcelain' to lend an up-market tone to their wares. Hence wares marked 'Stone China', 'Ironstone China', 'Semi Porcelain', etc. are not china or porcelain as the term is usually understood.

Distinguishing hard and soft

It is sometimes suggested that this is easy, for true soft-paste can be scratched with a knife or a nail-file which makes no mark on hard paste. Please don't buy this old trick. Take our word for it, this test is unreliable. At best you will mark a perfectly good piece of porcelain and probably be banished for ever from any shop or auction room where you seek to test porcelain in this way. Various books (including the first edition of this one) contain statements such as 'A broken piece can be identified easily enough, as hard paste fractures like glass or flint, leaving clean, sparkling edges of compact texture, while a soft past fracture is granular, like fine lump sugar.' These statements are fine until you seek to put them into practice. Do you purposely break a piece in order to discover if it is hard or soft-paste? Also do remember that there are degrees of hardness and of softness, much depends on the firing temperature or on the position in the kiln of the piece in question.

The feel and appearance of hard and soft porcelain will come to you with practice. Study your porcelains, fondle them. Buy a damaged, inexpensive piece of Chinese hard-paste porcelain and a Derby or Pinxton specimen as representing the two extremes of hard and soft-paste. Live with them, get on the same wavelength.

Above all do not be too carried away with the idea that you cannot collect until you can distinguish between hard and soft. This is nonsense. The only time you need to distinguish between the two classes is when you collect very expensive types of eighteenth-century English soft-paste porcelain, for copies were made in Europe in the nineteenth century in a hard paste. However, the later copies are usually rarer than the genuine article and the whole appearance of the later Continental copy should give the game away. Whilst writing of fakes do be warned not to put all your trust in a mark, especially in a gold anchor device.

If you collect only nineteenth-century or later pieces there is really no need to distinguish between hard and soft porcelain. Certainly no need if you buy only what you like – the best test of all.

Glazes

Glaze is applied to a porcelain or pottery body to make it waterproof, enhance colour, and add brilliance to its surface. Glazes may be clear, opaque, or coloured to various degrees.

Hard-paste porcelain was given a glaze made of powdered china-stone mixed with lime, potash, sand, or quartz. Being of similar composition, body and glaze fused intimately together. Pottery and soft-paste porcelain were treated in various ways. Early English soft-paste and earthenwares such as creamware were coated in a transparent glassy lead glaze (sand or silica fused with a lead oxide), a process which caused lead poisoning among the workmen. The proportion of lead, at first as much as 40 per cent, was therefore steadily reduced, and as early as 1820 Coalport won an award for introducing an excellent leadless glaze, using felspar. In delftware calcined tin oxide was added to the lead glaze, giving an opaque white finish. Saltglaze was used on some pottery; salt was thrown into the kiln at high temperature and fused with the clay. Glazes may be stained by the metallic content of the clay, natural or introduced; coloured glazes were used on earthenware by Thomas Whieldon, Ralph Wood, and many others.

The glazed surface of most hard-paste porcelain, when properly prepared, has a brilliantly white hard glitter and a cold touch; any overglaze decoration tends to stand out slightly from the surface. By contrast, soft-paste looks and feels warmer and softer, like unused toilet soap or candles; overglaze decoration sinks slightly into the glaze and the overall effect of subdued colours and mellow richness is preferred by many to the relative garishness of, for example, German porcelain. In figures the difference is particularly noticeable; the thin close-fitting glaze on hard-paste makes for finer detailed modelling, while the thicker richer soft-paste glaze produces softer unsharp outlines, often with pools of surplus glaze forming in hollows.

Various imperfections can occur, especially in the earlier porcelains. The pieces, particularly large dishes, can warp, while figures can lean, cracks may open, or bubbles form and burst during the high-temperature firing processes. In moderation these are points to welcome as a sign of genuineness, but unsightly blemishes will certainly affect the value of a piece and its saleability.

The covering glaze too can run or bubble and develop small black spots as if it were dusted with black pepper. More seriously, the glaze can break up over the years into a network of fine cracks. This is called 'crazing'. It is quite common even on relatively late wares. In basic English the glaze does not 'fit' the body and the glaze will expand and contract to a slightly different degree than the underlying body as the piece is used and is warmed and cooled over a period of time. This crazing can result in the underlying slightly porous body becoming stained.

Colour decoration

This may be overglaze, underglaze, or obtained by use of coloured glazes. Overglaze decoration used elaborately prepared mixtures of pigments from metallic oxides with (at first) flint-glass, to form what were virtually colour glazes; these are technically known as enamel colours. Each colour might have to be fired separately, at specific but relatively low temperatures (in the 700–950°C range). On soft-paste porcelain, during the firing, the enamels melted and sank slightly into the softened glaze. On hard-paste this was not so; the layers of colour stand slightly proud. Decoration in several colours is called polychrome. Among the sources of enamel colours are manganese (purple), copper or chromium (green), iron (red), uranium or antimony (yellow). The shades of colour differ with the temperature used.

To avoid the high cost of hand-painting, transfer-printing, an English speciality, was introduced on porcelains, probably by Robert Hancock at Worcester (1756) and later became standard practice elsewhere; designs were engraved on copper plates from which impressions were taken on specially treated very thin but strong paper, and transferred to the already glazed wares.

Some very fine printing was carried out mainly, but not exclusively, in the early nineteenth century by the bat-printing process. Here the design was transferred from specially engraved or etched copper plates by means of bats of pliable glue-like material which picked up from the plate not pigment but oil. Once the oil had been transferred to the glazed object, finely ground ceramic colour was dusted on. This was retained by the oil and the surplus colour cleaned away. A further firing fixed the colour to the glaze. Typical examples are shown in Plates 9 and 66.

In underglaze decoration the colours were painted (or transfer-printed) on to the unglazed (biscuit) wares and had therefore to withstand much higher firing temperatures. At first the easiest colour to manage at high temperatures was cobalt blue, hence the prevalence of underglaze blue decoration from the Ming period onwards, and its popularity for English printed nineteenth-century table-wares, since the glaze protected the decoration from wear. Underglaze blue transfer-printing was pioneered or perfected at Worcester c.1760 and was adopted almost everywhere except Chelsea and perhaps the Vauxhall factory.

Blue and white decoration not only seems 'right' for ceramic decoration, it had the added advantage of being relatively inexpensive. It did not need the extra firings necessary for enamel decoration and normally it does not bear any gilt enrichment, so saving the cost of applying the gold, of firing and burnishing this metal and the cost of the gold itself.

Gilding
Gold has been used to enhance porcelains from at least the seventeenth century as far as Chinese and Japanese wares are concerned, and some of the earliest imports were even mounted in gold.

Various types of gilding have been used on English ceramics from the 1740s onwards, for example honey gilding in which gold leaf was ground up with honey and, after firing at a low temperature, burnished. This gave a dull finish; a brassy finish resulted from mercury gilding ('best' gold), introduced c.1790, in which the mercury of a gold amalgam was vaporized. From the 1870s 'bright' or liquid gold was used on some less costly porcelains and earthenwares, such as flatback figures. It was a very thin film of colloidal gold, so brilliant that it needed no burnishing; but it did not wear well. This fault also occurred on some of our earliest gilding which was 'cold' or unfired or at least fired at a temperature which did not ensure its permanent fixing to the body.

Surprisingly little attention has been paid by collectors to ceramic gilding. It dresses the more expensive porcelains, enriching them in more senses than one. It is not so much the cost of the gold used but rather the time and skill in applying it in an artistic manner coupled with the fact that this gilding has to be fired and then burnished by hand before the piece can be marketed. Some eighteenth and nineteenth-century porcelains were embellished only with a gilt pattern. Mighty tasteful they can be too. But don't get carried away by the wording of some advertisements for modern so-called limited edition plates, etc. where it is claimed that a simple gilt edge has been painstakingly hand-applied in pure (or nearly pure) gold. The gold may have cost tenpence but is not recoverable!

A to Z of British Pottery and Porcelain

ADAMS FAMILY. A line of Staffordshire potters stretching from the claimed date of establishment in 1657 to today. Among the most notable were William Adams of Tunstall and Greengates (1779–1805), who made various types of earthenware including Wedgwood-style blue jasper with white reliefs, the blue being more violet than Wedgwood's; his son Benjamin (1805–12), who made high-quality blue transfer-printed pearlware; and William Adams of Stoke (1804–29), who specialized in blue-printed earthenware with appropriate scenes (e.g. the 'Landing of Columbus' set) for the US market. The Adams products closely rivalled Wedgwood's in style, quality, and in the various types of earthenware in demand both in the British home market and in the export markets enjoyed by the British potters. From about 1780 the impressed name mark 'Adams' can occur.

The Adams wares (which included some porcelains) were extremely varied and the mid-nineteenth-century printed earthenwares are not rare. From about 1891 the marks have included the word 'England'. Many present-century productions bear the date of establishment '1657'. A selection of the Wedgwood-style jasper wares are shown in Geoffrey Godden's *British Pottery. An Illustrated Guide* (Barrie & Jenkins, 1974), Plate 243.

Standard books on the older Adams wares include: *William Adams, an Old English Potter* by W. Turner (Chapman & Hall, 1904); *A History of the Adams Family in North Staffordshire* by P. W. L. Adams (St Catherine Press, 1914); *Ten Generations of a Potting Family* by R. Nicholls (Lund Humphries, *c.*1925); and *A Pride of Potters – Adams* by D. Peel (A. Barker, 1957).

AGATE WARE. Earthenware made to look like agate by building up irregular layers of clays coloured white, brown, green, and blue. The layered mass was then cut and each block rearranged at a different angle. This process was repeated many times before the pieces were pressed into moulds or turned on the potter's wheel to form objects such as those illustrated in Plate 1. It differs from tortoiseshell ware as the veining is in the clay, not the glaze. Agate table-wares were made by Thomas Whieldon from about 1740 and then by Wedgwood and other Staffordshire potters until *c.*1820; small figures of cats, pigs, birds, etc. in agate veined earthenware were very popular but as these have been collectable for a long period they have been copied.

Some modern Studio Potters have reintroduced agate-type earthenwares.

SAMUEL ALCOCK. Worked *c.*1822–59. A Staffordshire manufacturer of pottery and porcelain with a wide range of wares, notably

Rockingham-style table-wares, moulded jugs in Parian ware, porcelain animal models, and decorative vases.

In recent years much research has been carried out on the Alcock wares, in particular the decorative porcelains. A remarkably large range of shapes was produced by the Alcock firm, first at Cobridge and later at the Hill Pottery at Burslem.

Many, mainly printed, marks, were employed several including the name 'S Alcock & Co.' (as Plate 2) but others include only the initials 'S A & Co.' Many examples are, however, unmarked but the characteristic shapes or the form of fractional pattern numbers help to identify the Alcock products. Several of the shapes were registered and bear the registration device (see Registration Marks) as does the vase shown in Plate 3. Each such registered shape could be made in several sizes and decorated with very many different designs.

There is we believe good scope for the collection of the quite plentiful Alcock wares. For further information the reader is referred to Dr and Mrs Geoffrey Barnes's contribution in *Staffordshire Porcelain* (Granada, 1983), chapter 21 and the *Encyclopaedia of British Porcelain Manufacturers*, pp. 76–85.

1 *A Staffordshire 'Agate ware' small teapot and a similar creamer of typical early forms. The agate-like effect was obtained by mixing and chopping together various coloured clays. Teapot 5¼in high. c.1750.* **(Christie's)**

2   Rare printed Alcock mark giving
the name and address with the date of
publication of a parian bust. Most
examples are unfortunately unmarked.

3   A typical Samuel Alcock porcelain
vase of a form registered on 15 February
1844, with fractional pattern number
2/6113. 11¾in high. c.1844–7.

AMATEUR DECORATION. There was a great vogue for the amateur decoration of both pottery and porcelain, particularly in the 1870-90 period.

However, much non-factory decorated wares were produced in the early 1800s and several factories seemingly engaged in selling white porcelains to these often very talented painters, often young ladies. In some cases the pieces were returned to be fired and to have gilt borders, etc. added.

Amateur work was very often signed and dated, as, for example, a water-colour drawing would be, but factory painting was seldom signed before the 1860 period and extremely rarely dated. The dish shown in Plate 4 is a typical amateur example of the 1880s, the colours are rather dull, the painting rather wooden and there is, in this case, a lack of gilding.

For further information on the often decorative but seldom valuable amateur decoration, the reader is referred to Geoffrey Godden's article in *Country Life* of 2 October, 1958.

4   *An amateur decorated earthenware dish, painted by Florence M. Gibbs. Signed and dated and exhibited in 1883. Diameter 13½in. 1883.*

ANIMALS AND BIRDS. Interesting collections can be built up from the immense variety of these models produced in pottery and porcelain up to the present time. Porcelain examples, often Meissen-inspired, were made by most eighteenth-century manufacturers, particularly Chelsea and Bow; these can now fetch extremely high prices. Native species predominate, usually pets, farm animals, or sporting (both the hunter and the hunted). Pugs seem to have been the favourite pet, cosily ensconced on tasselled cushions. Pointers and setters standing over game are the commonest sporting subjects. 'Rockingham' poodles and sheep with coats of shredded porcelain are not now thought to have come from the Rockingham factory. A Derby pair of figures, often seen in pottery versions, are the 'Welsh' Tailor and Wife mounted on goats (an oddly popular animal in those days) carrying everything but the kitchen sink; despite the assumed name, it is copied from Meissen. Classical themes are represented by Leda and the Swan, Europa and the Bull, numerous paw-on-globe lions (copied from Roman sculpture), and groups inspired by Aesop's fables.

Many nineteenth-century potters or large firms such as Samuel Alcock & Co. produced good quality porcelain animal models, as did the Chamberlain and Grainger firms at Worcester. The earthenware potters too produced flocks of animals, for they were popular saleable articles. Prices now relate to the age and quality of the specimen but some animals have special interest to individual collectors. Some folk collect monkeys, others elephants, and so on.

The reader should bear in mind that porcelain models bearing a gold anchor are more likely to be Continental than Chelsea.

A noteworthy twentieth-century development at Worcester is a series of limited-edition studies of birds in their natural habitat, inspired by Audubon's *Birds of America* but also modelled from life. These were made from 1935 by Charles Doughty's daughter Dorothy (d.1962).

Potters covered a far wider range, in earthenware, brown stoneware, saltglaze, and creamware, from at least the seventeenth century. Whieldon Ware, the Walton School, and Sherratt-type wares, account for many basic types or styles. The exotic is represented by a Chinese-inspired boy-on-water-buffalo group (Whieldon), dromedaries, lions (with their tamers), the London Zoo's first giraffe (1830; 'I don't believe it', said one lady firmly), and its famous Jumbo (1860). From bear-baiting days come numerous Nottingham and Derby brown stoneware beer jugs in the form of a sitting bear hugging a terrier, the head detachable as a cup; also owl-jugs – both coated with shredded clay. Equally odd are the early nineteenth-century Sussex pig-mugs, also with detachable heads. Cats are relatively rare; most notable are those in solid agate, but later forgeries have been produced. Dogs abound, especially the greyhound couchant, with or without its kill, and including Waterloo Cup winners; and dalmatians, the Regency carriage-dogs. The 'comforter', an extinct breed of spaniel-like lap-dog, has been immensely popular from the 1850s, sitting up, wearing a gold chain and a puzzled expression, and decorated with red or lustred spots; pairs of such dogs are still being produced. And, of course, there are the late Victorian Martinware 'birds' that never were on land or sea!

Most general books illustrate some ceramic animals but specialist books include *Animals in Pottery & Porcelain* by John P. Cushion (Studio Vista, 1974) and Dr D. Rice's *English Porcelain Animals of the 19th Century* (Antique Collectors' Club, 1989).

ANTIQUE. This word is so often grossly misused. So-called 'antique shops' or 'antique fairs' abound in which one is hard put to find any object over sixty years old let alone a hundred years! The legal (and generally accepted) definition of an antique is an object made a hundred or more years ago. It should be borne in mind, however, that the word has no magic qualities: a badly produced ugly object made ninety-nine years ago does not become a superb thing of beauty in a year's time. It is merely a year older! Admire or reject a piece on its qualities not on its age alone – antique or not!

APOSTLE JUGS. Relief-decorated stoneware jugs so called after a mock Gothic design registered in March 1842 by the Staffordshire potter Charles Meigh which showed a frieze of the apostles standing in niches beneath pointed arches (a variation was also issued without the figures). These moulded stoneware jugs were extremely popular in the 1840s and were made in various sizes and coloured bodies. The basic Gothic style was much in vogue at this period (and also at the 1851 Exhibition) and similar teawares can also be found. The Meigh examples usually bear a clear mark indicating the date of the initial registration; examples, of course, post-date this.

These Apostle jugs and the related Gothic-type designs were copied by other firms such as Ridgways. Examples are still not all that rare or costly.

ARMORIAL CHINA. From the late seventeenth century onwards there was a vogue for teawares, dinner sets, punch-bowls, etc. embellished with the family arms. At first these were made and decorated in China, sometimes with quaint results as the Chinese were inclined to rearrange armorial details, or even to copy instructions to the decorator onto the plate.

These oriental armorial porcelains are highly collectable and a surprisingly large number of families ordered their armorial porcelains from China, see Geoffrey Godden's *Oriental Export Market Porcelain* (Granada, 1979). The standard book on armorial porcelains is David S. Howard's *Chinese Armorial Porcelain* (Faber & Faber, 1974).

Some eighteenth-century English porcelain manufacturers also produced individual orders for armorial or crested wares, but these Worcester and other wares were greatly outnumbered by the fashionable oriental imports. However, by about 1820 even the English East India Company was ordering its armorial service from

Worcester. Some English porcelain armorial sets are magnificent (see Plate 5) and the Daniel sets made in 1827 for the Earl of Shrewsbury were reputedly the most expensive ever manufactured in Staffordshire (see *Staffordshire Porcelain*, Plates 417, 419–21).

5   *A magnificent and very costly Worcester tureen, cover and stand from the famous 'Stowe' service made for the second Marquess of Buckingham, and bearing his family armorial bearings. 7½in high.* **(Sotheby's).**

Apart from the magnificent quality porcelains, the tin-glaze earthenware potters and various makers of the ever popular creamwares catered for those who ordered ceramics embellished with their armorial bearings, although Josiah Wedgwood disliked such one-off orders that could not be sold to others should the order be cancelled for any reason.

Such prestige orders are still received by our leading manufacturers, from Heads of State, or others able and willing to pay for such costly services.

ART DECO (1925–1930s). A style evolved in the Jazz Age, partly in reaction to Art Nouveau (q.v.), influenced by the severe functionalism of the German Bauhaus school and characterized by crisp lines, strong colour, highly stylized flowers and themes from nature (e.g.

rising sun, lightning, rainbow). It also absorbed motifs from current discoveries (Tutankhamen's tomb, Aztec ruins, and the Diaghilev ballet). The style was reputedly introduced at the 1925 Paris Exhibition. In ceramics the functional side was typified by the cubic teapot with recessed handle, lid, and spout – almost unbreakable and easily stacked – with matching teacups on square saucers. The Cube teapot was introduced *c.*1925 but was licensed to several manufacturers by the introducing Company.

Perhaps the best known Art Deco earthenwares are the shapes and bold designs introduced by Clarice Cliff (q.v.). These once inexpensive designs were produced by Messrs A. J. Wilkinson Ltd over a long period. A large team of ladies was employed to hand-paint the bold patterns, which are now very much back in favour.

The Art Deco style was mainly confined to earthenwares and was quite widespread in the 1930s, see *British Pottery. An Illustrated Guide* (Barrie & Jenkins, 1974) pp. 385–93. A good specialist book is Judy Spours's *Art Deco Tableware* (Ward Lock, 1988).

ART NOUVEAU (1890–1910). A fin-de-siècle style evolved in reaction against the ugliness of the Industrial Age, characterized by sinuous designs derived from plant life and by a love of extravagant detail for its own sake. It drew inspiration, through William Morris's arts and crafts movement, from Japanese designs and the Pre-Raphaelites.

More prominent on the Continent and deriving its name from a Paris shop, L'Art Nouveau (1895), its chief manifestations were in architecture (Otto Wagner), illustration (Beardsley; Mucha's theatrical posters), glass (Lalique, Gallé, Tiffany), fabrics (Liberty & Co. of Regent Street); ceramic examples of the style are found on William De Morgan, Doulton, and Martinware vases, on Royal Lancastrian lustreware, and rarely on some Minton and Royal Worcester porcelains. The Art Nouveau style is often seen on tiles of the period. Several rather costly art books give a good overall picture of the period but few feature British ceramics. Some specimens are, however, shown in Geoffrey Godden's book *British Porcelain. An Illustrated Guide* (Barrie & Jenkins, 1974).

ART POTTERY. This term is used to embrace an interesting and varied group of small potteries which flourished in the late nineteenth century and in some cases continued up to the period of the Second World War.

Most are very individual in style and do not reflect the taste of the larger very commercial potters. They are nevertheless very typical of their period and today there is a reawakening of interest in such Art Potteries, many of which were situated in the West Country.

Several recent books have been written on these including M. Haslam's *English Art Pottery 1865–1915* (Antique Collectors' Club, 1975) and A. W. Coysh's *British Art Pottery 1870–1940* (David & Charles, 1976).

ASTBURY WARE (*c*.1720–50). A convenient generic label for two classes of Staffordshire lead-glazed earthenware, made by John Astbury (*c*.1689–1743) of Shelton and by others. Many innovations have been tentatively attributed to this member of the large Astbury family.

1. Redware teapots, jars and other tableware, decorated with applied reliefs. The body was fired before glazing, given a transparent cream-coloured glaze and refired, the result being a warm brown colour.

2. Figurines, in the same styles as those made in saltglaze, but using clays of two colours (red or brown and white). They include musicians, horsemen, soldiers, milkmaids, and some animals and birds.

The early Astbury earthenwares are not marked and the name is used in a very general sense to indicate a type and general style and period, much as we use the name Chippendale when referring to furniture.

ASTBURY-WHIELDON WARE (*c*.1740–50). A convenient generic label for Astbury-type figurines in which the transparent glaze is replaced by glazes stained green, brown, purple, blue, or black by various metallic oxides, usually in mottled or 'tortoiseshell' mixtures; the clay was either white or a combination of white and brown. They were made by many Staffordshire potters.

Most general books on British pottery will feature illustrations of good typical examples, which can be seen in many of our large museums, such as the Victoria & Albert in London or the City of Stoke-on-Trent Museum and Art Gallery at Hanley.

BARGE TEAPOT (*c*.1880–1910). A vast brown-glazed teapot often recognizable by having a miniature replica of itself as a lid knob. Coloured applied decoration (birds, flowers, etc.) added a final touch of the bizarre to these wares, made chiefly in the Burton-on-Trent area and especially favoured by bargees' wives. There were also jugs and bottles in similar style. These and the large teapots (as Plate 6) were sometimes personalized with names and dates, features which add interest.

A known maker of these usually unmarked wares was William Mason of the Pool Pottery, Church Gresley.

HANNAH B. BARLOW. Miss Hannah Barlow, a student from the Lambeth School of Art, was one of the most celebrated artists taken on by (Sir) Henry Doulton to decorate his Lambeth stonewares in the early 1870s. Reputedly she was the first of a long succession of such students to be employed by Doultons.

Hannah Barlow's working period was 1871–1913. Her speciality was incised studies of animals or birds. The incised lines were then accentuated with ceramic pigment (see Plate 7). The technique is

6 *A large teapot and jug of Barge teapot-type with treacle-coloured glaze and relief motifs. Teapot 12in high. c.1880–1900.*

known as 'Sgraffito' but Hannah Barlow also occasionally painted her animal studies in the conventional manner.

Her work will bear her monogram made up of the initials HBB but arranged with the Bs back-to-back, each side of the H, as shown in *Handbook of British Pottery & Porcelain Marks*, p. 66. Her work will also bear a standard Doulton-Lambeth mark, often the year of production, and a reference number relating to the design – each one of which was unique.

Hannah Barlow's work is highly collectable and important or rare types may be costly. Typical examples are shown in Geoffrey Godden's *British Pottery. An Illustrated Guide* (Barrie & Jenkins, 1974), Plates 404–7, or in specialist books on Doulton wares.

Hannah's sister Florence specialized (c.1873–1909) in bird studies usually built up in coloured clays, see *British Pottery. An Illustrated Guide,* Plates 408–9. Her brother Arthur, who died in 1878, also decorated Doulton stonewares. All the Barlows' work is collectable.

7 *An early Doulton stoneware jug and two vases bearing Hannah B. Barlow's free-hand incised drawings of animals. Doulton trade marks and Barlow monogram. c.1873–80. Jug 7¾ high.*

BAROQUE, ROCOCO, NEO-CLASSICAL. The first of these styles is of minor importance in English ceramic history. Emanating from Roman Catholic southern Europe and watered down in the (pre-Sèvres) France of Louis XIV (1643–1715), Baroque in ceramic terms chiefly spells symmetry and strong colours (red, black, gold).

The more frivolous Rococo style, by contrast, was manifested in asymmetry, feminine colours (rose-pink, mauve, pale yellow), and wild curvaciousness seen e.g. in the elaborate scrolled bases of Bow figures (1760). Rococo is associated with the France of Louis XV (1715–74) and Sèvres (moved from Vincennes 1756), and came to England (via Meissen at first) about the time when the earliest porcelain factories began in the mid or late 1740s.

Soon, however, the very different Neo-Classical influence also appeared, derived from discoveries made at Pompeii and neighbouring Herculaneum from 1748. At first these finds were thought to be Etruscan art (hence Wedgwood's 'Etruria' factory), but in fact they were Roman and Graeco-Roman. In 1758 the architect Robert Adam brought from Italy the ideas typically embodied in his austere classical fireplaces, with their swags or festoons, urns, etc. In English ceramics the Neo-Classical fashion coincided with the Chelsea-Derby period (1770), and Wedgwood at Etruria (1769) found it most suitable for his unglazed stonewares, with classical reliefs, modelled by Flaxman among others, and the Adam-style motifs and shapes. A further development was the heavier Regency styles (roughly 1790–1830, corresponding to the French 'Empire' style) in which Egyptian and other exotic inspirations were added to close copies of Ancient Greece and Rome. There was also a Revived Rococo fashion (*c.*1820 onwards), typified by the Rockingham-style porcelain shapes of 1826–42.

BARUM WARE. Slip-decorated earthenware has been made over a very long period at Barnstaple (Latin name Barum), Devon. It became very popular when Queen Victoria bought some from Liberty & Co. in London. It may be in sgraffito decoration on white over brown, or in coloured slipware, or in high relief.

Some very decorative and ornate pieces have been produced from the nineteenth century onwards. Pieces are often incised 'C H Brannam. Barum', but other marks can occur.

An interesting account of these wares was published in 1982 entitled *A Family Business, the Story of a Pottery,* by Peter Brannam. (No publisher is given but the ISBN is 0-950824-70-4.)

BASALT WARE (*c.*1767 onwards). A fine black vitreous unglazed stoneware developed by Josiah Wedgwood I from the cruder 'Egyptian Black' made by many Staffordshire potters. It was ideal for the 'Etruscan'-style vases favoured by Wedgwood; these were often painted with red and/or white designs in the Greek classical tradition. It was also used for library busts, figures, plaques (with historical scenes in relief), tea-sets, mugs, inkstands, etc. Black basalt was copied by many other potters, notably by Neale and Spode (Plate 8). Wedgwood preferred the Latin form of the name 'basaltes'.

The old term 'Egyptian Black' was also used and vast quantities of Basalt or Egyptian Black useful wares, mainly teapots, covered sugar-basins, and creamers were produced well into the nineteenth century. These wares were easily produced from moulds and they needed no expensive painted decoration – they also met a good demand. Unfortunately, few specimens bear a maker's mark except for important specimens by the leading makers Wedgwood, Palmer, Neale, etc. These unmarked basalt useful wares are not expensive. A glazed shiny version was introduced in the 1830s, which is not now considered a success.

The standard (and expensive) book on the subject is M. H. Grant's *Makers of Black Basalt* (W. Blackwood & Sons, 1910). A new work including much new information is promised but in the meantime the reader may study Mrs P. A. Halfpenny's article 'Black Basalt Ware' published in *Antique Collecting*, April 1989. Most good general books on British pottery or on Wedgwood wares will also be helpful.

8   An impressed-marked SPODE oval teapot in the black basalt body. Most leading and many small firms produced such basalt wares from about 1790 onwards. 5¼in high. c.1795–1805.

BAT PRINTING. This technique for printing small-size delicate designs was much used in the 1800–40 period. Such prints may occur on fine porcelains as well as on less costly earthenwares.

   The name arises from the fact that a pliable glue-like bat or hand-size slab was used to transfer oil from the engraved (or etched) copper plate onto the object. The oil then held a finely-powdered pigment which was dusted onto the ware and the surplus cleaned away. A final firing fixed the colour onto the glaze. As oil rather than a thick colour pigment was used the designs could be finely worked on the copper, the lines and shading being mainly formed of small dots rather than straight lines. The result was a delicate picture. As the process did not require the heating of the charged copper plates, production costs were also reduced.

The Spode factory produced some extremely fine bat-printed designs, as the jug shown in Plate 9, but nearly every firm produced some bat-printed designs. For further information on the process the reader is referred to *Spode Printed Ware* by David Drakard and Paul Holdway (Longman, 1983).

9   A Spode bone china jug with good-quality bat-printed panels – a delightful and relatively inexpensive form of decoration. Unmarked. 6in high. c.1810–20.

THOMAS BAXTER (1782–1821). Thomas Baxter (junior) was one of the most celebrated ceramic artists in British ceramic history. Signed examples of his work in the approximate period 1800–10 were produced at his father's decorating studio at 1, Goldsmith Street, Gough Square, London, before this painter went to Worcester (*c.*1814). After his experiences there he moved to Swansea in the 1816–18 period. He had returned to Worcester where he was employed at the Chamberlain factory from at least July 1819. He died at Worcester in April 1821.

Baxter paintings in the London period from c.1800 to about 1814 comprise fine figure subjects, floral studies as well as superbly-painted shells and fruit compositions. These are mainly painted on Coalport blanks but his work can also occur on French and even on Chinese porcelains. It is probable that Thomas Baxter was also a gilder, indeed that he was an all-round decorator.

Baxter's signed work is rare and rightly costly but much other Baxter studio-decorated porcelain can be identified from the standard gilt borders employed, by the background designs or by the characteristic groups of tightly posed flowers (see Colour Plate I).

For further information the reader is referred to Geoffrey's Godden's three books: *Coalport & Coalbrookdale Porcelains* (Antique Collectors' Club, revised edition 1981); *Chamberlain-Worcester Porcelain, 1788–1852* (Barrie & Jenkins, 1982); or his *Encyclopaedia of British Porcelain Manufacturers* (Barrie & Jenkins, 1988).

BELLARMINES. Globular, handled Continental bottles or jugs in brown saltglaze stoneware; on the narrow neck is the mask of a bearded man. They were so named to deride the Italian Jesuit and future Cardinal, Bellarmine, whose theological teachings at Louvain University (1569–76) gravely upset Protestant Netherlands, but they descended in fact from a long line of masked bottles. Dwight of Fulham copied them but the English examples are far outnumbered by the imported examples. These originally utilitarian containers were not marked, but early examples in good condition are decorative and costly, especially the very rare pieces with armorial bearings added. Beware, however, of later reproductions.

An interesting article on Bellarmines written by Robin Hildyard of the Victoria & Albert Museum was published in *Antique Collecting*, September 1989.

BELLEEK WARE. The Belleek factory, Co. Fermanagh, Ireland, became famous for parian ware coated with an iridescent glaze resembling mother-of-pearl. Characteristic was the decorative use of marine motifs such as shells, seaweed, mermaids, dolphins, and coral, see Colour Plate II. Products included eggshell-thin tea services and openwork baskets with extremely fine flower incrustation made possible by the strength of the parian body. The basket shown in Plate 10 is typical of this characteristic class of Belleek glazed parian. These were made in various sizes and designs, over a long period. The pair of figures is uncommon but the other objects shown are characteristic.

Some doubt exists over the date of establishment of the factory, 1858 is often given but 1863 may be nearer reality. Certainly finished wares were shown at the 1865 Dublin Exhibition.

The factory has continued now for well over a hundred years and is still in production. The older examples in particular are very collectable and the rarer models quite costly. Most examples bear a clear printed trade mark. Examples including the wording 'Co Fermanagh Ireland' date from at least 1890 but from 1965 only the world 'Ireland' appears. The separate circular device with 'Deanta in Eirinn' occurs after about 1927. A ® appears as part of the trade mark from 1955.

Specialist books include Richard K. Degenhardt's *Belleek. The Complete Collector's Guide and Illustrated Reference* (Portfolio Press, USA, 1978). Details of the various marks are given in Geoffrey Godden's *Encyclopaedia of British Porcelain Manufacturers*. The price and desirability of a piece is very much dependent on the period of manufacture.

10 *A selection of typical Belleek porcelains, the marine forms are characteristic, the figures rare. Printed Belleek marks. Shell centrepiece 8¼in high. c.1885–1920.* **(Phillips)**.

BESWICK. One of a relatively new collecting class is Beswick ware which may be either china or fine earthenware. Many readers must be familiar with the well-modelled Beswick horses or other animal models. These are but a very small part of the large range of wares made by the firm of J. W. Beswick of Longton between *c.*1894 and 1920. Production of earthenware then continued under the style John Beswick or after 1938 as John Beswick Ltd. The china was produced by Beswick & Son(s) under the trade name 'Aldwych China'. The Beswick Company was taken over by Doulton & Co. Ltd in 1969 and production continues under the Beswick name.

The Beswick wares are decorative and reasonably inexpensive but not 'antique'. The standard book on the subject is *The Beswick Collectors Handbook* by Harvey May (Kevin Francis Publishing, 1986).

WILLIAM BILLINGSLEY (*c*.1785–1828). Porcelain decorator particularly famous for his roses. He introduced a naturalistic style of flower painting, using a heavily-loaded brush and then wiping out the highlights. Apprenticed to Derby, he later partnered Coke at Pinxton (*c*.1795–99) and worked at Worcester (1808) before founding the Nantgarw China Works (*c*.1813). He devoted much of his life to costly attempts to improve the quality of porcelain and eventually at Nantgarw and Swansea was able to manufacture the very white and highly translucent soft paste that won those factories renown, and the secret of which he seems to have handed on to Rose at Coalport. Nevertheless, he died poor.

Most books on Derby porcelain give an account of Billingsley's early work. The standard specialist work is W. D. John's *William Billingsley* (Ceramic Book Co., 1968). An outline of his very varied career is given in Geoffrey Godden's *Encyclopaedia of British Porcelain Manufacturers* (Barrie & Jenkins, 1988).

It should be noted that William Billingsley was not the only talented rose painter in the 1790–1810 period; all the major porcelain factories would have employed several trained flower painters. Billingsley also painted landscape designs and may have turned his hand to gilding.

BIN LABELS. Pottery bin labels came into use in the eighteenth century and are still used to identify sections of a well-stocked cellar. The earliest are in delftware; creamware labels made by Wedgwood and Spode are sometimes marked on the back. The vintage year is sometimes given, and there are some interesting names: 'Orange Shrub', 'Marcella' (presumably Marsala), and even 'Teneriffe'. The humbler drinks are not forgotten – there is one marked 'Elder Flower'. These ceramic labels are interesting rather than decorative but are quite rare and collectable.

BIRD-WHISTLES. Pottery birds with a whistle in the tail. One attractive form is a cuckoo in glistening yellowish glaze marbled with brown, and a hole in the breast that can be 'stopped' to produce a two-note call. A Yorkshire earthenware group has children under a treeful of bird whistles. Apparently it was an old Sussex custom to place a wind-operated bird-whistle on the chimney to scare hobgoblins. Various other forms of ceramic whistles were made; some porcelain examples are in the form of a dog's head.

BISCUIT. 1. A term of Italian origin (also 'bisque' when applied to Continental wares) applied to a stage in production when pottery or porcelain has been fired once and is still unglazed.

2. Specifically applied to wares (usually porcelain figures) sold in an unglazed (or only very slightly glazed) state. They were made from *c.*1750 at Vincennes in France (the future Sèvres) and other Continental factories, and in England at Derby from *c.*1773. The composition of the body and the firing temperature were most important in achieving the requisite, slightly matt surface, ivory-tinted at first and after *c.*1795 given a velvety feel by volatilizing a little glaze in the kiln. Very sharp modelling of detail was made possible by the absence of glaze. Most of the figures copied classical or contemporary sculpture; they were modelled at Derby by Stéphen, Spängler, and others. A typical example is shown in Plate 11.

11   A Derby classical group in biscuit porcelain, showing the sharp modelling, devoid of glaze. 13½in high. c.1785. **(Sotheby's).**

Chamberlain's Worcester, Minton, and some other early nine-teenth-century factories produced biscuit figures, animal models or small groups before the introduction of the parian body in the early 1840s superseded the white biscuit porcelain.

BLANC-DE-CHINE. The nineteenth-century French term for the Chinese white or near-white richly-glazed porcelain of great beauty which was made in the Fujian province. Buddhist figures were made, particularly of Kuanyin (Guanyin), the graceful goddess of mercy. Other useful wares were made, often with applied prunus blossom motifs in relief. These undecorated Chinese porcelains were extremely popular imports from the late seventeenth century onwards. The standard book is P. J. Donnelly's *Blanc de Chine* (Faber & Faber, 1969) but chapter 8 of Geoffrey Godden's *Oriental Export Market Porcelain* (Granada, 1979) is also helpful.

The popular Chinese white porcelains were much copied by the early Continental porcelain manufacturers and in England princi-pally at the Bow and Chelsea factories in the 1745–55 period. The English copies can be much more costly than the Chinese proto-types, especially in the case of marked Chelsea examples.

'BLIND EARL' PATTERN. A famous Worcester relief pattern of the 1760s, with moulded leaves and buds. It was reputedly named after an Earl of Coventry blinded in a hunting accident but this is dis-proved by the dates. A version can occur decorated only in under-glaze blue, but most examples have enamelled decoration and added sprays of flowers. The design has been produced over a long period up to modern times and other firms such as Minton have emulated the popular pattern. The same style has been reintro-duced by Royal Worcester in post-war years.

BLUE AND WHITE. A name given to porcelain or earthenware painted or printed underglaze in blue. The original purpose of this development in Europe was to emulate the Chinese blue and white ('Old Nankin') which flooded the eighteenth-century market for medium-price domestic wares, and pseudo-Chinese designs were extremely popular. The glaze protected patterns from damage by knife, fork, or spoon, and cobalt blue was, at first, the only colour that could be relied on to withstand the temperature required in the first firing before the piece was glazed and refired.

Blue-painted wares were produced by all eighteenth-century English porcelain factories (although Chelsea examples are very rare). All except Chelsea and perhaps Vauxhall also adopted blue transfer-printing, especially Worcester, Caughley, Derby, and Lowestoft.

Staffordshire earthenware potters were slow to take up painting in underglaze blue on a commercial scale. The best-selling 'Stafford-shire blue' owes its existence to Josiah Spode, who from *c*.1781 applied printed blue patterns successively to his creamware, pearlware, bone china and stone china with such success that Davenport, Wedgwood, and eventually hundreds of Staffordshire and other potters followed his example, but as most of it was unmarked early examples tend to be lumped together as 'Staffordshire blue'. Patterns were freely pirated and attribution of unmarked pieces is extremely difficult. The heyday of Staffordshire blue was 1800–25.

Blue and white is a vast subject. The early English porcelains such as Worcester tend to be very costly but are charming and highly collectable. Some of the later Liverpool examples are less expensive but lack the 'oomph' of Worcester. The standard book on our blue and white decorated porcelains is Dr Bernard Watney's masterpiece *English Blue and White Porcelain of the 18th Century* (Faber & Faber, revised edition 1973). The many Worcester blue patterns are illustrated in *Worcester Blue and White Porcelain 1751–1790* by L. Branyan, N. French, and J. Sandon (Barrie & Jenkins, revised edition 1989).

The blue and white earthenwares (except the tin-glazed Delft-type wares) are later than the porcelains but they are usually much less costly. Enormous amounts were produced by hundreds of firms over a long period. Relatively inexpensive blue-printed dinner services were made as standard products so that odd plates and dishes from such sets are now relatively common. Of course, some patterns are rare and the work of some firms is scarce, but in general there is no shortage of nineteenth-century blue-printed pottery, especially of Willow pattern type.

It must be remembered that by no means all blue and white is of British origin. Masses of Chinese and to a lesser degree Japanese porcelains have been pouring into the British Isles and into Europe from the eighteenth century onwards. These are of hard-paste porcelain and are hand-painted rather than printed – the earlier examples inspired our copies. Likewise much tin-glazed blue-painted pottery is of Continental origin.

Probably the most helpful of several books on the subject is A. Coysh and R. Henrywood's large *Dictionary of Blue & White Printed Pottery 1780–1880* (Antique Collectors' Club, 1982, vol. II, 1989) but on a more modest scale, Robert Copeland's book *Blue & White Transfer Printed Pottery* (Shire, 1982) is extremely helpful.

BOCAGE. The name given to the background of stylized leaves and flowers on some porcelain and pottery figures and groups (see Plate 12). In the early days of porcelain there had always to be some device to prop up a figure (otherwise it was liable to collapse in the firing). From the usual tree-trunk support Meissen developed the light bocage (French for 'grove', 'copse') which Bow, Chelsea, and later Derby turned into an elaborate arbour-like background. These old type bocages, however, appear on later copies also. The early nineteenth-century earthenware potters also tended to copy the porcelain makers' use of mock-trees to support the figures and to form an attractive backcloth.

12   *A gold anchor marked Chelsea porcelain candlestick group (one of a pair) with leaf and floral back-cloth or 'bocage'. 13½in high. c.1765.*

BOOTHS. Messrs Booth Ltd of Tunstall produced in the early years of the present century a good decorative range of reproductions of old Worcester and other porcelains in a refined white earthenware body, called 'Silicon China'.

The CB monogram mark which appears on some of these wares was registered in 1907. This can be taken for an old Worcester crescent mark but many other examples are unmarked or have had the Booth mark erased or covered. These earthenwares are of good quality and are decorative and collectable in their own right – but not as genuine Worcester or Chelsea.

We illustrate a typical bowl (Plate 13) and the monogram device. Further details are given in Geoffrey Godden's *Encyclopaedia of British Porcelain Manufacturers* (Barrie & Jenkins, 1988).

13   A Booth earthenware bowl decorated in the manner of an eighteenth-century porcelain example. Diameter 8½in. c.1910.

BOOT-WARMER. An astonishing mid-Victorian item, shaped like a boot, which can be filled with hot water and placed inside a boot to warm it. They are found in 'Rockingham'-glazed pottery. These should not be confused with smaller shoe-shaped ornaments, trinkets or inkpots of this popular form.

CHARLES BOURNE. This Staffordshire earthenware potter of The Foley (Fenton) produced in the approximate period 1817–30 a range of very good quality porcelains, rather in the Spode manner. His earthenwares have not as yet been identified.

Most Charles Bourne porcelain examples (but not all) bear the pattern number expressed under the initials 'C B', as shown in Plate 14.

These Charles Bourne porcelains which include ornamental items as well as tea and dessert wares are very collectable. An assortment of typical specimens is shown in Plate 15.

For further information the reader is referred to *Staffordshire Porcelain* (Granada, 1983), chapter 16.

14   *A Charles Bourne bone china spill vase showing the initials 'CB' written over the pattern number in a typical manner. 5in high. c.1825.*

15 *A selection of Charles Bourne's high-quality bone china, each piece marked with 'CB' usually written above the pattern number. Diameter of plates 9in. c.1820–30.*

BOW (*c*.1748–76). Bow, in what is now east London, probably started as a small workshop where Thomas Frye, with others, experimented on various ingredients to find a porcelain body competitive with Chinese imports. If its existence is dated from his first patent (December 1744), Bow preceded Chelsea, but there is no firm evidence of commercial production until 1748 and the factory did not really get going until after Frye's second patent (November 1749) for a porcelain which included calcined bone. Bow remained innovatory to the end; its vast output varied greatly in quality and appearance, making identification at times difficult, the only constant being the high bone-ash ('phosphatic') content. The glaze, often laid on thickly, varying from greyish to bluish, reached its best in a soft creamy colour (*c*.1750). The porcelain, often thickly potted, was heavy and not very translucent.

16   *A pair of Bow porcelain Harlequin and Columbine figures, with typical floral boc-age. 6½in high. c.1760.* **(Christie's).**

Bow at first copied its designs from Chinese and Japanese wares and to underline this point the concern was called 'New Canton'. It concentrated consistently on durable tablewares which probably undercut Chelsea's in price; from 1750, figures became the other mainstay. During the first decade much of the tableware was undecorated with only applied white sprigs in the style of Chinese 'blanc de Chine' imports. Tea-sets were a speciality, especially those decorated in underglaze blue with mock Chinese designs. Enamelled wares were also produced. Octagonal plates and bell-shaped mugs were especially typical of Bow.

The early figures, modelled by the so-called 'Muses Modeller' (1750–4), are mostly on plain bases and designed to be left white – hence the exaggeration of the eyebrows, open mouth, and garment folds which are his hallmarks; they include actors in popular roles (Garrick, Peg Woffington, etc.). In general Bow went its own way and many of its figures break with the mainstream Meissen-Chelsea tradition of courtly sophistication. From c.1754, bases evolved from plain to increasingly rococo styles and finally the elaborately scrolled four-footed base with frontal swag typical from c.1760 to the end, the later Neo-Classical vogue being ignored; this adherence to the rococo long after it had become unfashionable may have contributed to Bow's downfall. The figures themselves were increasingly boldly, even garishly, coloured. Square holes at the back of the base for metal accessories (flower-holders, candle sockets) are a Bow feature.

The later 1750s saw more ornate wares: partridge tureens; animal and bird figures (dogs, hares, owls, hens); Meissen-style sprigs and insects; and the typical Kakiemon quail pattern. Some of these developments are attributed to an influx of Chelsea artists at the close of its Red Anchor period. As elsewhere, more elaboration and more gilding marked a general decline in taste, though some excellent pieces were still made, e.g. plates painted with Fragonard or Boucher themes; some seems to have been decorated elsewhere, in a palette in which light blue and crimson predominated. The factory was probably bought by William Duesbury of Derby in about 1776, but no evidence has been found to prove this.

An anchor and dagger device usually painted in red occur on some late examples of the 1760s or 1770s. Such pieces have sometimes been attributed to James Giles's London decorating establishment, though this seems doubtful.

For further information on the highly-regarded Bow porcelains the reader is referred to modern works such as E. Adams and D. Redstone's *Bow Porcelain* (Faber & Faber, 1981) or A. Gabszewicz and G. Freeman's *Bow Porcelain – the Collection formed by Geoffrey Freeman* (Lund Humphries, 1982). Most standard general reference books will also illustrate some typical Bow porcelains.

BRISTOL. Bristol, a thriving port, was also one of the many centres of the ceramic industry. Tin-glazed (Delft-type) earthenwares, porcelains, and stonewares were all made here at various periods.

The earliest Bristol porcelains are called 'Lund's Bristol' (q.v.) and were produced c.1749–51 by Benjamin Lund and William Miller. Examples are very rare and occasionally bear the relief-moulded mark 'Bristol'. The Worcester Company was formed in 1751 to buy up the Bristol manufactory. These scarce early Bristol porcelains were probably only decorated in underglaze blue with some white, undecorated examples. Present thoughts are that no overglaze enamel decoration was undertaken at Bristol in this first period. The mix, like the later related Worcester porcelains, contains soaprock.

For illustrations of typical examples and for historic background information the reader is referred to Franklin A. Barrett's *Worcester Porcelain and Lund's Bristol* (Faber & Faber, 1966 edition), to Dr Bernard Watney's standard book *English Blue & White Porcelain of the 18th Century* (Faber & Faber, revised edition 1973), to Henry Sandon's *Worcester Porcelain 1751–1793* (Barrie & Jenkins, London, 1980). Also Geoffrey Godden's *Eighteenth-century English Porcelain* (Granada, 1985) may prove helpful.

The second period of Bristol porcelain manufacture was commenced in the early 1770s when William Cookworthy moved to that city from Plymouth (q.v.). Cookworthy had patented his hard-paste porcelain mix and these Bristol porcelains of the approximate period 1772–81 are of this type.

William Cookworthy handed over management and sold his patent to Richard Champion, a shrewder businessman and a fellow Quaker. A complete change in style (to 'near-Dresden') is indicated in a November 1772 advertisement; the hard-paste porcelain was improved, better artists were employed, and Sèvres-style Neo-Classical decoration replaced rococo. Champion concentrated chiefly on tea and coffee sets (see Plate 17), including some expensive commissioned armorial services. More figures were made, but these are

17 *A selection of Bristol hard-paste table porcelains decorated in typical styles. Mock Dresden crossed-swords mark on coffee-pot. 7½in high. c.1770–80.* **(Victoria & Albert Museum).**

generally regarded as rather coarsely modelled and stiff. A Champion speciality was miniature oval biscuit plaques, modelled in relief with armorial bearings, portraits, flowers, or classical figures, framed and sold or given to influential friends. These are now extremely rare.

Champion's high ambitions were partly based on the potentialities of a market in the American colonies; the Revolution and the capture of his ships by the French were severe blows and, together with costly litigation over the extension of his patent (opposed by Wedgwood) and competition from newcomers such as Caughley in addition to older rivals such as Worcester and Derby, led to losses. Champion therefore sold his patent in 1781 to the group of Staffordshire potters who were to found the partnership later known as the New Hall Company, at Shelton in the Staffordshire Potteries.

Various, rather scarce, specialist books show a good range of Bristol porcelains, such as F. Severne MacKenna's *Champion's Bristol Porcelain* (F. Lewis, 1947) but representative examples are featured in general modern reference books such as Geoffrey Godden's *Encyclopaedia of British Porcelain Manufacturers* (Barrie & Jenkins, 1988).

The earthenwares are featured in rather older works, such as Hugh Owen's *Two Centuries of Potting at Bristol* (Bell & Daldy, 1873) and W. J. Pountney's *Old Bristol Potteries* (J. W. Arrowsmith, 1920). The tin-glazed earthenwares are well covered by Frank Britton in his book *English Delftware in the Bristol Collection* (Sotheby's Publications, 1982). The excellent local museum and art gallery has a good display of the products.

BROWNWARE. Saltglazed brown stoneware of the kind made since the seventeenth century in Nottingham, Derbyshire, London, and elsewhere. The colour might be brown, buff, or chocolate, and the decoration carved or with impressed designs. Brownware was used in making countless Posset-pots, loving cups, Toby jugs, candlesticks, figures, and the wares mentioned under Stoneware and Nottingham Ware. A favourite form was the hunting jug (and the similar mugs) bearing well-executed hunting scenes in relief. The reader is referred to *English Brown Stoneware 1670–1900* by A. Oswald, R. J. C. Hildyard and R. G. Hughes (Faber & Faber, 1982) and to the very comprehensive 1985 Victoria & Albert Museum exhibition catalogue *Browne Muggs, English Brown Stoneware* by Robin Hildyard.

WILLIAM BROWNFIELD (& SONS). In November 1850 William Brownfield set up his own Pottery at Cobridge in the Staffordshire Potteries, in succession to Wood & Brownfield. From 1850 to 1871 he produced a wide range of good quality earthenwares and was especially known for his many relief-moulded ornamental jugs, such as that shown in Plate 18.

In 1871 he added porcelains to the range of products and some very fine quality pieces were produced. In 1876 '& Sons' was added to the style. The Brownfield's Guild Pottery Society continued from 1892 to 1900.

The varied and often underrated Brownfield wares often bear 'W.B.' or 'W.B & S.' initial marks or the name in full. For further details the reader is referred to *Staffordshire Porcelain* or to Geoffrey Godden's *Encyclopaedia of British Porcelain Manufacturers* (Barrie & Jenkins, 1988).

18 A typical William Brownfield earthenware jug. One of hundreds of different moulded designs. Registration mark for April 1856. 8½in high. 1856–9.

BROWN-WESTHEAD, MOORE & CO. This firm occupied the celebrated Cauldon Place Works at Hanley in the 1861–1904 period, in succession to John & William Ridgway, 1814–30; John Ridgway (& Co.) c.1830–55; J. Ridgway, Bates & Co., c.1856–58; and Bates, Brown-Westhead, Moore & Co., c.1858–61.

The new partnership continued the very high standard achieved by the previous firms and some first-rate porcelains were produced. These are mainly unmarked, especially before about 1880, but the letter prefixes to the pattern numbers are helpful guides. The porcelains are featured in Geoffrey Godden's *Staffordshire Porcelain* (Granada, 1983) and in the *Encyclopaedia of British Porcelain Manufacturers* (Barrie & Jenkins, 1988).

A wide range of earthenwares, stonewares, and even majolica-type wares was also produced. Leading artists and designers were employed and even the inexpensive printed earthenwares can be novel and attractive. The various marks either incorporate the names in full or the initials B W M & Co.

19 *A Brown-Westhead, Moore & Co. bone china plate of a form registered in February 1870. Printed registration mark. Diameter 8½in. c.1870.*

C. The reader will often come across a small 'c' placed in front of a date or dates in reference books, catalogues, or on descriptive labels. This initial in this context is an abbreviation for the Latin word *circa*, 'about', indicating an approximate, rather than a precise date of manufacture.

It is reasonable to use a description '*c*.1810' or '*c*.1810–15' when the limits are within a few years, but sometimes the abbreviation is used to give a rather unlikely early dating to give a false enhanced importance or value to a specimen. The description '*c*.1810' used on an object that was really made in the 1830s or 1840s is misleading, at best. The writer has even seen the meaningless description '*c*.19th century'! It might be more accurate if the letter 'h' was used, meaning 'hopefully'!

CADOGAN TEAPOT. A lidless teapot filled through a hole in the base which was the end of a spiral tube reaching to near the top of the pot. It was so called after the Hon. Mrs Cadogan who commissioned the Rockingham pottery to make a teapot in imitation of a Chinese peach-shaped wine-pot she admired. Cadogans reputedly became a vogue (when the Prince Regent started drinking wine from them) and were also made by Davenport, Copeland, and others, often covered with the characteristic 'Rockingham' purplish-brown glaze. A typical example is shown in Plate 20.

20 *A typical shape 'Cadogan' teapot, with a so-called Rockingham all-over glaze. 7in high. c.1830–40.*

CANDLE SNUFFERS. See Extinguishers.

CANDLESTICKS. Bow, Chelsea, and Derby made some very elaborate porcelain candlesticks with animals or figures holding up flower-shaped sockets, the sepals forming the necessary grease-pans (see Plate 12). Others might be shaped much like silver models, but flower-encrusted, and there were also some very austere Neo-Classical models in creamware. Bow figures might have square sockets at the back to take branched metal candelabra. The chief uses were for the dining-table, dressing-table, and desk.

The chamber candlestick, to light the way to bed, could also be a very delicate concoction of flower encrustation. The taperstick was shorter, with a narrow socket, and could be used at the desk for sealing letters, or brought in with the tea service, partly to give light but mainly for its perfumed beeswax. These are very small and often very decorative and collectable (see Plate 21).

21   *A Coalbrookdale-type chamber candlestick with carrying handle and housing for the separate candle extinguisher. 3½in high. c.1825–35.*

CANE (AND BAMBOO) WARE (*c*.1785 into the nineteenth century). Wedgwood perfected the tan-coloured stoneware in the mid 1780s. It is usually decorated in relief and sometimes further embellished with touches of blue, green, or red. Wares shaped and coloured as if made of sections of bamboo were called Bamboo ware. Tea wares, jugs, pot-pourri bowls, bulb-pots, candlesticks, etc. were made; also imitation 'pie-crust' covers and dishes when flour was in short supply during the Napoleonic Wars.

This unglazed body usually displays the potters' skills to perfection, the turning, moulding etc. Most of the leading late eighteenth-century and early nineteenth-century Staffordshire potters produced good quality cane ware, which in general tends to be under-appreciated and is relatively inexpensive when compared to similar articles in Jasper or Basalt.

CARLTON WARE. Wiltshaw & Robinson (Ltd) of the Carlton Works at Stoke produced a very decorative range of high grade earthenware under this trade-name in the 1920s and 1930s. Some of these wares based on earlier shapes and styles are particularly fine (see Plate 22). The firm was retitled Carlton Ware Ltd in January 1958.

CARPET BALLS. Earthenware (or rarely stoneware) balls for a Victorian game of bowls played preferably in a carpeted corridor. A full set consisted of one plain ball and six with coloured rings or other identifying patterns. These may be very decorative displayed in a shallow bowl.

Such objects were made by the smaller firms, especially those engaged in the inexpensive figure trade. A Kent & Parr (c.1880–94) advertisement in *The Pottery Gazette Diary* of 1882, for example, lists 'Carpet balls, number balls, Marbles, Painted and clay, all sizes, &c. &c.', amongst Staffordshire dogs, figures, hens, and suchlike, with a note 'Special Attention to Carpet Balls and Nest Eggs for export'.

CASTLEFORD (c.1790–1821). A South Yorkshire factory near Leeds founded by David Dunderdale, who had been apprenticed at Leeds Pottery; best known for its fine white scantily-glazed stoneware teapots, often with panels outlined in blue, and with moulded reliefs. A very few are marked 'D Dunderdale': similar teapots, some marked '22', were made by other (perhaps Staffordshire) potters. The lids may be sliding or hinged rather than the usual sit-on type.

Castleford, however, produced much else; other teaware in the same thin semi-translucent felspathic stoneware; good creamware, much of it exported; transfer-printed earthenware in blue or brown; some black basalt; large jugs with a wide dark brown collar and classical reliefs. As so little is marked, 'Castleford' is more a generic than a specific name.

See Godden's *An Illustrated Encyclopaedia of British Pottery & Porcelain*, Plates 256–7 and the specialist work *The Castleford Pottery 1790–1821* by Diana Roussel (Wakefield Historical Publications, 1982).

CASTLE HEDINGHAM (c.1870–1905). Essex art pottery making fantastically designed teapots, urns, 'Essex jugs', etc. in pottery which chipped easily. The relief mark is a castle, usually with the name of the potter Edward Bingham. Typical wares and a photograph of Bingham are shown in Geoffrey Godden's *An Illustrated Encyclopaedia of British Pottery & Porcelain*, Plates 53–6.

22   *A decorative 'Carlton Ware' fine-quality earthenware 'Persian' styled vase by Wiltshire & Robinson. Printed W & R mark. 11¼in high. c.1930.*

CAUGHLEY (1775–99). A Shropshire porcelain factory (pronounced calf'ly) established near Broseley and Coalport by Thomas Turner; its wares are sometimes called (and marked) 'Salopian'. Turner had reputedly learned engraving at Worcester under Robert Hancock. This Thomas Turner should not be confused with the Staffordshire potter John Turner. The new factory used the same type of soapstone body as Worcester (Davis/Flight period) and copied many of their printed patterns. The tradition that porcelain from the main

Worcester factory was decorated at Caughley seems unfounded; but much Caughley was sold to, and some decorated by, the separate Worcester firm of Chamberlain.

Many patterns are Chinese-style landscapes printed or painted in underglaze blue, but those with disguised Chinese numeral style marks have been shown to be Worcester. Some of the designs used by both factories are distinguishable by differences of detail, e.g. the fishing line in the 'Fisherman' pattern (see Plate 23) is taut on Caughley, slack on Worcester; the familiar cabbage-leaf mask-jugs have the eyes of the face-mask open on Caughley, closed on Worcester; the filled-in or shaded crescent mark is usually (perhaps always) Worcester. The initial 'C' with a clear serif is a standard Caughley mark. Gilding is found on Chinese-style printed designs and underglaze blue-painted European landscapes or floral sprays; some of the overglaze enamel and gilt decoration seems to be the work of Chamberlain or London decorators. A print of the world's first iron bridge (1779) at neighbouring Coalbrookdale is found on some rare Caughley (and later Coalport) porcelains.

23   A typical Caughley teapot and stand decorated with the underglaze blue printed Fisherman pattern – a design by no means unique to Caughley. Impressed 'Salopian' mark on stand. Teapot 5¾in high. c.1780–5.

Defeated by ill-health, and competition from bone china and Staffordshire blue-printed earthenwares, Turner sold the factory to his former apprentice, John Rose (see Coalport) in 1799. Possibly during Turner's last few years, and certainly under Rose, hard-paste porcelain was made at Caughley and is provisionally termed Caughley/ Coalport hybrid hard-paste.

Contrary to old thinking, much Caughley porcelain and its decoration is of very high quality, often as good or better than Worcester of the same, rather late, period. Note also that many of the shapes and patterns are unique to Caughley, not all by any means were mere copies of Worcester wares.

For further information see Geoffrey Godden's standard book *Caughley and Worcester Porcelain, 1775–1800* (Antique Collectors' Club, revised edition 1981) or the same author's general work *Encyclopaedia of British Porcelain Manufacturers* (Barrie & Jenkins, 1988).

CAULDON LTD. Many good quality post-1905 earthenwares and fine porcelains bear the name Cauldon. Messrs Cauldon Ltd succeeded Brown-Westhead, Moore & Co. at the famous Cauldon Place Works at Hanley in 1905 and continued the high standards of earlier firms. In 1920 the company was retitled Cauldon Potteries Ltd. In 1962 the earthenware side was acquired by Pountney & Co. Ltd and later by the Perks Ceramic Group. The porcelain side of Cauldon was acquired by E. W. Brain & Co. Ltd, later Coalport China Ltd, and now part of the Wedgwood group.

CHAMBERLAIN'S WORCESTER (c.1788–1852). A breakaway firm founded on the site of the present Royal Worcester Porcelain Co. by Robert Chamberlain, after Flight bought the main Worcester factory; Chamberlain had reputedly been Dr Wall's first apprentice. At first Chamberlain decorated wares bought, usually in the white, from Caughley. In about 1791 Chamberlain began making his own porcelain, at first a compact hybrid hard-paste body. The porcelain and the decoration had so greatly improved by 1800 as to constitute a threat to the main Worcester firm, which was absorbed in 1840 (and styled 'Chamberlain & Co') the better to meet rivalry from Staffordshire bone china. Wares were in many ways similar to those of Flight & Barr. Thomas Baxter decorated for both, and several Flight artists joined Chamberlain, whose son also painted some superb pieces. In addition a very fine porcelain ('Regent china') was developed in 1811.

From 1840 there were financial troubles and unsuccessful experiments which led to the management being taken over by Kerr & Binns (1852–62). New artists and ideas were introduced, e.g. Renaissance-style designs painted in white enamel on deep blue grounds ('Limoges enameis'), which suited contemporary taste. Kerr retired and Binns was left to form a new company, parent of today's Royal Worcester Porcelain Co.

The full, long story of Chamberlain's factory, porcelains, decorators, and a list of nearly five thousand patterns is given in Geoffrey Godden's standard work *Chamberlain-Worcester Porcelain, 1788–1852* (Barrie & Jenkins, 1982).

CHELSEA (*c.*1744–69). It is uncertain whether Chelsea or Bow was the earliest English porcelain factory; Chelsea is generally more highly esteemed and offered a wider range of forms, but quality varied. Founded by a Flemish silversmith, Nicholas Sprimont, and relying heavily for its figures on another Fleming, Joseph Willems,

24 *An early Chelsea cream or milk jug of typical leaf form. Incised triangle mark. 5in high. c.1745–9.* **(Sotheby's).**

Chelsea alone aimed at the luxury market tapped by Meissen and Sèvres, usually imitating the former until Sèvres became dominant in the 'Gold Anchor' period c.1756–69. By contrast Bow was chiefly influenced by Oriental designs.

The marks used divide Chelsea into brief but indeterminate periods: Triangle (c.1745–9), Raised Anchor (to 1752), Red Anchor (to 1756) and Gold Anchor (1756–69). These dates are approximate only and some overlap of use may have occurred. It is said that genuine Chelsea is outnumbered by reproductions (e.g. Coalport, Minton) and fakes (especially Samson's hard-paste examples with oversize gold anchors). Table-wares predominated; but very little blue and white was made.

The first paste was a milk-white, translucent glassy frit, with a soft glaze. The body was prone to warping and 'pinholes' or 'moons', seen when held to the light, are characteristic. Triangle products were mostly tea and coffee sets, with moulded decoration (as Plate 24) or 'raised' flowers; painted sprigs and insects often concealed defects. One of the earliest (and often reproduced) models is the famous Goat and Bee jug.

The typical Raised Anchor period body was less glassy, slightly greyish, and had an opaque look due to tin in a glaze often so thick that it formed pools. The stronger paste permitted elaborate figures and groups to be made; enamelled birds are especially attractive but extremely rare.

Red Anchor marked wares are highly prized; the small anchor mark is often difficult to spot. Translucency was good; moons continued; spur or stilt marks (three or more small blemishes) are found under plates, as in the next period. Characteristic products are sparsely-decorated moulded plates and leaf-shaped dishes; tureens in the form of hen and chickens, other birds, animals, fish, or vegetables; a wide range of figures (Plate 25) was made – peasants and the best Chelsea classical figures – some to be used as flower-holders, candlesticks, or sweetmeat stands.

The Gold Anchor period was characterized by Sèvres rococo styles; increasingly elaborate form and decoration, especially mercury gilding; and richly coloured grounds, notably turquoise, claret, and several blues. Bocages were much used but figures in general are inferior to the less ornate Red Anchor examples. Wares were thickly potted in a bone-ash paste; the glaze tended to craze.

The Chelsea factory specialized in charming toys – seals, scent-bottles, and suchlike small, delicate feminine objects.

Although the various periods of Chelsea's production are known by the type of mark used, it must be remembered that much of the porcelain was unmarked and that some marks – especially the gold anchor – have been extensively faked. Beware of an anchor over a quarter of an inch in height.

The most up-to-date specialist book is Mrs Elizabeth Adams's *Chelsea Porcelain* (Barrie & Jenkins, 1987). See Plates 12, 24–5 and 54 of the present book for other illustrations.

25 *An attractive Chelsea Italian Comedy figure. Small red painted anchor mark. 6¼in. c.1750.* **(Sotheby's).**

CHELSEA-DERBY (1770–84). The name generally applied to wares made at Chelsea after William Duesbury of Derby bought Sprimont's Chelsea factory in 1770. It is often difficult to tell if the porcelains were made at the Chelsea works or at Derby. The Chelsea gold anchor was continued and sometimes this appears with a large cursive 'D'. Various mutually contradictory criteria have been suggested, but it appears that the factories (Chelsea and Derby) exchanged both raw materials and undecorated pieces, making them to all intents and purposes a single producer.

The Chelsea-Derby wares are characterized by a thinly potted bone-ash body and craze-free glaze, both an improvement on Gold Anchor. Restraint in style (except gilding) was restored with the coming of Neo-Classical fashions. The Chelsea factory was closed in 1784 and the moulds and other working materials sent to Derby.

The so-called Chelsea-Derby porcelains can be most attractive but they are in general rather neglected by collectors. Typical examples are featured in Geoffrey Godden's *Eighteenth-century English Porcelain* (Granada, 1985), Plates 153–7 and his *Encyclopaedia of British Porcelain Manufacturers* (Barrie & Jenkins, 1988), Plates 106–8.

CHILDREN'S PLATES. Small earthenware plates, some octagonal, with transfer-printed scenes etc., often with an embossed border and a title or text. Some subjects were purely decorative (birds, flowers, children's games), others educational (alphabetical borders, Biblical scenes, pious texts, nursery rhymes).

These originally low-cost plates were made mostly between 1830 and 1850 in the Staffordshire Potteries, Sunderland, Wales (as Plate 26), and Scotland. These often charming plates are very collectable and sometimes bear the marks of little-known makers.

26   *A pair of Swansea earthenware children's plates of typical small size. Impressed mark. Baker Bevans & Irwin. Diameter 4½in. c.1825–35.*

CHINA GLAZE. A term used in late eighteenth-century directories for a type of earthenware. Typical entries from William Tunnicliffe's *Survey of the County of Stafford* of *c.*1787 include: 'William Adams & Co. Manufacturers of cream coloured Ware and China glazed Ware painted'; 'Bourne & Malkin. Manufacturers of China glazed, blue, and cream colour Ware'; 'John Robinson. Enameller and Printer of Cream colour and China glazed Ware'; 'Ambrose Smith & Co. Manufacturers of Cream coloured Ware and China glazed Ware painted Blue'; 'Thomas Wedgwood. Manufacturer of Cream coloured Ware and China glazed Ware, painted with Blue &c'.

It is therefore clear that the wares referred to were not the standard cream coloured earthenwares, yet the 'China glazed' objects were popular and of a general type, often decorated in underglaze blue.

It is thought that the term 'China glaze' referred to what we now call 'Pearl Ware', a creamware-type mix made to appear white by the addition of a glaze slightly tinted blue. This type of earthenware was seemingly in production by at least 1775.

For further information see *Creamware & Pearlware,* the catalogue of the 5th Northern Ceramic Society exhibition held at Stoke-on-Trent City Museum & Art Gallery in 1986. Terry Lockett's chapter 'The Later Creamwares and Pearlwares' discusses this problem and refers to the American authorities who first discussed the meaning of the old term, notably the researches of George L. Miller.

CHINESE LOWESTOFT. An old name for eighteenth-century Chinese hard-paste export market wares, once mistakenly thought to hail from Lowestoft. Vast quantities were shipped to Europe and, although the myth that they had any connection with Lowestoft was exploded long ago, some Chinese hard-paste export market porcelain is still described as 'Lowestoft'. Chinese porcelain decorated with armorial bearings is still called 'Armorial Lowestoft' in error.

The true English soft-paste Lowestoft porcelains of the 1757–99 period are discussed in Geoffrey Godden's *Lowestoft Porcelains* (Antique Collectors' Club, revised edition 1985), the Chinese imports in his *Oriental Export Market Porcelain* (Granada, 1979).

CHINOISERIE. The name given to Chinese-styled European designs such as 'Chinese Chippendale' and lacquered furniture decorated with mock Chinese scenes. In ceramics, the vogue had reached Meissen and French porcelain centres by 1725 and in the 1740s and 1750s came to Chelsea, Bow (which called itself 'New Canton'), Worcester (the 'Tonquin' Company), and the Vauxhall factory. Other sources were Dutch Delftware (an influence on blue-and-white), the chinoiserie paintings of Watteau and Boucher, among others, and travel-book engravings.

Chinoiserie features ranged from Long Elizas to particular flowers (chrysanthemum, prunus, paeony). Especially striking among polychrome designs are the Ho-ho-bird, said to be the phoenix; the hermaphrodite Kylin with dragon head and not very deer-like scaly body; and the Dog of Fo, a temple guard-dog breathing out fire in all directions through its fearsome teeth.

The taste for chinoiserie succumbed on the Continent before the Neo-Clasical onslaught, but in England it has lingered on, increasingly mixed up with japonaiserie. The early chinoiserie designs on ceramics can be delightful and amusing, if costly.

CHOCOLATE CUPS. 'Jocalatte', as Pepys called it, was at first more popular than tea, and was drunk at breakfast or in coffee houses. Chocolate pots were generally smaller than coffee pots and sometimes followed the silver shape in having the handle at right angles to the spout (a feature later transferred to coffee pots). The cups were often elaborate, resembling caudle cups. They were generally larger than tea or coffee cups. In general the vogue for chocolate had declined by the 1780s.

CLARICE CLIFF (1899–1972). The mass-produced Art Deco-style earthenwares introduced by Miss Clarice Cliff in the 1920s have returned to favour in recent years. Once the standard hand-painted patterns on tablewares were very inexpensive; now rare shapes or patterns can command hundreds of pounds, and in some cases thousands. This, however, is far from true for the normal run of wares which so many people purchased new in the 1920s and 1930s – it was colourful and novel, attractions that still hold good today.

Clarice Cliff was the designer of the shapes and added decoration but did not paint ware herself. There was a large team of lady painters working to reproduce the broadly painted patterns.

Recent specialist books on the earthenwares produced by Messrs A. J. Wilkinson at Burslem include *Clarice Cliff* by P. Wentworth-Sheilds and Kay Johnson (L'Odeon, 1976) and *Collecting Clarice Cliff* by H. Watson (Kevin Francis Publishing, 1988). In addition, Judy Spours's *Art Deco Tableware* (Ward Lock, 1988) is helpful and shows how other firms sought to emulate the Clarice Cliff styles.

There is also a Clarice Cliff Collectors Club – write to Fantasque House, Tennis Drive, The Park, Nottingham, NG7 1AE for details.

CLOBBERED. A derogatory adjective for blue and white underglaze painted or printed wares which a faker has tried to make look richer, and therefore more valuable, by adding enamel colours, usually in execrable taste in reds, greens, yellows, and gilding. The practice goes back to the early nineteenth century.

27 An eighteenth-century Worcester vase painted in underglaze blue but with later (nineteenth-century) 'clobbering' – the addition of overglaze enamels and gilding in an effort to make the piece more saleable. The reverse was the result and such pieces are now disliked. Vase 6½in high.

This term is sometimes incorrectly applied to the Imari-type designs so popular in the 1720–60 period, where underglaze blue was used in conjunction with overglaze enamels to complete the design. With the later clobbering the blue design was complete before later attempts were made to enhance(!) the piece. The Worcester vase shown in Plate 27 was originally only decorated in underglaze blue. Probably in the nineteenth century the excessive enamels and gilding were applied, making it a typical case of clobbering.

COALBROOKDALE. A synonym for nineteenth-century English flower-encrusted bone china (c.1820–60), a 'revived rococo' fashion inspired by the floral encrusted Dresden porcelains. In the best specimens each applied flower has individually moulded and naturalistically coloured thin petals and leaves; there was a later descent to mass-moulded work. A great range of flowers was copied, from tiny forget-me-nots to inch-wide roses. Favourite wares were scent bottles, pierced edge baskets with fruit and flowers in full relief, pot-pourris, pastille-burners, candlesticks, trays, spill and other vases (Colour Plate III).

They were made by Minton, Rockingham, Coalport, Bloor Derby, Grainger's Worcester, Davenport, and Spode, to name only the larger firms. Such Dresden-style floral encrusted wares often bear a mock cross-swords device in blue or abbreviations for Coalbrookdale – 'C.D.', 'C. Dale', etc.

For further information and illustrations of typical examples see Geoffrey Godden's *Coalport & Coalbrookdale Porcelains* (Antique Collectors' Club, revised edition 1981).

COALPORT (c.1796–present day). A Shropshire factory founded by John Rose, it was sited on the east bank of the Severn opposite Jackfield. In the period prior to c.1811 hybrid hard-paste porcelain was made. There is a tradition that in 1820 Rose ended competition from Nantgarw and Swansea by buying their equipment and moulds and engaging Billingsley and Walker to come to Coalport. An 1860s factory mark incorporated the initials C, N, S, standing for these three factories, but there remains considerable doubt about the terms of any agreement with the two latter. The last of the Rose family retired in 1862, and the firm moved in 1926 to the Staffordshire Potteries, where Coalport continues to this day as part of the Wedgwood group.

Coalport's best period opened in about 1820 with the introduction of a brilliantly white and very translucent felspar china and a new leadless glaze. Thereafter the factory became, as it remains, famous for high-quality tablewares with distinctive ground colours, e.g. maroon, *gros bleu*, several greens, the Sèvres *rose pompadour*, and a dark underglaze blue. Also notable were ornamental wares made to suit the revised fashion for rococo (1820–40), including flower-encrusted Coalbrookdale pieces; parian figures (1850s); and copies (some with faked marks) of Chelsea (including the Goat and Bee jug), Meissen and, from about 1840, very decorative Sèvres-type and shapes.

Although most collectors think only of John Rose (& Co.) when speaking of Coalport there were, in the *c.*1800–14 period, two distinct factories, one situated on each side of the narrow canal. The short-lived one was owned by Reynolds, Horton & Rose (*c.*1800–3) and then by Anstice Horton & Rose (*c.*1803–14). Both firm's products are featured in Geoffrey Godden's specialist book *Coalport & Coalbrookdale Porcelain* (Antique Collectors' Club, revised edition 1981) or his *Encyclopaedia of British Porcelain Manufacturers* (Barrie & Jenkins, 1988).

COFFEE CANS. Straight-sided coffee cups or 'cans' were very fashionable in England particularly in the period *c.*1800–20. All, or most, porcelain manufacturers included such coffee cans in their services as a standard form, the fashion having crossed from the Continent.

These cans are very collectable and examples can be found with a very large range of added patterns. The handle form will change from manufacturer to manufacturer. The examples here shown as Plate 28 are a small selection of Spode.

Standard reference books on each factory will illustrate that firm's basic characteristics. The reader is further recommended to consult Michael Berthoud's book *An Anthology of British Cups* (Micawber, 1982).

COMFIT-HOLDERS. Pairs of porcelain figures holding small baskets, bowls, or shells in which were placed tiny sugared breath-sweeteners – Shakespeare's 'kissing-comfit' – for use after drinking, smoking, or eating far-from-fresh meats. Made of aniseed, celery, coriander, caraway, etc., these comfits ('confections') were thus the precursors of today's chlorophyll cachous. The comfit-holders – traditional shepherdesses, Turks, gardeners, etc. – were part of the elaborate decoration of the eighteenth-century dessert table. They were made well on into the nineteenth century by most of the leading porcelain factories, but mainly in imitation of earlier styles.

COMMEMORATIVE CHINA. Strictly, this term is confined to pieces which commemorate an event within a short time after its occurrence; this definition rules out, e.g. Waterloo replicas issued at Wellington's death and many Nelson jugs, as well as recent limited-edition issues commemorating centenaries, etc.

Commemorative ceramics became especially popular after the introduction of transfer printing and cheaply produced creamware. Main categories are: Royal births, weddings, coronations, jubilees, and deaths; great victories; disasters; political campaigns (Reform, 1832; Free Trade, 1840), electioneering, and occasionally satire. The usual forms are mugs, jugs, plates, teapots, and teacups, transfer-printed often in black, sometimes on lustreware.

Much was generated by misguided public (and malicious Whig) support for George IV's wife Caroline, whom he barred from his coronation (1821) after evidence of her adulteries had been presented to the House of Lords, also by the popularity of the fruit of their single and singular union, Princess Charlotte, who married Leopold of Belgium and died young. Coronation mugs for Queen Victoria are now very rare; after Prince Albert's death (1861) she became almost a recluse and few royal commemorative pieces were issued until the Golden Jubilee (1887) and the Diamond Jubilee (1897). These late commemoratives were mass-produced and are still not all that rare or expensive. Modern commemoratives too are often made in large numbers and may have a limited resale value.

The standard book on the older examples is John & Jennifer May's *Commemorative Pottery 1780–1900* (Heinemann, 1972). The Mays (of Kensington Church Street) are two of the several dealers specializing in commemorative wares.

SUSIE COOPER (OBE). 'Susie Cooper has become the most important and influential ceramic designer of her generation to emerge from Staffordshire', so correctly wrote Mrs Ann Eatwell in her excellent catalogue of the 1987 exhibition of Susie Cooper's designs from the 1920s to the present-day. Miss Cooper was born in 1902 and has been engaged in ceramic painting and design from 1920 onwards. Her taste was modern, clean-cut, attractive wares normally decorated in pastel shades.

From about 1930 her designs (made for various firms) have borne her name, although the pieces usually 'speak for themselves'. Her work cannot be regarded as rare – being popular it was produced in vast quantities – but it is fit for its purpose and attractive. Susie Cooper China Ltd was taken in 1966 into the large Wedgwood group who continue to produce several characteristic designs.

Mrs Eatwell's 1987 catalogue *Susie Cooper Productions* should be available from the bookshop at the Victoria & Albert Museum.

W. T. COPELAND (& SONS) (1847–1970+). William Taylor Copeland took over the former Spode Works in Stoke when his partner, Thomas Garrett, retired in June 1847.

He continued the Spode and the Copeland & Garrett tradition of fine quality porcelain and various types of earthenware. Copeland was Minton's great rival in Stoke and by 1861 the factory employed over 800 persons. In the production of superb parian figures and groups Copeland led the considerable field.

The Copeland products usually bear a clear name-mark and they can often be dated to narrow limits: see Geoffrey Godden's *Handbook of British Pottery & Porcelain Marks* (Barrie & Jenkins, 1972), *Staffordshire Porcelain* (Granada, 1983), or *Encyclopaedia of British Porcelain Manufacturers* (Barrie & Jenkins, 1988). Mr R. Spencer C. Copeland has published *The Copeland China Collection* by Vega Wilkinson.

In 1970 the Copeland company reverted to the name Spode Ltd.

28   A selection of Spode bone china straight-sided 'coffee cans' of the 1805–15 period. A wide range of patterns between 343 and 1409 is shown on these collectable cans. Average height 2½in. c.1805–15.

COPELAND & GARRETT (1833–47). This partnership between William Copeland and Thomas Garrett took over the Spode works.

A very good diverse range of both earthenware and fine porcelain was produced and the wares are usually marked in full, making identification simple. For their uniform high quality and relatively early period these quite scarce Copeland & Garrett wares are rather neglected. As yet no book has been devoted to this period but some typical examples are shown in *Staffordshire Porcelain* (Granada, 1983).

CORNUCOPIA. A horn of plenty, usually flat-backed to hang on a wall, made in many kinds of pottery and porcelain; fashionable *c.*1750–1870, they were used for flowers or ivy. Some have moulded bird or floral decoration, others are in blue and white.

The origin of the shape lies in Greek mythology. The infant Zeus, kept alive by a Cretan princess with goat's milk, in gratitude (not to the goat) broke off one of its horns and gave it to the princess, promising that it would always be filled with whatever its possessor wished. The early examples are rare and highly collectable.

CORONATION WARES. An interesting subdivision of commemorative wares (q.v.). However, one must remember that from the coronation of Edward VII onwards these wares were produced in

29 'Coronation Ware' made for the intended Coronation of King Edward VIII by the New Chelsea company. Reproduced from the Pottery Gazette, *1937.*

extremely large numbers – one or more for every child in the land. Such wares given by schools or towns were mass-produced to a low price and most were treasured and handed down from generation to generation.

There is consequently little rarity value in such printed earthenware souvenirs. However, some of the leading firms have produced special high-grade coronation pieces, often in porcelain and in limited editions. These often have great merit and rarity and may be considered as collectors' pieces.

Our illustration (Plate 29) shows a selection of pieces made for King Edward VIII's coronation that was to be held in 1937. These are relatively rare but it must be remembered that the potters had designed and produced their special wares well before the Abdication. The pots were produced even if the event did not take place!

COTTAGES. A convenient term covering china cottages, castles, toll-houses, or churches, often made to burn pastilles emitting pungent smoke through the chimney – a useful function when sanitation was primitive. These may have lift-off roofs, and gables (as Plate 30), dormer windows, occasionally human figures, or a dog. Some were nightlight holders whose cut-out windows gleamed comfortingly in children's bedrooms. Money-boxes, broken to retrieve the pennies, are rarer.

Some were in early Prattware; the better porcelain examples of 1820–40 are usually called 'Rockingham' but this attribution is most unlikely; Coalport, Worcester, Minton, and Derby made them, and many are in Staffordshire bone china. Later, cruder pottery models came from Staffordshire, Yorkshire, and Scotland.

Some 'cottages' merely represent a building and have no function. All types are decorative and usually attractive, but many late copies exist and some models are still in production.

COW-CREAMER. A ceramic milk-jug modelled in the form of a cow (as Plate 31), with curved tail as handle, mouth as spout, and detachable 'saddle' on the back as lid. They were made in every kind of ware and colour by many potters. They probably emulate the early silver models.

Most survivors are from Staffordshire or Swansea, the former often with black or brown markings, some in lustre. Identification is difficult, but Staffordshire characteristics possibly include a tail curving on to the back, oval green base with a large moulded daisy, and an added milkmaid figure. Early specimens had thin flat rectangular bases. Later Swansea models were often transfer-printed, had a rectangular moulded base and the tail curving to the flank. After c.1850 cow-creamers were made for decoration rather than use since, being impossible to clean properly, they were unhygienic.

The Stoke-on-Trent City Museum at Hanley has an unusually large herd!

30   A good-quality marked 'Spode Felspar Porcelain' cottage pastille-burner. These attractive ornamental items were made in pottery as well as in porcelain. 7in high. c.1821–30.

CRADLES. Miniature pottery imitations of wicker basket cradles made as christening presents c.1700–1850. The earliest were in slip-ware and might contain a crudely hand-modelled baby; a few were inscribed. Later cradles were moulded in saltglaze or other stone-ware or in earthenware; decoration might be tortoiseshell, the Wedgwood green glaze, or bright painted colours. These usually small toys are attractive and very collectable.

31   A typical cow-creamer (missing the flat cover which should cap the filling hole).
Such earthenware novelties have been made from about 1760 up to the present day.
Recommended for display rather than for use! 5½in high. c.1800.

CREAMWARE (*c.*1720–present day). Lightweight thinly-potted lead-glazed cream-coloured earthenware, made with the same basic ingredients as the saltglaze body but fired at a lower temperature. Its invention is attributed both to one of the Astburys and to Enoch Booth, the latter responsible (*c.*1740) for the characteristic butter-coloured fluid glaze (of ground lead, flint, and pipeclay) in which the wares were dipped. In the late eighteenth century it displaced saltglaze and delftware as the staple earthenware product, and was exported in very great quantity. It was perfected by Wedgwood and called Queen's Ware. Neale, Turner, Enoch Wood, Spode, Davenport, and practically all earthenware potters from 1770 produced creamware.

Typical forms of decoration were pierced work (plate-rims, baskets, etc. with various openwork patterns punched out by hand); basket work (openwork basket designs); intertwined handles on jugs; free-painted flowers, often in red and black or a distinctive green; teapots with crabstock handles and spouts, decorated with scenes, portraits, birds, etc. in underglaze blue, transfer-printed, enamel-painted or with tortoiseshell glazes; jugs and loving-cups with a name or dedication in elaborate scrollwork. Many pieces were sold to the public market in the less expensive undecorated state.

Quality copies of old Leeds styles and shapes are still made today and some eighteenth and nineteenth-century examples were made on the Continent.

Like any standard type of ceramic, quality and desirability varies greatly, but for the rare old forms well-decorated and marked speciments are in great demand, as are inscribed and dated examples.

The standard work is Donald Towner's *Creamware* (Faber & Faber, 1978) but even this specialist work is now out of date in some respects. Although most creamware found in the British Isles is of our own manufacture, various foreign potters and firms did produce their own creamware-type wares. A good modern general book is *European Creamware* by Jana Kybalová (English edition, Hamlyn, 1989).

CRICKET THEMES. The game is ceramically depicted from at least 1820 – a blue and white dish showing top-hatted cricketers with baseball type bat – down to the heyday of Hobbs and Bradman. Flat-back figures show named cricketers (Pilch and Box) before a wicket and tree-trunk spill-holder resembling at first glance a five-handed wicket-keeper. These two celebrities and Lillywhite also appear in relief on Prattware jugs, Minton mugs, and in silver lustre – the Pratt-type jugs reproduced at Leeds as recently as 1906. Flatbacks of helmeted Volunteer officers at the wicket in full regimentals appeared in 1859; as there was a war scare at the time they were presumably ready to wield what look like canoe paddles to hit either ball or Frenchman for six. Transfer-printed pieces commemorate specific matches of this period, and a Coalport porcelain mug W. G. Grace's hundredth century (1895). Being highly collectable some figure models have been reproduced and even 'aged'.

Various sporting activities have been depicted by the potters over the years, the cricket subjects being the most popular. Strangely, football was seldom featured.

CROWN STAFFORDSHIRE (*c.*1889–present-day). This company produced a varied array of good quality decorative bone china, including figure models, bird subjects, and much floral-encrusted work, apart from useful tablewares.

The Crown Staffordshire Porcelain Company succeeded T. A. & S. Green at the Minerva Works at Fenton in 1889. Their wares and those of the succeeding firm – Crown Staffordshire China Co. Ltd (*c.*1948 onwards) – are usually fully marked and these devices include the trade-name 'Crown Staffordshire' or 'Staff's' or 'Staffordshire' with a crown.

For further information and illustrations of typical examples the reader is referred to Godden's *Staffordshire Porcelain* (Granada, 1983) and the *Encyclopaedia of British Porcelain Manufacturers* (Barrie & Jenkins, 1988).

DAMAGE. A few personal words on damage may be helpful to the new or would-be collector. Some highly respected old books will tell collectors only to purchase perfect specimens. This is still good advice especially if your purse is bottomless and if you are buying purely for investment.

However, if you are forming an interesting representative collection for pleasure or for study, this same advice is bad. In endeavouring to follow this ideal you will miss the opportunity to add to your collection many pleasing or even beautiful specimens and many rare, even dated, examples.

As long as you are aware of the damage and if the price takes such faults as there may be into account, then there is often a case for buying a damaged example. Obviously there are degrees of damage. Few serious collectors would reject a good specimen because of a small chip or a hair-line crack. On the other hand a missing head or limb from a figure or an unsightly crack across the middle of a plate may well put that piece out of court – unless you are willing to have such a piece repaired (see 'Repairs').

H. & R. DANIEL. Staffordshire potters at Stoke. Henry and Richard Daniel (*c*.1822–54) made high-quality decorative porcelains notable for colour grounds and rich gilding. Henry, prior to 1822, had been responsible for the decoration of Spode's porcelains at workshops

32   A typically ornate Daniel porcelain covered sugar-bowl of characteristic form. Pattern number 4661. 5¾in high. c.1827–35.

within the Spode factory before the agreement was terminated and Henry Daniel and his son established their own factory. Apart from the finely-decorated porcelains, less expensive earthenware and stone china were also made. The Daniel wares are seldom marked but several key shapes or border forms as Plate 32 help identification. The London retailer's mark is sometimes mistaken for the Stoke manufacturers, but the London firm was spelt Daniell.

For further information on this important firm and for illustrations of typical wares the reader is referred to Michael Berthoud's specialist work *H. & R. Daniel 1822–1846* (Micawber, 1980) or such general works as Godden's *Staffordshire Porcelain* (Granada, 1983) or the *Encyclopaedia of British Porcelain Manufacturers* (Barrie & Jenkins, 1988).

DAVENPORT (1794–1887). A Staffordshire firm founded at Longport by John Davenport and carried on by his sons. For the first few years only earthenware was made, including creamware and later stone china; much of it was attractively decorated with underglaze blue transfer-prints, or painted landscapes. Porcelain was first made c.1805. Then artists were engaged from Derby and elsewhere, leading to the addition of more expensive lines of fine porcelains, often heavily gilded and with elaborate landscapes, well-painted roses and other flowers, or still lifes etc; an apple-green ground was particularly successful and the dessert services of the 1850–70 period are especially admired. In the last two decades 'Japan' patterns were much favoured.

The Davenport complex trading under various names produced a very wide range of products, including glass. Much of the early porcelain was unmarked and in general the pre-1850 Davenport wares are little understood and are probably undervalued.

T. A. Lockett's pioneer book *Davenport Pottery & Porcelain 1794–1887* (David & Charles, 1972) has now been superseded by his new work (written with Geoffrey Godden) entitled *Davenport China, Earthenware and Glass* (Barrie & Jenkins, 1989).

DELFTWARE. In England the name given to tin-glazed earthenware; the tin (added to lead) gave an opaque white surface finish on which in its unfired absorbent state decoration, usually in blue, had to be painted quickly, giving a characteristically spontaneous quality. One type of this ware, called 'blue-dash chargers', took the form of large shallow dishes of which the rims were decorated with dashes of blue; these were probably intended for decoration rather than for table use.

The origin of delftware goes back to a Mesopotamian technique brought by the Moors to Spain (Hispano-Mauresque ware) and thence to Italy (Maiolica, 'from Majorca'; faience, 'made at Faenza') and the Low Countries (Delft) and brought to England (Norwich) by two Dutchmen c.1571. It was made in London at various potteries, at Bristol, Liverpool, Dublin, Glasgow, and elsewhere. Too fragile to be really serviceable (surviving examples are usually chipped or cracked), it was eventually displaced by creamwares, although tin-glazed earthenwares were produced in decreasing quantities up to, at least, the 1780s.

Early, unusual, or inscribed and dated examples (as Plate 33) may be very costly. Correctly, when referring to the English examples, a small 'd' is used, underlining the point that the term is used in a generic sense.

Recent standard reference books on the British types are Frank Britton's *English Delftware in the Bristol Collection* (Sotheby's Publications, 1982) and *London Delftware* (Jonathan Horne, 1987), and L. L. Lipski and M. Archer's *Dated English Delftware* (Sotheby's Publications, 1984).

33 A very rare English 'delft' or tin-glazed earthenware cup or mug, painted with the likeness of Charles II, who had been restored to the throne in 1660. This was probably produced at one of the several London delftware manufactories. 3in high. 1661. **(Christie's).**

DELLA ROBBIA WARE (1893–1906). Art pottery of striking, some-times grotesque, shapes decorated with a mixture of painting and sgraffito, usually with a vivid green glaze, made by the Della Robbia Company Ltd, Birkenhead. The name implied a revival of the opaque-glazed and enamelled terracotta made by the Della Robbia family in fifteenth and sixteenth-century Florence. The old Liberty & Co. advertisement reproduced in Plate 34 shows typical *c.*1900 wares and the original prices.

The marks comprise the Della Robbia name or the head-on outline of a sailing vessel with the initials 'D R' and the initial of the decorator placed above the mast. Typical examples are shown in *British Pottery. An Illustrated Guide* (Barrie & Jenkins, 1974).

Della-Robbia Pottery (English).

No. 1. Della-Robbia Flower Vase.
Quaint and effective for Table Decoration.
4½ inches high.
Price 3/6 each.

No. 2.
Della-Robbia Bowl and Cover.
For Batter or Muffins.
Prices 6/6 and 7/6 each.

No. 3. Della-Robbia Jar.
For Jam or Preserves. In quaint designs and effective colourings.
Price 5/6 each.

No. 4. Della-Robbia Jug.
Tall and graceful shape. Quaintly and artistically decorated in colours. Very effective for Sideboards and Overmantels.
12 inches high.
Price 15/6 each.

No. 5. Della-Robbia Plaques.
Highly decorative and unique. In varied designs and colourings.
18 inches diameter.
Prices 30/-, 32/6 to 63/- each.
Many other shapes and sizes in stock.

No. 6. Della-Robbia Vase.
In conventional designs and artistic colouring. For Overmantel and Sideboard Decoration.
12 inches high.
Prices 10/6, 12/6 and 21/- each.

34 *A Liberty & Co. 'Della-Robbia' advertisement showing typical forms and styles of decoration with the original retail prices: vase top left priced at 3/6d or 18p. c.1900.*

WILLIAM DE MORGAN (1839–1917). The versatile inventor, novelist, and potter who set up a studio-type pottery or decorating workshop in Chelsea and elsewhere in London (1872–1907). His friendship with William Morris and Burne-Jones linked him to the Arts and Crafts movement and the Pre-Rapahelites.

He tried to revive Hispano-Mauresque iridescent lustreware and to recapture the shapes and colours (turquoise, other blues and greens, and red) of Persian pottery. He bought white tiles, large dishes, and pots from Staffordshire and painted them in majolica style with strange but attractive designs, in harmonious colour schemes, of fantastic beasts and birds, fabulous ships under full sail. Tiles formed the bulk of his output but he made many vases and plaques and some beautiful dishes, some triple-lustred in copper, silver, and gold. The original designs were given to the Victoria & Albert Museum in 1917, published in Martin Greenwood's *The Designs of William De Morgan* (R. Dennis & W. E. Wiltshire, Shepton Beauchamp, 1989), with illustrations of related finished wares.

In recent years the De Morgan earthenwares which are usually marked with various devices including the name De Morgan or the initials 'D.M.', have become very collectable and often costly.

Typical specimens are shown in Godden's *British Pottery, An Illustrated Guide* (Barrie & Jenkins, 1974), Plates 436–41. The standard work is W. Gaunt and M. D. E. Clayton-Stamm's *William De Morgan* (Studio Vista, 1971).

DERBY (*c*.1749–present day). Little is certain about Derby's origins as a small porcelain-producing workshop where, in the 'Early Derby', 'dry-edge' or 'Planché' period (*c*.1749–55), many unmarked figures were excellently modelled, traditionally by a young Huguenot, André Planché, possibly financed by John Heath. Paste and glaze were milk-white, the latter wiped away round the base to prevent sticking to kiln furniture – hence the term 'dry-edge figures'. They included chinoiserie-style figures, sophisticated shepherdesses, and some boars and bulls. Many early figures were left in the white. There is also a mysterious white cream-jug marked '1750 D[erby]'.

The factory proper was established in Nottingham Road (1755) by William Duesbury, who had previously decorated for Chelsea, Bow, and Derby in his London studio. His partners were Heath and possibly Planché (unmentioned after 1756). A shrewd businessman, Duesbury realized that it paid to advertise – as 'the second Dresden' (1757); he bought up the Chelsea works *c*.1770, giving rise to the Chelsea-Derby (q.v.) period (1770–84).

At Derby in the first few years he produced a transitional 'pale-coloured family' of delicate doll-like figures in lightweight, rather chalky paste with blued glaze, decorated in pastel colours. Figures and groups were always Derby's mainstay, and the next generation was the 'patch family' (1758–70), typically with three or four patches marked on the base by clay balls or pads on which figures rested in the kiln – a substitute for the dry-edge precaution. These figures, thought until 1926 to be Chelsea, have numerous characteristics: almost knife-edge garment folds, sharp nose, flushed cheeks, and a dominant dirty turquoise enamel. They imitated Chelsea Gold Anchor trends, and included classical groups and 'Ranelagh' figures (couples in fancy dress), some with bocages. Useful wares include attractive tea-sets, sauceboats, openware baskets, and elaborate Meissen-style vases which became another Derby speciality, particularly of the Crown Derby period.

Derby employed good ceramic artists, including Askew (cupids), Duvivier (landscapes), Billingsley, and latterly Boreman (landscapes). A highly successful innovation was the first, and best, English biscuit figures (Plate 11), some modelled by Spängler; 'smear' glazing imparted an ivory sheen, the glaze being smeared not on the figure but on the kiln or saggar walls, and volatilized. Figures were often marked on the base with a script 'N' and model number. High-quality useful wares were made, often with Neo-Classical decoration, probably mainly for the cabinet, especially coffee cans.

On Duesbury's death his son, also William, inherited, initiating the Crown Derby period (1786–1811), named from the mark used. During the ten years before his death he put Derby in the forefront of English porcelain, helped by a finer translucent porcelain and clearer glaze, decorated by artists of the preceding period and by newcomers. His successor Kean upset the staff, the artists left and a general decline followed; bone china was introduced, permitting greater concentration on table wares; much Imari decoration was used.

The final period is called Bloor Derby (1811–48), although the date that Richard Bloor bought the factory may have been 1814, and when he became insane in 1828 control passed to a useless manager. Bloor's main preoccupation was to pay off the mortgage by indiscriminate marketing of vast quantities of substandard old stock often painted in heavy Imari patterns to hide defects, and to suit popular taste of the period. But he also produced fine ware painted by artists such as Thomas Steel (fruit), Moses Webster (Billingsley-style flowers), and Daniel Lucas (landscapes). There were also sentimental gaudy figures and well-painted plaques.

After the main factory closed for good in 1848 some employees started an independent factory in King Street, the Old Crown Derby China Works (1848–1935), which under various managements copied old Derby patterns and used old moulds. The Stevenson & Hancock regime, continued by Sampson Hancock alone (c.1865–98), was the most successful, producing many figures, old and new, and hand-painted Japan pattern tea-sets etc., as shown in Plate 35.

In 1876 an entirely new concern, the (Royal) Crown Derby Porcelain Co., was established at Osmaston Road, and continues to this day. In 1935 it bought the King Street factory giving the new company a link with the eighteenth century.

The over two-hundred-year story of Derby is a vast one and the reader is recommended to consult one of the several specialist books on this factory's products. Recent works include: *Derby Porcelain* by John Twitchett (Barrie & Jenkins, 1981); *Derby Porcelain. The Golden Years* by D. G. Rice (David & Charles, 1983); *Royal Crown Derby* by

John Twitchett and Betty Bailey (Barrie & Jenkins, 1976); and *Derby Porcelain Figures 1750–1848* by Peter Bradshaw (Faber & Faber, 1990). Geoffrey Godden's large *Encyclopaedia of British Pottery & Porcelain Marks* (Barrie & Jenkins, 1964) gives details of the many types of mark used at the various period. It should be noted, however, that Derby porcelain made before about 1775 is unlikely to bear a mark. The reader is also warned that clever fakes exist!

35   *Typical early twentieth-century Derby Japan pattern porcelains made at the small King Street works. Reproduced from the firm's undated catalogue. c.1910.*

DESIGN(S) COPYRIGHT ACT. See Registration Marks and Numbers.

DESSERT SERVICES. After tea wares the most often found examples of English porcelain are dessert wares. The often richly decorated dessert services included not only plates but variously shaped dishes, a centrepiece, and often a pair of tureens (for cream and sugar) and rarely a pair of fruit coolers.

All our major porcelain makers and the leading potters produced dessert services in various styles from the 1750s onwards. In the eighteenth century it was also the fashion in wealthy circles to dress the dessert table with various figures and groups, or with boxes or tureens in the form of fruit or animals.

It is impossible to generalize on the range of dessert wares produced in England in the eighteenth and nineteenth centuries but most general reference books will illustrate typical examples: see, for example, *Staffordshire Porcelain*. Most specialist books on the products of individual factories will also show the wealth of that firm's dessert wares.

DINNER SERVICES. The standard eighteenth-century sets would include soup and meat plates, meat platters, salad bowls or junket dishes, sauceboats, and a covered tureen with stand and ladle.

However, few eighteenth-century English porcelain manufacturers were able to compete with the quality and relatively low cost of the Chinese dinner wares imported in large numbers by the English East India Company and at this period, before 1780, there were far more Chinese dinner services in use in England than those of our own manufacture.

In the nineteenth century our porcelain manufacturers specialized in very richly decorated large dinner services. The products of one typical factory are well illustrated and explained in Geoffrey Godden's specialist book *Chamberlain-Worcester Porcelain 1788–1852* (Barrie & Jenkins, 1982). The price list of Chamberlain patterns also shows the high cost of complete porcelain dinner services (or 'Table Services' as they were called); in one pattern a complete tea-set may have been ten guineas, a matching dessert service thirty guineas, whilst the dinner service was priced at one hundred and fifty guineas – at a period when the average weekly wage was little more than one pound or guinea (£1.05).

In contrast the earthenware dinner services were relatively cheap but they were not richly decorated. The blue-printed Staffordshire earthenware sets were, however, very decorative and fit for their purpose.

All large plates with a diameter of ten inches or so, all soup plates and the large platters, etc. were originally part of a large complete dinner service.

The fashionable dinner-time advanced from about 3 p.m. in 1700 to 6 p.m. in 1770. Since breakfasts were minimal and there was no luncheon, dinners were gargantuan; a bishop in 1783 laid on two 'courses' of twenty dishes each followed by a dessert of twenty dishes. There might also be a supper at about 10 p.m.

DOE AND ROGERS. The porcelains shown in Plate 36 bear the written name-marks 'Doe & Rogers Worcester'. These represent one of several examples where factory-trained painters set up their own decorating studio and marketed wares under their own name or names.

In this case we have Enoch Doe and George Rogers, both former painters for Chamberlain of Worcester, decorating blanks possibly purchased from the Coalport management. They firstly practised in London in the 1806–7 period but later ran a business at 17 High Street, Worcester. George Rogers had died by 1835 but the partnership with Enoch Doe was continued by Rogers's widow and son until 6 October 1835. Enoch Doe continued and exhibited at the 1851 Exhibition.

For further information see Godden's *Encyclopaedia of British Porcelain Manufacturers* (Barrie & Jenkins, 1988).

36   A selection of porcelains (probably of Coalport make) decorated by Doe & Rogers in Worcester and bearing their painted name and address mark. Spill vase 4¼in high. c.1825–35.

DON POTTERY (*c.*1801–1983). A south Yorkshire pottery at Swinton, near Doncaster, founded by members of the Green family who were also connected with the Leeds Pottery, and sold in 1834 to the Barkers of Mexborough Pottery. They made good Leeds-type creamware and whitewares, also earthenware tea-sets with red or chocolate line-rims and painted decoration. Hand-painted and also attractively printed (including classical figure patterns) dessert services were also made but are now very scarce. Green-glazed dessert services with moulded patterns, and blue and white wares with named and well-executed scenes of ancient Italy. Marks may include the names Don, Green, or Barker, or initials S.B. & S but many examples are unmarked.

Information on this pottery and on the many others in Yorkshire is given in Heather Laurence's excellent book *Yorkshire Pots and Potteries* (David & Charles, 1974).

DOULTON (1815-present day). A very well-known Lambeth firm which manufactured brown saltglaze stoneware, at first for utilitarian purposes only. Later they also made decorative spirit flasks and other decorative articles.

Doultons are celebrated for their revival (*c*.1870) of individually designed and decorated collectors' pieces, a first step towards the Studio Pottery movement; Henry Doulton, through friendship with the head of the Lambeth School of Art, was able to employ its students as decorators. These wares included stoneware vases, tankards, jugs, classical urns, etc. decorated with coloured patterns of flowers and foliage in incised outline; rows of applied beads in white slip became an increasingly prominent feature.

Hannah Barlow, one of the most famous students, specialized in spirited animal sketches done in economically used incised outlines filled in and accented with pigment; later she lost the use of her right arm and trained herself to use the left. Her sister Florence painted bird studies in coloured clays and also did incised work. George Tinworth made excellent terracotta plaques of biblical scenes, and also

37   *A selection of small Doulton stoneware ornaments modelled by George Tinworth and bearing his incised TG monogram mark. Punch & Judy group entitled 'Playgoers'. 5¾in high. c.1900.*

amusing animal groups in stoneware – e.g. of mice watching a Punch and Judy show (see Plate 37), and others illustrating Aesop's fables. All pieces bear the artist's signature or monogram, factory mark, and (usually) date.

Doultons also made (1875–1914) what they called faience, i.e. creamware vases, dishes, tiles, plaques, etc. painted underglaze; 'Silicon' (1880s), i.e. unglazed brown stoneware carved and decorated in various ways; 'Carrara', a dense white stoneware; 'impasto' thickly painted on unfired clay; and, later, stoneware Toby-style 'character' jugs depicting celebrities.

In 1882 an earthenware factory at Burslem, Staffordshire, was taken over, where high-quality porcelain has been made ever since; stoneware was discontinued in 1956 when the Lambeth division was closed.

The Burslem branch continued and is perhaps best known for the wide range of decorative bone china figures and groups made there.

In recent years there has been much interest in the collection of Doulton wares of all types, but the reader should bear in mind that the output of the Doulton factories was very large and that not all marked Doulton wares are valuable or especially desirable. There are several very good specialist books to guide the Doulton collector, including some price guides. These works include D. Eyles's *Royal Doulton 1815–1965* (Hutchinson, 1965), *The Doulton Lambeth Wares* (Hutchinson, 1975), and *The Doulton Burslem Wares* (Barrie & Jenkins, 1980), and *Royal Doulton Figures* by D. Eyles, R. Dennis, and L. Irvine (Royal Doulton Ltd, revised edition 1987). A pleasingly helpful little book in the Phillips Collectors Guides series is *Royal Doulton* by Catherine Braithwaite (Boxtree Ltd, 1989). There are also several price guides which are up-dated from time to time.

DRESSING-TABLE SETS. These porcelain sets were extremely popular from about 1850 onwards. Typically they comprise a porcelain tray (for brush and comb), a pair of porcelain candlesticks, powder and trinket bowls, or covered boxes and a ring-stand.

These sets were normally unmarked and were generally made cheaply by the smaller manufacturers.

Many are of Continental (French) origin, made in a hard-paste porcelain. Few sets are now found in an undamaged, complete state but the individual components can be decorative and are useful for their original purpose.

DR SYNTAX (*c*.1815+). An accident-prone clergyman-schoolmaster whose tours on his nag Grizzle were depicted in a series of engravings after Thomas Rowlandson; William Combe, in a debtors' prison, wrote verse for each plate as it was finished, and the final result was three bestselling books, parodying the popular travel books of the day.

Incidents from the series appear on Staffordshire blue and white earthenwares (and later reissues) and on several makes of porcelain in the approximate period 1816–30. Earthenware and porcelain small figures depicting Dr Syntax were also made and are very popular with collectors.

DRUG-JARS. Made from the seventeenth century (in delftware), these jars stood in chemists' shops marked in abbreviated Latin with their contents. These and jars of succeeding centuries are found in many shapes and often bear elaborate decorations, such as Apollo as god of healing, cherubs, and much scrollery. Originally there were no lids (they were covered with parchment if necessary). Those for oils and syrups had handles and spouts, but these were not needed for electuaries (powders in honey) and treacles (for poisonous bites).

Genuine seventeenth and eighteenth-century drug-jars are rare and costly but many later examples have decorative merit even if not antique.

DUDSON (c.1800–present day). The reawakening of interest in the Dudson wares is largely due to the publication of an excellent deeply-researched book by Audrey M. Dudson entitled *Dudson. A Family of Potters since 1800* (Dudson Publications, 1985). The best-known Dudson wares are Wedgwood-styled jasper-type jugs, vases, and useful wares of above average quality. The early examples are unmarked, but from about the 1870s name-marks were used. Incised shape numbers occur climbing into the thousands. Various impressed size numbers or potter's marks occur, also names such as 'PAXTON' (see Plate 38).

38   A chocolate-ground Dudson-type stoneware jug with moulded white 'Tropical Bird' reliefs. Incised model number 1530. Impressed name PAXTON. 7½in high (size 12). c.1870–80.

JOHN DWIGHT (1633–1703). One of the most celebrated potters in England. A highly educated man, rather than a run of the mill potter. He produced at Fulham wonderful figures (Plate 39) and portrait busts in a high fired stoneware, and also useful wares such as bottles. He took out a patent in the early 1670s for a 'transparent earthenware commonly called porcelane or china' but is mainly known for his (now rare) stonewares.

Several E.C.C. Papers deal with various aspects of the Dwight story, as does *The Journal of Ceramic History,* no. 6 (1974).

39   An exceedingly rare high-fired stoneware figure by John Dwight of Fulham. 12¼in high. c.1690–1703. **(Victoria & Albert Museum).**

EARTHENWARE. Porous non-vitrified baked clay; to make it of practical domestic use it has to be rendered impervious to liquids by glazing. Used from ancient times, its main forms in England, as the result of successive modifications, were Slipware, Delftware, Creamware, Pearlware, Stone China, Mason's Patent Ironstone, and similar hard, durable bodies but the basic pottery body remained standard over very many years.

In general earthenwares could be produced much cheaper and with less trouble than porcelain and the lower cost of earthenware ensured that its production was vast. There were very many more firms producing earthenware than porcelain.

E.C.C. (English Ceramic Circle). Readers may well come across references to E.C.C. Transactions and Papers. These initials relate to the English Ceramic Circle, a private society formed in 1933 (arising from the earlier English Porcelain Circle).

The printed and published Transactions contain a wealth of material contributed by past and present authorities and specialists. The main Papers published between 1928 and 1986 are listed in Godden's *Encyclopaedia of British Porcelain Manufacturers* (Barrie & Jenkins, 1988), pp. 834–8.

Other like societies exist such as the Northern Ceramic Society (q.v.) and the serious collector is recommended to join such groups and to exchange knowledge and meet new collecting friends.

EGG CUPS. Of all the useful tablewares, egg cups today tend to be the most popular with collectors. Eighteenth-century examples are now extremely rare but Worcester, Caughley, Bow, Lowestoft, and Derby examples certainly exist. The main earthenware manufacturers, Wedgwood, Leeds, etc. also made them in creamware.

In the nineteenth century the porcelain examples tended to be very richly decorated and the major firms sold them in sets, often in elaborate stands. Geoffrey Godden in his book *Chamberlain-Worcester Porcelain 1788–1852* (Barrie & Jenkins, 1982) shows such stands and quotes from that factory's records. Egg cups were included in the costly breakfast services, not in the standard tea services.

ELERS WARE. Unglazed smooth-surfaced red stoneware, typically in the form of teapots with applied reliefs, originally made in imitation of Chinese wares. Traditionally attributed to David and John Elers, who came to England from Holland about the time of William of Orange (1688) and worked in London and Staffordshire, they may also (or first) have been made by Dwight of Fulham, who patented an opaque red 'porcelain' in 1684 and later accused the Elers, among others, of infringing his patent. Elers-type wares were later made by several other Staffordshire potters and today the term is usually used in a generic sense.

Wedgwood attributed to the Elers the idea of using a lathe to achieve the exceptionally smooth finish on these pots, and other innovations which later became standard in the industry.

The reader is referred to a serious study 'Staffordshire Red and Black Stonewares' by G. W. Elliott (*Transactions of the English Ceramic Circle*, vol. 10, part 2, 1977).

ELTON WARE. In the early 1880s Sir Edmund Elton (1846–1920) of Clevedon Court in Somerset started to produce a very individual type of 'Art Pottery'. This venture was on a relatively small scale as Sir Edmund and his estate workers (notably George Masters, d.1921) had no training in pottery making or decoration. Yet these novel wares attracted wide attention and were reviewed in *The Magazine of Art* in 1883. Formal floral motifs were popular on jugs, vases, and similar ornamental objects. All over gilt and silvered effects with a crazed surface were distinctive. Most examples bear an impressed or painted 'Elton' name mark. A cross was added to the mark on pieces produced after Sir Edmund's death in July 1920, when the small pottery was continued up to *c.*1930 by Sir Ambrose Elton, assisted for a period by W. F. Holland. The Elton wares enjoyed favourable publicity at various exhibitions, no doubt on account of the novelty and the standing of the owner, but the Elton pottery must be considered as the hobby of a rich landowner rather than as a successful commercial enterprise.

Nevertheless the wares are decorative and typical of their period and their West Country origin. Certainly in recent years they have returned to favour and they may be considered to be one of the less expensive collecting lines open to the new collector.

Clevedon Court is a National Trust property open to the public and it houses a notable collection of the earthenwares made in the outbuildings in the 1881–1930 period. An interesting article 'Elton Ware Rediscovered' by John Bartlett appeared in *Antique Collector* magazine of July 1985, but the main source of information is undoubtedly Malcolm Haslam's book *Elton Ware – the Pottery of Sir Edmund Elton* published by Richard Dennis in 1989 (144 Kensington Church Street, London W8).

EXTINGUISHERS. Some colourful little figures or ornaments were made as candle extinguishers, often called snuffers (originally devices for trimming wicks). These have a conical hole in the base so that the flame could be extinguished without the fingers being soiled or burnt – a charming decorative novelty.

40   *A rare pair of Minton candle extinguishers, with their original stand displayed upright behind the small hollow-based figures. Such complete units are very scarce. Figures 4in high. c.1840–5.*

Minton made delightful examples *c.*1840–50, which were sometimes mounted on a tray or base (see Plate 40) or form part of a decorative candlestick. For examples of this rare and costly type the reader is referred to Geoffrey Godden's *Minton Pottery & Porcelain of the First Period 1793–1850* (Barrie & Jenkins, 1968).

Later in the century the Royal Worcester company produced a long series of charming extinguishers (Plate 41) which normally bear a Royal Worcester mark on the inside. Examples of this collectable type are featured in Henry Sandon's *Royal Worcester Porcelain from the 1862 to the Present Day* (Barrie & Jenkins, 1973). Some Royal Worcester models have been reissued in recent years. These are not as highly valued as the original examples.

41   *Examples of the decorative Royal Worcester hollow-based candle extinguishers sold without stands, as novelties. Printed Royal Worcester marks. 3½ and 4⅛in high. c.1880–1900.*

EYE BATHS. These small, high-stemmed, very utilitarian objects are highly collectable, especially if they were made in the eighteenth century at a well-known factory such as Worcester.

Like other utilitarian objects they are now rare because they were very prone to damage in use, and once broken they were discarded and not retained as perhaps a favourite decorative teapot might have been. A Worcester or Lowestoft porcelain eye bath would be a lucky find, but later examples or a pottery example are less valued. Eye baths in glass can be quite recent.

FAIRINGS. Small mass-produced porcelain figure groups made in Germany for the English and other markets as sixpenny presents sold or won at a fair. Archly humorous inscriptions on the base tended to be on bedroom themes (hence the nickname 'Early-to-beds'). 'The last in bed to put out the light' is the commonest; others are 'Shall we Sleep First or How', 'Mr. Jones, remove your Hat' (said by a woman abed to a man in his nightshirt). Some were designed as match-holders. Rare specimens, e.g. those featuring velocipedes, fetch high prices, but other common subjects can be bought for a few pounds. Early examples usually have an incised or impressed number (starting at 2850); others have a trade mark and, after 1891, are marked 'Germany' or after 1921 'Made in Germany' to conform to US import regulations. Other guides to dating include the style of lettering and gilding.

Some present-century examples appear to be of Japanese manufacture: these are less desirable than the German originals.

The standard book on these once inexpensive novelties is W. S. Bristowe's *Victorian China Fairings* (A. & C. Black, 1964).

FAKES AND FORGERIES. Strictly speaking, while ceramic *forgeries* are totally fraudulent, the much commoner *fakes* began life as genuine pieces, bought in the white or sparsely decorated, then given new or additional decoration (any existing unwanted decoration being removed) designed to increase their value. For example, the rare yellow ground might be added to a genuine early Worcester plate. A third category is the reproduction, a copy possibly made with honest intent but turned into a fake by removing a manufacturer's mark or adding a false one. In practice these terms tend to get mixed up.

There are degrees of deceit: thus the 'C' on Caughley is suspiciously like the Worcester crescent; Worcester sometimes used Meissen or pseudo-Chinese marks, while Lowestoft used the Worcester crescent device. In a sense most early English porcelains were made to emulate the Chinese imports. However, these eighteenth-century English porcelains are not regarded as forgeries but as original high-quality ceramic work and they are very desirable in their own right.

Soft-paste porcelain is difficult to imitate, and most Continental forgeries of English eighteenth-century porcelain are in hard-paste (as Plate 42) and are thus relatively easy to detect. Samson of Paris from at least the 1870s made accurate copies of Plymouth and Bristol hard-paste, Chelsea, Worcester, or Derby. Some Samson copies were so good that they are now collected on their own merits.

42 *A pair of Continental hard-paste porcelain figures, one turned to show the over-large fake Chelsea anchor device. Note the arrowed small vent hole, not present on Chelsea models. 2¾in high. c.1900+.*

Worcester was the chief victim, especially scale-blue; it was even reproduced in earthenware, by Booth of Tunstall. Red Anchor Chelsea was copied in bone china at Tournai, but most Chelsea forgeries are of Gold Anchor period pieces, with the anchor too large and prominent. Nantgarw and Swansea forgeries occur usually with overglaze painted marks. In recent years forgeries have been made of Chelsea and Derby birds and animals, also of porcelain and pottery cottages. Many were, we believe, made by Creative Studios of Torquay, see Godden's *Encyclopaedia of British Porcelain Manufacturers*, p. 267.

There have also been forgeries of Ralph Wood, Astbury, and Whieldon figures. Most forgeries in pottery are difficult to spot, and most types of commercially valuable ceramic have been imitated –

delft, slipware, saltglaze, creamware, Wedgwood wares, and even lustre decorated wares.

For the beginner the best protection against buying a fake or forgery is to purchase from a knowledgeable source, a dealer who is prepared to give a full written descriptive receipt. This should include the claimed factory of origin and the date of production, e.g. Chelsea, c.1760.

FAMILLE ROSE AND VERTE. *Famille rose* is the nineteenth-century French name given to a 'family' of Chinese porcelain painted in a palette based on a new range of opaque pink enamels (derived from gold) invented in Europe but borrowed by the Chinese for use on their export porcelains. It was decorated in a delicate style of miniature-like refinement, with the addition of other semi-opaque enamels, especially blue and yellow. The basic rose-pink could be changed to rose-purple or violet by altering the kiln temperature. This basic Oriental style was copied by Meissen, Bow, Chelsea, Worcester, etc.

Famille verte was an earlier, Kangxi period (1662–1722), 'family' decorated in transparent enamels, with green and iron-red predominating, supplemented by yellow, violet-blue, and aubergine. Introduced c.1700, it was imitated on Continental and English porcelain.

Although the terms are correctly applied to Chinese porcelains they can be used to describe the same style and range of colours copied in England (see Plate 43) or on the Continent.

*43 A Bow porcelain sauce-boat and stand decorated in the 'famille rose' palette. 8¼in long. c.1755. **(Sotheby's New York)**.*

FEEDING CUPS. Like eye baths these once common everyday household objects can now be quite desirable and costly. A Lowestoft porcelain model could command several hundred pounds but a nineteenth-century earthenware example would be in a much lower price bracket. Still, all are collectable and scarce. There are many basic designs, but most have a long spout intended to feed children or invalids with various semi-liquid foods.

FIGURES. The high fashion for porcelain figures was extraordinarily short-lived. From about 1750 there was a sudden outburst of figure production at Chelsea, Bow, Derby, Longton Hall, and Vauxhall but by 1777 only Derby survived, to continue making enamelled porcelain figures on a large commercial scale. Worcester in its earlier days made very few as did the Lowestoft factory. In 1768 Plymouth began to make some not very satisfactory hard-paste examples, followed by Bristol.

The fashion had been to group these figures on dining or dessert tables, but *c*.1760 a new type was introduced, intended to be viewed from the front only and used as cabinet exhibits or chimney-piece ornaments. Thus the bocage background came into favour; the ultimate development of this trend was to be the Victorian flatback. From the early 1840s figures in parian came to be preferred; in nineteenth-century porcelain the chief names are Derby, Rockingham, Minton, and Royal Worcester.

The range of subjects was very wide. There were Chinese groups and figures, classical gods and heroes; the inevitable 'Dresden' shepherdesses, Turks, huntsmen, gardeners, cooks, fishermen, usually paired off with 'mates'; religious subjects, nuns; Matrimony, Liberty, Charity, etc. There were sets of Seasons, represented by men, women, children, or putti – Spring holding flowers, Summer a wheatsheaf, Autumn fruit, Winter skating or a figure huddling from the cold. Sets of 'Continents show Asia as a lady with a dog-sized camel, America as an 'Indian' huntress with prairie dog, Africa as a negress with lion and crocodile, Europe with a horse and crowned. There were also sets representing the Elements and the Senses. Numerous animal models were also produced.

The making of a figure or group was very complicated. The modeller's wax original was cut into sections from which separate plaster moulds were taken. Hollow moulds (e.g. for the body) had slip (liquid porcelain) poured into them ('slip-casting'), which left a thin coat of porcelain on the plaster. At other factories (Bow etc.) the figures were press-moulded, such pieces are heavier than the slip-cast examples. All these casts, while still moist ('cheese-hard') had to be assembled by the 'repairer' and bonded together with slip.

The first firing followed, during which the porcelain would shrink by an eighth; the main difficulty was that all the parts had to shrink by the same amount, otherwise the figure would crack. This was why all these operations required great skill, encouraged in the bad old days before 1871 by the refusal to pay for work done on pieces that did not survive the kiln. After firing, glaze was painted on and fired; then enamels and gilding were applied, each fired separately according to its resistance to heat. Bow figures in 1760 were sometimes sold undecorated to an enameller elsewhere. Other, mainly early figures, were left in the white, i.e. undecorated, and were still saleable. Some now white figures, however, originally had cold (unfired) colours added to enhance the appearance, which have long since worn away.

It is now difficult to find pairs of perfect and unrestored eighteenth-century porcelain figures. Attractive models can be costly, rare examples extremely costly. Copies abound, especially hard-paste examples bearing a Chelsea gold anchor device, but many other fakes occur and the reader should tread warily.

Many of the older figures are completely unmarked – this can be a good sign! Peter Bradshaw's book *18th Century English Porcelain Figures 1745–1795* (Antique Collectors' Club, 1981) is a very good guide to English figures and groups. The various recent books on our main factories – Bow, Chelsea, Derby, etc. – include illustrations of typical examples from that factory. The reader is referred to the relevant entries in the present book.

Other, originally less expensive, figures were made in various earthenware bodies, but the range is so vast that to attempt the task of listing them in this book would probably be more confusing than helpful. Most earthenware figures are unmarked and in price they can range from tens of thousands of pounds for a very rare early eighteenth-century model to ten or twenty pounds for a Victorian flatback figure of a common subject.

FLIGHT & BARR etc. (1783–1840). In 1783 Thomas Flight purchased the Worcester porcelain factory. Owing to changes in partnership we have three separate periods and marks of Flight & Barr (1792–1804), Barr, Flight & Barr (1804–13) and Flight, Barr & Barr (1813–40). The factory was then absorbed by Chamberlain.

The Worcester soapstone type body continued in use. In conformity with fashion, Neo-Classical styles of decoration (urns, festones, scrolls) were adopted. From *c.*1807 shell motifs printed or painted by talented artists were popular; also, as at Derby, elaborate cabinet pieces, e.g. two-handled vases, open or covered, on square plinths, sometimes richly decorated with japan patterns or naturalistic flowers, many pieces being heavily gilded. Large dinner and dessert services, vases, jardinières, inkstands, etc. were sometimes decorated with named local landscapes, as Plate 44.

As a good general rule the Flight period Worcester porcelains are of superb workmanship, and neatly potted, well painted and attractively gilt. Not all pieces are richly decorated but all are neat and attractive. Clear name or initial marks were generally used and these help to date the article into previously mentioned periods.

The standard reference book is Henry Sandon's *Flight and Barr Worcester Porcelain 1783–1840* (Antique Collectors' Club, 1978) but other modern general books, such as Godden's *Encyclopaedia of British Porcelain Manufacturers* (Barrie & Jenkins, 1988) are helpful.

44   *A typically superb Worcester covered vase of the Barr Flight & Barr period (c.1804–13), painted with a named Sussex view. Impressed crowned 'B.F.B.' mark, also written Barr Flight & Barr mark. 8¾in high. c.1804–13.*

FLOWER-HOLDERS AND BULB-POTS. Bowls with perforated covers were used both for growing bulbs and for arranging flowers. They were made in a great variety of shapes and wares. 'Quintals' or finger vase five-socketed fan-shaped holders on square or oblong bases made in earthenware rather than porcelain. Similar holders were flatbacked to hang on walls, see Cornucopia. One popular Victorian form was the vase-in-hand, a small vase held in a lady's hand, her cuff forming the base. A representation of a baby's hand was also popular.

Flower-holders were made at all periods and in all ceramic bodies. Some are reasonably plain and neatly decorated, especially the earthenware examples of the 1770–1820 period made by Wedgwood and other leading potters. The porcelain examples are more fanciful, the Chelsea factory even produced a model ornamented with three dolphins. The range of models produced by the larger factories can be judged by consulting Godden's book *Chamberlain-Worcester Porcelain 1788–1852* (Barrie & Jenkins, 1982), Plates 337–45.

Most of these bulb-pots, flower-holders, and cornucopia were sold in matching pairs. Perfect decorative pairs are now very costly.

FLOWN (FLOW) BLUE. The name given to a muzzy form of printing (usually in underglaze blue) where the blue is induced to flow or run slightly. This technique was (strangely) popular in the 1840s and 1850s when applied to inexpensive earthenwares. It was especially popular in the overseas markets and several American books deal at length with such wares. In the British Isles the flown blue wares get a mixed reception, see *Davenport China, Earthenware, and Glass* by T. A. Lockett and G. A. Godden (Barrie & Jenkins, 1989), chapter 15.

FOOD WARMERS. A bedside device (of Continental origin) to provide light and to keep drinks or semi-liquid foods warm through the night; made in England from the 1760s to 1840s in delftware, creamware (Plate 46), porcelain, etc. and often elaborately decorated. A nightlight-type candle or wick-type burner was placed in a large opening at the side of the base component (as Plate 45) on which rested the covered pot containing the liquid. Sometimes a vessel of hot water was interposed between pot and lamp; in later types ('tea-warmers') the top element might be a teapot.

The Continental examples (called a Veilleuse) are generally more

45   A rare Lowestoft porcelain food-warmer or veilleuse, decorated in underglaze blue. painter's number 5. 10¼in high. c.1760–70. **(Sotheby's).**

common and decorative than the English examples but all are desirable objects especially when complete with all their components. The standard book is Harold Newman's *Veilleuses* (A. S. Barnes & Co., South Brunswick, NJ, 1967).

Another variety of food warmer was the double-thickness plate or dish with a hole in the rim, into which hot water or hot sand could be poured.

46   An undecorated creamware food-warmer or veilleuse, the units separated for display. Wedgwood and many other potters produced such elaborate articles for the sick. Main unit 6in high. c.1810.

FOOTBATH. A pottery oval bowl about 9–14in deep and perhaps 28in long and 15in wide, sometimes with end handles. Made by most potters in the nineteenth century, when our forebears were addicted to mustard baths for tired feet, many footbaths were surprisingly well decorated. Now that such objects have gone out of fashion or been superseded they make attractive containers for plants and flowers. Early (c.1790–1830) specimens have straight upright sides; after about 1830 they tend to become more ornate with shaped sides. By about 1900 earthenware footbaths ceased to be made.

Some high-quality footbaths were made in porcelain rather than in earthenware but these costly examples are the exception.

FROG-MUGS. Quaint reminders of eighteenth-century tavern humour. Theoretically the guileless toper would be startled as he lowered his ale to see a frog (often gaudily spotted) peering out of the dregs or crawling up the drinking side; in early mugs the frog might be hollowed to produce gurgling sounds as the beer spouted from its open mouth. These mugs were made from c.1750 to the 1880s, particularly in Sunderland and Staffordshire and have since been reproduced. Some had more than one frog, a few had toads, snakes, or newts.

Frog-mugs tend to be in earthenware rather than porcelain, the additional frog device being added to a variety of designs so that a collection of such novelties can be quite varied.

FRUIT AND VEGETABLE. These have often been reproduced in porcelain and pottery, sometimes as dishes (e.g. a Chelsea apple sliced so that the top half can be lifted by its stalk) or just for fun and decoration.

Other lidded forms are cos lettuce, globe artichoke, cauliflower, lemon, orange, bundle of asparagus, and melon. Some of these novelties can be of eighteenth-century English or Continental porcelain and such rarities are rightly expensive. Other specimens are Victorian or even modern for such decorative accessories have always been popular.

FULHAM. This district of London is rightly famous, mainly for the stonewares made there from the early 1670s onwards. In April, 1672, John Dwight, then of Fulham, took out a Patent to make 'transparent Earthenware . . . also . . . the stone ware vulgarly called Cologne ware' and was soon able to claim to make 'as good and as much Cologne ware as would supply England'. These brown stonewares were mainly useful objects such as bottles and jugs, but Dwight is also famous for some sharply-modelled figures and portrait busts. The early Dwight stonewares are very rare. After his death in 1703 the Fulham pottery was continued by a succession of owners. C. I. C. Bailey owned the Pottery in the 1864–91 period. In the present century it was owned by the Fulham Pottery and Cheavin Filter Company Ltd.

Whilst stonewares were made at the Fulham pottery for over 300 years, similar wares were made at other centres and the term Fulham pottery or stoneware tends to be a generic term. No. 11 of *The Journal of Ceramic History* (Stoke-on-Trent City Museums, 1979) is devoted to 'John Dwight's Fulham Pottery 1672–1978'. The reader is also referred to A. Oswald, R. J. C. Hildyard and R. G. Hughes's joint work *English Brown Stoneware 1670–1900* (Faber & Faber, 1982).

GAUDY WELSH (*c*.1830–60). American name for once inexpensive pottery ware made mainly for the US market. It was gaily decorated with a few characteristic formal floral designs in orange, blue, and gold. These mainly useful wares are very seldom marked and it is by no means certain that all examples have a Welsh origin. The name is really a generic one, relating to a popular colourful but inexpensive style of decoration.

GIRL-IN-A-SWING FACTORY (*c*.1749–54). The name given to a mystery class of early English porcelain which was probably made in London. No marked examples are known and the name arises from a white figure of a girl in a swing (Plate 47) in the Victoria & Albert Museum. Little is known of the factory, but some of its products are now confidently identified, mainly consisting of attractive small figures and the delightful miniature 'Chelsea toys' (e.g. scent bottles, bonbonnières, seals, etc. in the form of animals, birds, putti, etc.) of the type that the main Chelsea factory also manufactured. The very thin glaze permitted great clarity of detailed outline, resulting in a distinctive style, especially in modelling faces and drapery. The porcelain body contains on chemical analysis a high lead content. The pieces attributed to this factory are very rare and costly.

Information on these early porcelains is given in Arthur Lane and Robert Charleston's joint E.C.C. Paper 'Girl in a Swing Porcelain and Chelsea' (*Transactions of the English Ceramic Circle*, vol. 5, part 3, 1962), in Mrs Elizabeth Adams's book *Chelsea Porcelain* (Barrie & Jenkins, 1987) and her articles 'The Sites of the Chelsea Porcelain Factory' (*Ceramics*, November 1985) and 'A Mysterious Masterpiece' (*Collectors Guide*, May 1989).

47   *The early white porcelain group of a girl in a swing, a very rare model that gave the name to this small group of mid eighteenth-century London unmarked porcelains. 6¼in high. c.1750+.* **(Victoria & Albert Museum).**

GOSS (1858–1939). William Henry Goss made his reputation at Copelands before setting up his pottery at Stoke in 1858. Here, in 'ivory porcelain' (a glazed parian), he made portrait busts, statues, ear-rings, and brooches shaped as flowers, and 'jewelled' pieces in which gems were embedded. He also produced some very good parian figures. To most people Goss means the mass-produced and inexpensive crested or heraldic china started c.1884, miniature pieces transfer-printed with the crest of some popular seaside resort or other town or village – the poor man's cabinet piece. The range of shapes was great; those who like oddities may look for e.g. models of a Cornish pasty marked Lostwithiel, or of Queen Victoria's first little shoe, bought by father at Sidmouth and so bearing the Sidmouth crest.

Various other tourist type wares were made including a series of model cottages, houses, etc.; some but by no means all of these models are now rare.

In general the Goss china ornaments were mass-produced and sold in their thousands. The more common designs are still plentiful and are inexpensive. On the other hand, some designs and forms are rare and are keenly sought after by collectors. By no means all crested china of Goss-type was made by this firm; many others sought to share the market.

A good general book is Sandy Andrews's *Crested China. The History of Heraldic Souvenir Ware* (Springwood Books and Milestone Publications, 1980). Milestone Publications have also published several specialist books and Price Guides on Goss wares.

GRAINGER'S WORCESTER (c.1805–89). Founded by Thomas Grainger who had decorated for his father-in-law Robert Chamberlain (see Chamberlain's Worcester). Like him, Grainger at first decorated porcelain bought from other factories, but by about 1805 he had started to make his own porcelain and produce wares in the Chamberlain and, later, Royal Worcester styles; early specimens are not easily identifiable as they were usually unmarked.

Grainger's traded under varrious styles, the main ones sometimes reflected in the marks being: (T) Grainger & Co (c.1805–39), as Plate 48, Grainger, Wood & Co (c.1805–March 1811), Grainger, Lee & Co (c.1820–37), George (or G) Grainger & Co (c.1839–89). The later Grainger porcelains sometimes bear initial marks G & Co or G. W (for Grainger Worcester). In 1889 the Grainger firm was taken over by the main Worcester firm generally known as Royal Worcester although production continued under the Grainger name until 1902. Many of the old Grainger shapes and styles were continued by Royal Worcester for many years, the model or pattern numbers being prefixed 'G'.

For further information the reader is referred to Godden's *Encyclopaedia of British Porcelain Manufacturers* (Barrie & Jenkins, 1988) and to Henry and John Sandon's specialist work *Grainger's Worcester Porcelain* (Barrie & Jenkins, 1989).

*48   A rare marked Grainger porcelain jug painted with a coaching scene. Painted mark 'Grainger & Co., Worcester'. 8½in high. c.1820. **(Christie's).***

GREEN-GLAZED WARES. Josiah Wedgwood, while working with Whieldon, perfected the first of several semi-translucent green lead glazes, *c.*1760. These were later used as an all-over glaze on dessert and other wares moulded with leaf designs, etc., the green glaze accentuating the moulded designs.

These decorative wares were popular and inexpensive as no additional decoration was needed. Green-glazed relief-moulded wares were made by many firms – Brameld (Rockingham), Copeland, Davenport, Ridgway, and Wedgwood to name only a few of the many producers of this type of earthenware.

Whilst the dessert wares were the staple line, some fine ornamental pieces were made by firms such as Neale. In the Victorian period the quality of the wares made by the smaller firms declined both in the colour of the glaze and in the potting. The reader is warned that not all pieces are necessarily old and some may not even be English.

JAMES HADLEY (*c*.1838–1903). A noted modeller who worked for most of his life for the Royal Worcester Company. He produced a charming series of figures, groups, etc. of Kate Greenaway-style figures. He also excelled in Japanese-styled designs and forms in the 1870s and 1880s (see Plate 49 and Colour Plate VIII).

49　A rare pair of Royal Worcester figures modelled by James Hadley in the Japanese style, so popular in the 1870s. Printed Royal Worcester mark with year mark for 1874. 6½in high. 1874.

Many of these designs were supplied to the Worcester company on a freelance basis and he also ran his own porcelain producing firm at Worcester in the 1896–1903 period (Plate 50). Much of his work is signed and his own products bear special marks: see Geoffrey Godden's *Handbook of British Pottery & Porcelain Marks* (Barrie & Jenkins, 1972).

For further information the reader is referred to Henry Sandon's *Royal Worcester Porcelain from 1862 to the Present Day* (Barrie & Jenkins, third edition 1978) or Geoffrey Godden's *Encyclopaedia of British Porcelain Manufacturers* (Barrie & Jenkins, 1988).

50   Typical Hadley-Worcester vases produced from tinted clays and then hand-painted. Printed factory marks. Larger vase 8in high. c.1896–1903.

HEN TUREENS. Tureens in the form of a hen and chickens, partridge, other birds, rabbits, fish, etc. were copied from Meissen models by Chelsea, Bow, and Derby *c.*1750–70 for use on the table. They reappeared in the 1840s as vividly coloured 'hens-on-nests'; small models might originally have contained a Valentine gift. Most of those found today are Staffordshire pottery hens of the 1840s to 1890s (as Plate 51), but later reproductions occur.

These Victorian hen tureens or covered boxes were usually made by the firms that produced the flat-back type Staffordshire earthenware figures. For example *The Pottery Gazette Diary* of 1882 features advertisements for Kent & Parr (*c.*1880–94) of Burslem listing various types of Staffordshire, dogs, figures, and 'Hens'.

These decorative and once inexpensive pottery examples are very seldom marked but a Dudson example is shown in Godden's *Illustrated Encyclopaedia of British Pottery & Porcelain* (Barrie & Jenkins, 1966). These Staffordshire earthenware examples have a decorative charm; the earlier porcelain examples are collectors' treasures.

51   A typical Victorian earthenware hen tureen for eggs. These popular novelties were made in various sizes and decorated in different ways from about 1850 into the present century. 4½in high. c.1860.

HERCULANEUM. The Herculaneum factory at Liverpool in the period 1796–1840 produced a wide range of earthenwares, stonewares, and porcelains which were quite unlike the earlier Liverpool wares.

The porcelains in particular can be most attractive and well decorated, as can be seen from the oval covered sugar-bowl shown in Plate 52. The shapes are usually characteristic and a range of key shapes is shown in Godden's *Encyclopaedia of British Porcelain Manufacturers* (Barrie & Jenkins, 1988), Plates 195–9.

The impressed mark HERCULANEUM rarely occurs (the spelling HERCULANIUM has also been noted), the impressed capital letter 'L' is also recorded. These Herculaneum wares are all quite rare. The City Museum at Liverpool has a representative display of this distinctive manufacturer's work.

52   *A rare and superb Herculaneum Liverpool oval covered sugar-bowl of a characteristic porcelain form. 6½in long. c.1810.*

HILDITCH (*c*.1819–35). One of the smaller nineteenth-century Staffordshire porcelain manufacturers whose products have recently been researched and publicized and have therefore become popular.

William Hilditch of Church Street, Lane End, in the Staffordshire Potteries, may be considered a typical 'second division' manufacturer producing a wide range of mainly unmarked bone china of average quality.

The firm of Hilditch & Sons, later Hilditch & Hopwood (*c*.1835–59), catered well for the vast middle-class market and their porcelains have become very collectable.

For further information the reader is referred to Peter Helm's chapter 18 in *Staffordshire Porcelain* (Granada, 1983) or to Godden's *Encyclopaedia of British Porcelain Manufacturers* (Barrie & Jenkins, 1988).

HYBRID HARD-PASTE PORCELAIN. This term is a relatively recent one, used for quite a large quantity of English porcelain produced in the approximate period 1790–1815.

The porcelains are dense and relatively heavy and in appearance and feel they (and the covering glaze) seem to fall midway between hard and soft paste. It is possible that new mixes were introduced to avoid Cookworthy's original and then extended Patent Rights on true hard-paste porcelain using both china-stone and china-clay from Cornwall. By about 1815 and in some cases earlier the hybrid hard-paste porcelains had been superseded by the more pleasing and more dependable bone china.

The hybrid hard-pastes were usually unmarked and consequently the correct indentification of the various makes is extremely difficult and often a fruitless exercise! The main makes of English hybrid hard-paste porcelain are:

Caughley (*c*.1795–99)

Chamberlain-Worcester (*c*.1791–1815)

Coalport (*c*.1795–1815)

Davenport (*c*.1807–12)

M. Mason (*c*.1802–14)

New Hall (*c*.1781–1815)

Thomas Wolfe (*c*.1796–1800)

Factory X (*c*.1795–1815)

Factory Z (*c*.1800–10)

In addition many less well-known firms produced similar wares and it is now believed that even the Spode firm (the father of bone china) produced a small quantity of hybrid hard-paste porcelain, before leading the advance into the perfected bone china body, a lead followed by all.

INK POTS, INKSTANDS. When in the eighteenth and nineteenth centuries ink pots were in general use the porcelain manufacturers made a bewildering variety of such objects. The Bow factory, called 'New Canton', made some simple circular examples inscribed, perhaps for publicity purposes, 'Made at New Canton' with dates such as 1750 or 1751. Other simple drum-shape examples were made at Derby and at the Lowestoft factory. Here too they were regarded as perhaps suitable gifts and some were inscribed 'A Trifle from Lowestoft'. These are now of great rarity.

Other inkstands were more elaborate, especially those made at Chelsea or Derby, comprising an ornamental stand to hold the various component pieces – an ink pot, a sander (or pounce-pot), and perhaps a taper-stick. Such niceties might have graced a lady's writing-table or bureau.

In the nineteenth century a vast number of very elaborate inkstands were made although the inexpensive drum-shape remained the standard type. The range of such pieces can be gauged by consulting works on individual factories such as Godden's *Minton Pottery & Porcelain of the First Period 1793–1850* (Barrie & Jenkins, 1968) or *Chamberlain-Worcester Porcelain, 1788–1852* (Barrie & Jenkins, 1982), Plates 299–313. An interesting cabinet of inkstands is on show at Standen, a National Trust property in West Sussex.

JACKFIELD. A generic term used for a black and glossy-glazed earthenware. Strictly, the name refers to eighteenth-century red earthenware darkened with manganese and cobalt, thickly coated with very shiny glaze. The products, mainly tea wares, jugs, and other useful articles, were sometimes originally decorated with un-fired (or lightly fired) gilding or enamel decoration. In most cases this has long since worn away.

These wares were formerly believed to have been made at or near Jackfield by the river Severn in Shropshire, but most examples are now thought to have been made in Staffordshire. Examples are not marked and some Jackfield-type wares may not be eighteenth-century.

JAPAN PATTERNS. A term best reserved for designs on English porcelain and pottery derived (usually very distantly) from one of two quite different Japanese styles – Kakiemon and Imari. It is, how-ever, sometimes used in relation to other oriental, including Chinese, patterns all of which in the eighteenth century tended to be grouped together as 'Japanese'.

53 *A Coalport 'Japan pattern' plate with broken wasters from the factory site showing only the underglaze blue parts. This vase of flower pattern was loosely copied from the Japanese imports and was very popular with English manufacturers. Diameter 8¾in. c.1805–10.*

Kakiemon was the founder of a family of potters who worked in the Arita district of Japan *c*.1650–1720. His style was characterized by asymmetrical compositions of well-spaced flowering branches (especially prunus) with additions such as rocks, banded hedges, quails, and rarely figures (see Plate 54). These were painted in a pleasing palette of brick-red, green, and lilac, often supplemented by yellow, turquoise, or slight gilding. Sparingly applied, this decoration emphasized the perfection of white porcelain. It was copied by Bow, Chelsea, Worcester, and by early French and German porcelain manufacturers.

Imari is a later and much less refined style, named after the Arita district port from which the Japanese porcelains were exported in the eighteenth century. The palette was dark underglaze blue, with green and red enamel, combined with gilding in confused patterns covering most of the available space, see Colour Plate IV. It was inspired by oriental brocaded silks and lacquer which caught the European fancy. Imari ware was imported into Europe in large quantities and was copied by European manufacturers.

As all-over decoration it was useful in covering up defects on porcelains and became a Derby speciality under Bloor's management. Much was produced at Coalport and Chamberlain's Worcester while Spode and Mason's Ironstone also featured this style. The Davenport Company in the 1870s and 1880s also produced a very colourful range of such porcelain designs on a wide variety of objects. A central vase of flowers surrounded by an ornate colourful border is characteristic of the Japan patterns, as the Coalport example featured in Plate 53.

The Royal Crown Derby Company still produces a range of these designs which sell world-wide.

54   An early Chelsea plate painted in the seventeenth-century Japanese style in the Kakiemon manner. Not to be confused with the more colourful allover 'Japan patterns' as shown previously. Diameter 8¼in. c.1748–53. **(Christie's)**

JAPANESE-STYLE. The early English porcelain manufacturers at Bow and Chelsea (Plate 54) in particular, produced many attractive designs in the manner of Japanese painters who are believed to have been responsible for such restrained decoration. These porcelain designs are very different from the colourful broadly painted so-called Japan patterns. These attractive Kakiemon-style designs mainly date from the 1745–60 period. The popular style was also employed by Continental firms.

In the 1875–90 period there was a revival of interest in Japanese art and styles but these Victorian Japanese-style designs were mainly applied by printing techniques to relatively inexpensive earthenwares. Both types are attractive but quite different.

JASPER WARE (*c.*1774 onwards). A dense unglazed stoneware, translucent when thin; the white body was either colour-stained throughout or surface-coloured by dipping. It was perfected by Josiah Wedgwood I in about 1774 after many trials. Decoration was usually in white relief, classical themes predominating; wares included vases, tea wares, portrait medallions (Plate 113), plaques, and a variety of objects large and small. Whilst some fine examples date to the later part of the eighteenth century or to the early part of the nineteenth century, very many more pieces are much later, as Plate 115 illustrates. Other examples were made in the present century.

Wedgwood employed some famous artists (e.g. Flaxman, 1776–87) to design the reliefs. The commonest colour is blue, pale at first and today, but darker in the 1800s; there is also jasper in green, yellow, black, or a combination of colours, see Colour Plate XI. In the earlier examples the moulded clay reliefs are trimmed up by hand to obtain sharper relief. An outstanding example was a series of exact copies of the Portland Vase in blue-black (1790), reissued later in other colours. Jasper ware was imitated by many other potters, including superb wares by Neale, Turner, or Adams, but many early examples are unmarked.

The early jasper wares can be most attractive and show the potter's art to good effect. Many firms produced Wedgwood-style jasper in the nineteenth century, Dudson being but one of the major makers. The Wedgwood firm have produced the jasper body almost continuously from the 1770s. From *c.*1891, the word 'England' was added to their name-marks, to be replaced by 'Made in England' after 1921 to conform to US trade regulations for imported wares.

JET. This ceramic trade description relates to a glossy black-glazed earthenware, similar in appearance to the earlier 'Jackfield' wares. Jet was particularly associated with inexpensive teapots made in the approximate period 1875–1910. The trade advertisement reproduced in Plate 55 relates to a selection of Gibson & Sons 'Jet' teapots of the late 1880s which can be decorated with printed gold or other patterns.

   We have included these mainly non-antique teapots as examples of this type are so widely distributed and their owners tend to regard examples as antique and desirable. Decorative as they can be, they are not (as yet) valuable. Perhaps here lies a neglected field for further study.

55   A range of inexpensive 'Jet' (black glossy glazed) earthenware teapots as advertised by Gibson & Sons of Burslem in 1888. Matching kettles, coffee pots, sugar-bowls, creamers, and jugs were available. The added decoration was printed, often in gold.

GEORGE JONES (& SONS). This firm of the Trent Potteries at Stoke produced from 1861 a good range of decorative and useful earthenwares. From 1872 good quality bone china was also made. Perhaps the firm is best known for its novel and decorative majolica-type earthenwares. Decorative Pâte-sur-Pâte vases, dishes and plaques were also made. The trade-name 'Crescent' or 'Crescent China' was much used in marks from about 1893 and the address Crescent Pottery was used from 1907. After several changes of ownership the firm closed in 1951.

JUGS. Ceramic jugs come in all shapes and sizes. Some of the best known eighteenth-century examples are the sharp-pointed sparrow-beak cream jugs (Worcester, etc.), larger masked-lip jugs in moulded cabbage-leaf form (Worcester, Caughley, Lowestoft, etc.), the helmet-shaped cream-jug (New Hall, etc.), the octagonal jug in Mason's Patent Ironstone, and many examples in Brownware. Narrow-necked harvest jugs, taken out to the men at work at haymaking and harvest seasons, were made in stoneware or earthenware, sometimes covered with slipware and inscribed with appropriate doggerel.

56 *A Coalport porcelain jug, a one-off order bearing the owner's armorial bearings. Thousands of jug forms were produced as such articles were both decorative and useful. 4½in high. c.1810–15.*

In the nineteenth century hundreds of different moulded forms were produced in earthenware, in stoneware, and from *c.*1842 in the parian body. Originally these were often issued in sets of three or more, made in graduating sizes.

The variety of types is almost limitless – lustre, printed or painted decoration of various sorts. The shapes range from simple utilitarian traditional forms to fanciful ornate shapes such as the Toby jugs, the cow-creamers, or the Doulton-style character jugs.

Specialist books on jugs, mainly the later types, include *Jugs, a Collector's Guide* by J. Paton (Souvenir Press, 1976), *Relief-moulded Jugs 1820–1900* by R. K. Henrywood (Antique Collectors' Club, 1984), *The Character Jug Collectors Handbook* by K. Pearson (K. Francis Publishing, 1985), and *A Collectors Guide to Nineteenth-century Jugs* by Kathy Hughes (Routledge & Kegan Paul, 1985).

KERR & BINNS (1852–62). The Worcester partnership between William Henry Kerr and R. W. Binns succeeded Chamberlain & Co. In just ten years they produced a wide selection of very good quality porcelain, completely different in style to earlier types. Talented artists were employed, including Thomas Bott who specialized in white (or slightly tinted) decoration in the style of the old Limoges enamels (see Plate 57).

57 A typically superb Kerr & Binns period Worcester vase, decorated by Thomas Bott in the style of Limoges enamels. Printed shield-shape mark with year numbers for 1857. 12¾in high. 1857.

Kerr retired in July 1862 and Binns then founded the Worcester Royal Porcelain Company, which continues to this day as Royal Worcester. One neat printed shield mark includes the initials K & B and space for the last two numerals of the year to be filled in – i.e. 57 for 1857.

LEAF DISHES. Small moulded porcelain trays in the form of a leaf, made by most factories from the eighteenth century onwards to hold pickles etc. Bow and Lowestoft favoured vine or ivy leaves, Worcester overlapping cabbage leaves or a vine leaf with the stalk forming a handle, and Longton Hall twig handles. Very many of these leaf-shape dishes were decorated in underglaze blue and these are very popular.

Similar small dishes for use on the table were in the form of scallop shells.

LEEDS POTTERY (c.1760–1878). Chiefly noted for fine creamware, especially the pierced work of the 1780–1820 period. Unfortunately it was copied, together with the Leeds mark, by later firms or potters whose products have a pinkish tinge and are altogether too light; other late pieces were too thick (Plate 58), and badly crazed, and those with transfer-printed subjects of American interest were too brilliant.

Leeds made a wide range of creamware figures (some, in the 1790s, in Pearlware), including birds, animals, Derby-style gods, musicians, the four elements, Isaac Newton, making free use of Staffordshire models. The large piebald horses of the early 1800s are particularly well known; they originally advertised shops selling harness or veterinary drugs. This factory also made basalt and lustre wares. It went bankrupt in 1820 but was kept in production by other owners for many years. In recent times the traditional Leeds-style earthenwares have been reintroduced; at first these were made in Leeds but production has now been moved to Staffordshire.

Not all creamware traditionally attributed to Leeds was made there and the name is sometimes used in a generic sense.

Illustrations of typical Leeds wares will be found in the following standard books: *The Leeds Pottery* by Donald Towner (Faber & Faber, 1963), *Creamware and other English Pottery at Temple Newsam House, Leeds* by Peter Walton (Manningham Press, 1976), and *Creamware* by Donald Towner (Faber & Faber, 1978).

LINTHORPE POTTERY (1879–89). A Yorkshire art pottery at Middlesbrough, where the local coarse red clay was used for pottery (often of almost surrealistic shapes) decorated with beautiful iridescent multicoloured flowing glazes and sgraffito. The tone was set by Henry Toft, who was there for only three years. Artists drew inspiration from the ancient art of Egypt, the Far East or Central America, or from the Middle Ages, and each item was individually fashioned. C. W. Hart's book *Linthorpe Art Pottery*

I   A Coalport porcelain vase, decorated at Thomas Baxter's London studio. Note design of gilt borders, the red and gold striped ground, and the typical flower painting. 8¾in high. c.1805. (Private collection.)

II   A typical marine-form Belleek glazed parian teapot. Note iridescent glossy glaze. Printed Belleek mark and moulded Registration device for 22 February 1869. 6¼in high. c.1869–72.

III   A Coalport porcelain covered bowl decorated with applied hand-made flowers in the 'Coalbrookdale' style – a technique also used by many other firms. 4¾in high. c.1825–35.

IV   A typical Spode early nineteenth-century 'Japan pattern' in underglaze blue and overglaze enamels and gilding. Many firms copied or adapted such rich old Japanese designs. Painted Spode pattern number 967. 4½in high. c.1810–20.

V   One of a pair of typically fine quality Minton vases painted by the Sèvres-trained artist Anton Boullemier. Impressed MINTON name-mark with year cypher for 1871. 19in high. c.1871–2.

VI   A very typical Moorcroft earthenware covered jar with bold fruit and floral design worked in coloured glazes within raised outlines. Printed and impressed Moorcroft name marks. 11in high. c.1920–5.

VII A Minton tray decorated in Pâte-sur-Pâte style by M. L. Solon, for the 1878 Paris Exhibition. The use of tinted (rather than only white) slips is unusual. Signed 'L. Solon, 78'. Minton Globe mark and special exhibition wording. 18in long. 1878.

VIII A Royal Worcester vase, one of a pair modelled by James Hadley in the Japanese style so popular in this country in the 1870s and 1880s. Printed Royal Worcester mark with year mark for 1874. 10¼in high. c.1874.

IX   A superb quality Minton vase (one of a set of three) decorated in the eighteenth-century Sèvres-style. Printed Minton name-mark and ermine device. 12½in high. c.1850–60.

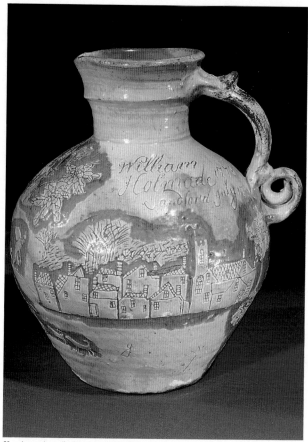

X   *A rare inscribed and dated West Country earthenware harvest-type jug, the added layer of slip cut away in the sgraffito technique. Dated 17 July 1778. 10¾in high. 1778. (I. T. Henderson collection.)*

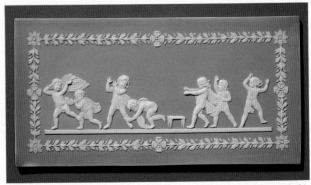

XI *A two-colour Wedgwood jasper-ware plaque or panel decorated with typical white relief designs. Impressed 'Wedgwood' name-mark. 12½in long. c.1850.*

(Aisling Publications, Guisborough, Cleveland (UK), 1988) gives a good account of these wares.

58   A 'Leeds creamware' covered sugar-box and a matching creamer, made to commemorate the 1908 Royal visit to Leeds. Most examples of Leeds are of late eighteenth or early nineteenth-century date, but many later examples exist and much creamware attributed to this factory was in fact made elsewhere. Examples are seldom marked.

LITHOPHANES (1827–c.1910). Thin white porcelain small panels of varying thickness which, when (but only when) held to the light, reveal a detailed black and white mezzotint-like picture (see Plate 59) that might be of a landscape, battle, or scene from fiction but was more frequently a religious subject. The effect was achieved by a laborious process of modelling a wax mould (from which successive plaster and metal moulds were taken) to obtain different thicknesses in the parian or porcelain slab – the highlights very thin, the shadows comparatively thick.

Lithophanes were incorporated in lamp shades, night-light holders, fire-screens, the base of a mug or tea wares, or were made to be hung in windows. Most rare are German (marked KPM, PPM, etc.) but at the height of their popularity in the 1850s some were made by Minton, Grainger, Copeland, Belleek, and other firms in Britain and elsewhere.

Most were left white, but some were carefully coloured by hand to add to the effect and to make a picture even when unlit.

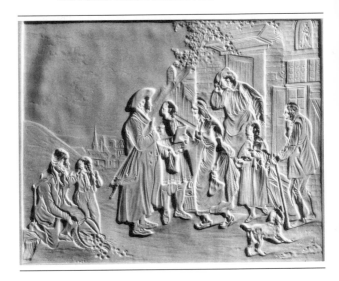

59   *A German porcelain moulded lithophane and below the same thin slab when illuminated from behind to bring the picture to life. Impressed initial mark 'P.P.M'. 7 × 5in. c.1860.*

LIVERPOOL. There were several porcelain factories in Liverpool, specializing mainly in blue and white useful wares. Very few examples were marked, and attribution to specific factories is particularly difficult as many features, though typical of Liverpool, are common to several of them. These include a greyish look, a slightly blue-tinted glaze, and a rather dull blacklish underglaze blue, but some Liverpool blue and white can be superb.

Soapstone porcelain was used by Richard Chaffers (1755–65) and his successor Philip Christian (1765–78); bone-ash porcelain by the Penningtons (c.1763–1805) and Samuel Gilbody (c.1754–61); bone china at the later Herculaneum factory (1796–1840); and near hard-paste porcelain by Thomas Wolfe (c.1796–1800).

Chaffer's products included overglaze transfer-prints, in black, brown, or red. Christian added to the Chaffers range elaborate moulded shapes and good enamel-painted wares. The Penningtons copied some of Christian's designs but in the 1790s turned to mass production of rather ordinary designs. Gilbody's porcelain can resemble Longton Hall; attractive bird designs and chinoiseries are attributed to this factory. The porcelains formerly attributed to William Ball are now (from 1988) believed to have been made at Vauxhall (q.v.) in London. Wolfe's porcelain, resembling some New Hall, was clumsily potted and usually decorated with transfer-prints in underglaze blue. The Herculaneum factory produced much transfer-printed earthenware; also urn-shaped vases, busts (in porcelain and stoneware), and also some delightful bone china tablewares.

Sadler & Green (1756–80) decorated wares with black or red transfer prints for other factories, including Liverpool firms and Longton Hall as well as Wedgwood and other Staffordshire pottery.

As to pottery, delftwares, notably punchbowls, were made from 1710; saltglaze, cream-coloured earthenware, and stoneware were also made.

For a good general account of Liverpool ceramics the reader should consult Alan Smith's *The Illustrated Guide to Liverpool Herculaneum Pottery* (Barrie & Jenkins, 1970). The porcelains are discussed in Bernard Watney's *English Blue & White Porcelain of the 18th Century* (Faber & Faber, 2nd edition 1973). A helpful more recent contribution is Maurice Hillis's paper 'The Liverpool Porcelains' published as the Northern Ceramic Society Occasional Paper no. 1 (1985).

Once the Liverpool porcelains were regarded as inferior to Worcester and other makes. This is not necessarily the case: some of the earlier examples are very attractive and of good quality. Often they have a charm lacking in the products of some other manufacturers.

LONDON DECORATORS. Independent enamellers and gilders of porcelain who decorated wares which they bought from, or which were sent to them by, the eighteenth-century manufacturers 'in the white' (i.e. glazed but not decorated). They tended to decorate in a more sophisticated Continental style than the factories' own artists.

Some of them seem eventually to have been lured into at least short-term employment by individual firms. Their activities have made life much more difficult for connoisseurs.

The most famous was the Giles studio (*c.*1760–78), established by James Giles in Kentish Town and later Soho. Giles's own work has not been identified, and his highly gifted artists are only known by such unsatisfying names as the 'spotted-fruit painter', the 'sliced-fruit painter', the painter of 'dishevelled birds' or of 'open-petalled tulips'. This studio was chiefly associated with Worcester, but also decorated for other factories. Their decoration included armorial, landscape, scenes taken from Watteau or Teniers, and ground colours, executed according to the instructions of private buyers, retailers, or the manufacturers. Some fine quality decoration was added to Chinese porcelains but this work was not necessarily all carried out in London.

Possibly a member of this group was Jefferyes Hamett O'Neale who specialized in Aesop's fables and landscapes; his work appears on Chelsea (*c.*1750) and Worcester. Another possible member was Fidelle Duvivier, who came from France *c.*1763; his style resembled that of O'Neale and he seems to have worked on (or at) Chelsea, Derby, Worcester, and New Hall.

John Donaldson was a miniaturist who came to London in 1760; his signed work appears on Chelsea and he also worked for Worcester and Derby.

Early in the nineteenth century the Worcester-born Baxters had a workshop at Clerkenwell and decorated Coalport porcelain. The son, Thomas, later worked at Worcester and Swansea (1814–21).

These porcelains not decorated at the original factory are generally speaking of very high quality and are highly collectable.

The standard book on the Giles porcelains is *In Search of James Giles* by G. Coke (Micawber, 1983). Information on Duvivier can be found in *New Hall* by David Holgate (Faber & Faber, 1987) and *Chamberlain-Worcester Porcelain 1788–1852* by Geoffrey Godden (Barrie & Jenkins, 1982). The last work also contains information on the Baxters. For information on the English decorated Chinese porcelains the reader is referred to Godden's *English China* (Barrie & Jenkins, 1985) or chapter 12 of the same author's *Oriental Export Market Porcelain* (Granada, 1979).

LONG ELIZAS. English nickname for the tall and elegant ladies who featured prominently on early eighteenth-century Chinese (Kangxi) blue and white porcelain exported to the West; they were copied on Delftware by the Dutch (who called them Lange Lijzen, 'tall stupids'; corrupted to 'Long Elizas'), on early Worcester, and much other blue and white and polychrome decorated porcelain.

LONGTON HALL (*c.*1749–60). One of the first Staffordshire porcelain factories; William Littler, who had worked in saltglaze, was the moving spirit of its brief existence, maintaining a large output despite financial crises. The Longton Hall body was usually heavy, thickly and unevenly potted, with greenish translucency. The glaze at first was thin, with a cold white glitter and many black specks.

Many pieces were decorated, even swamped, in a streaky underglaze dark blue ('Littler's blue'), e.g. a white plate might have a solid blue moulded border; a yellowish green was another characteristic colour. Leaf-shaped dishes and sauceboats moulded with high-relief overlapping leaves were common. Decoration (and general quality) improved in the middle years. The painters are unnamed but one is called the 'Trembly Rose' painter and another specialized in castles and classical ruins.

60   A Longton Hall oval dish with characteristic relief-moulded edge and typical bird painting. 13in long. c.1755.

Figures were important in the earliest and latest years. The early ones form a group ('snowmen') of white figures mainly of animals (e.g. bulls, horses), Chinese deities or Meissen models; the thick, exceptionally glassy glaze obscured the rather primitive modelling, and formed masses of bubbles; firecracks were prevalent. The later examples were quite different, better modelled, often large and massive figures, e.g. of the Continents, Seasons, musicians, with rather harsh colouring. Cookworthy appears to have obtained their moulds, for some models were produced at Plymouth and Bristol.

Littler went to Scotland and set up a pottery at West Pans near Musselburgh, where he decorated old Longton Hall stock and perhaps produced new porcelains in the 1764–77 period. He later returned to Staffordshire and reputedly died in poverty.

In recent years much porcelain attributed to Longton Hall has been reclassified as West Pans. It could also be that some Longton Hall figures should be reclassified as Vauxhall.

The reader is referred to Bernard Watney's standard work *Longton Hall Porcelain* (Faber & Faber, 1957), Godden's *Staffordshire Porcelain* (Granada, 1983), chapters 2 and 3 and Godden's *Encyclopaedia of British Porcelain Manufacturers* (Barrie & Jenkins, 1988).

LOVING-CUP. A two-handled cup usually urn-shaped like a sporting trophy; it developed from the grace cup passed round after grace at the end of a banquet. A silver version is still used at City of London functions.

Loving-cups were made at least from the 1740s in white saltglaze, slipware, creamware, brownware, etc., some transfer-printed in blue and white, or inscribed with the owner's name and a date, or the arms of a friendly society, etc. Their more homely use, confined to northern and midland counties, was to enable two cronies, the cup between them, to take turn and turn about, from hob and nob ('give and take') sipping hot toddy (rum, sugar, lemon, nutmeg, and water, much in favour 1780–1850).

Inscribed and dated examples are particularly valued but reproductions exist.

LOWESTOFT (c.1757–99). A small east-coast porcelain factory catering mainly for an undemanding local middle class, and specializing in tea services and other useful wares. The paste resembled Bow in its high bone-ash content, had a creamy appearance and was more open-grained than most of its contemporaries; the glaze was laid on thickly enough to pool, and much of it had a bluish tint.

Products of the first four years are rarely seen. For the first few years all wares were decorated in underglaze blue with 'Chinese' themes; some, e.g. sauceboats and tea-caddies, were additionally moulded in relief. Most typical are the dated and named mugs, inkwells (as Plate 61), etc., commissioned to commemorate some event or person, and pieces marked 'A Trifle from Lowestoft' (or other local town). Another curiosity was small circular plaques, apparently given to employees on the birth of a child.

Later, transfer-printed local views, ships, hunting scenes, etc., came in, together with a bid for the London market in the form of wares well painted in enamels with floral designs in which a tulip was prominent. There were also a few figures, and some animals and small swans.

The 'Trifles' and other pieces have been much reproduced; on the other hand Lowestoft in its later years copied both the wares and the marks of other factories. Further confusion was created by an employee, Richard Allen, who set up his own Lowestoft shop and decorated wares bought in the white from Leeds, Castleford, and Staffordshire; he decorated them in the Lowestoft style and even added 'A Trifle from Lowestoft' to some. The delightfully unassuming Lowestoft firm diversified into curing herrings! Production declined in 1799 due to competition from Staffordshire and the factory seems to have closed late in 1799, after a comparatively long life.

61 A unique Lowestoft inkpot and pen-holder decorated in underglaze blue and inscribed as shown. 2¾in high. c.1770. (Sotheby's)

62 A Lowestoft trio of saucer, tea-bowl, and coffee cup decorated in the so-called Red-grave style with an oriental landscape pattern in underglaze blue with overglaze red and green and slight gilding. Diameter of saucer 4¾in. c.1780–5.

For further information and illustrations of typical products the reader is referred to Godden's *Lowestoft Porcelain* (Antique Collectors' Club, revised edition 1985), *Lowestoft Porcelain in Norwich Castle Museum* by Sheenah Smith (Norfolk Museums Service: vol. I, *The Blue and White Wares*, 1975; vol. II, *The Polychrome Wares*, 1985), and *Early Lowestoft* by Christopher Spencer (Ainsworth & Nelson, 1981). Several other articles and papers on various aspects of Lowestoft porcelain are listed in Godden's *Encyclopaedia of British Porcelain Manufacturers* (Barrie & Jenkins, 1988).

LUND'S BRISTOL (*c*.1749–52). The predecessor of Worcester in the making of soapstone soft-paste porcelain, at a factory founded by Benjamin Lund on the site of Lowdin's glassworks (and hence formerly called Lowdin's Bristol). Not much has survived that can be definitely assigned to Bristol rather than the earliest Worcester years; a very few pieces are marked 'Bristol' or 'Bristoll'. The ware, usually greyish, is sometimes creamy white and very translucent.

Sauceboats are the most numerous, some moulded and decorated in underglaze blue; they always have a thumb-rest on the handle. There were also cream jugs, mugs, leaf-dishes, bowls, and similar useful wares. There are no transfer-printed wares, no gilding, and only one figure model is known (a Chinese Immortal), in white.

The firm and equipment were bought by the newly formed Worcester Company and Lund moved there for an initial period.

The blue and white Lund's Bristol porcelains are scarce and costly. The reader is referred to Bernard Watney's *English Blue & White Porcelain of the 18th Century* (Faber & Faber, revised edition 1973) and Godden's *Eighteenth-century English Porcelain* (Granada, 1985) which includes an illustration of a reproduction blue and white sauce-boat in Plate 47.

LUSTREWARE. In its accepted form an exclusively English ceramic decoration with pigments containing minute quantities of gold (for 'copper' and pink lustre) or platinum (for 'silver' lustre), together with various other ingredients. Lustre can be applied to bone china, creamware, and other kinds of pottery. There are several claimants to the invention, which was first put to commercial use *c*.1805, the main centres of production being Staffordshire, Sunderland, Swansea, Newcastle, and Leeds. All kinds of objects were lustred, including goblets, mugs, Toby jugs, animals, and all types of jugs.

The intention, to imitate the colour and shapes of gold and silver ware by all-over lustre, was later abandoned and lustreware developed as a thing of beauty in its own right. The most highly prized is silver resist, in which designs or reserve panels were formed, before the lustre was applied, by treating them with wax or grease that would protect them from (or 'resist') the lustre. These reserves might be left white or given a coloured ground (canary or blue are most sought), and further embellished by painting or transfer printing flowers, foliage, birds, landscapes, sporting scenes, etc. In a reverse process, lustre was stencilled on.

The lustre was laid on as a very thin film; thus the colour of the body of the ware was important. Most copper lustre is painted on brown-glazed earthenware, as on the familiar copper lustre jug. A thin gold solution on white produced pink lustre, which could be deepened to purple by additional coats. 'Splashed' (mottled) pink or purple lustre was produced by dropping oil on to a wet gold lustre; this type is mainly associated with Sunderland. Wedgwood produced a 'variegated lustre' of pink or purple, marbled with grey, brown, or yellow.

In Staffordshire, Spode, Wood & Caldwell, Davenport, Wedgwood, and many others made lustreware, but attribution is difficult as much is unmarked.

Among the delights of lustreware are the doggerel and mottoes dealing with anything from the sailor's farewell to trade, political elections, pious admonitions, and plain bawdy. 'Sweet, Oh! Sweet is that Sensation, When two hearts in union meet' may serve to indicate the form. Some pieces celebrated current events and personalities. The best quality or dated specimens must be sought with patience; much of that seen is undistinguished or far from antique, and reproductions abound.

A new detailed book on British lustre wares is in preparation by Geoffrey Godden and Michael Gibson. This will be published in 1991 and illustrates a wide range of lustreware.

MADELEY (c.1825–40). A small factory near Coalport founded by Thomas Randall. He catered successfully for a revived vogue for eighteenth-century soft-paste Sèvres, making excellent imitations of it but, being a Quaker, refusing to fake the Sèvres mark. Among his decorators were his nephew John Randall, whose bird-paintings won him fame at Rockingham and Coalport, and William Cook (flowers), who also went on to Coalport.

The Madeley porcelains are unmarked with the exception of one figure of a lion, but recently discovered site wasters may well help to identify more of the factory's products.

For further information the reader is referred to Godden's *Encyclopaedia of British Porcelain Manufacturers* (Barrie & Jenkins, 1988).

MAJOLICA (1850–1914). Minton's name for a family of earthenware moulded in bold relief and coated in various coloured glazes. The modelling and painting, in academic style, was done by leading artists; dishes with vegetable shapes, jardinières, and figures were among the more notable items made. Very little had any resemblance to Italian Renaissance *maiolica*, on which the body, glaze, and decoration were initially based.

After the success of Minton's colourful new Majolica wares in the 1851 Exhibition various firms commenced producing similar wares.

The examples by leading makers such as Wedgwood, Copeland, Royal Worcester, and George Jones could be extremely good quality but (as with parian) a host of small firms made lesser work.

The earlier Majolica by the leading makers is highly collectable, mainly for its decorative merits. Similar wares were made elsewhere, particularly in America where Majolica is very popular.

For further information see *Majolica* by Victoria Bergesen (Barrie & Jenkins, 1989).

MANSION HOUSE DWARFS. A pair of grotesquely fat little figures first made at Derby in the eighteenth century copied (through a Chelsea red anchor figure) from etchings by Jacques Callot. They carried advertisements on their high hats and were so named after dwarf figures that stood outside the London Mansion House similarly decorated with announcements of sales, plays, etc. There are many reproductions, particularly by Samson, and later Derby examples were produced by the Royal Crown Derby Company (Plate 63).

63   *A pair of Derby 'Mansion House Dwarfs', popular models which have been produced from the eighteenth century onwards. Fakes can occur. Printed Crown Derby mark. 6¼in high. c.1880–90.*

MARTINWARE (1873–1915). Art pottery made by four brothers Martin at Southall, London, chiefly vases and jugs, in saltglaze stoneware. They are generally considered to be the first Studio-type potters in England. Their most famous handiwork, made almost throughout their career, were the grotesque leering birds (Plate 64), resembling a cross between an owl and a vulture with a human expression, soberly coloured in brown, grey, and blue; the heads are detachable. Jugs were also modelled as human faces (reproductions occur). Other more conventionally shaped jugs and vases of the middle period were incised or coloured in a wider palette with designs derived from vegetable or marine life, sometimes with birds (realistic birds) or dragons. No two pieces were the same, not even the pawns of a chess set. Each piece was signed and dated. The grotesqueries repel some, but values have greatly risen in recent years.

The brothers' output of these handmade stonewares was very large and varied considering that only stonewares were made. A good specialist book is *The Martin Brothers Potters* by M. Haslam (Richard Dennis, 1978). Typical specimens may be seen in Godden's *British Pottery. An Illustrated Guide* (Barrie & Jenkins, 1974), pp. 310–22.

*64 Two typical Martin Brothers stoneware two-piece birds and a face-jug – popular Martinware lines. Incised name-marks with dates (left to right) 5–1903, 10–1898, 4–1899. Birds 13in high. 1898 to 1903. **(Louis Taylor & Sons, Hanley).***

MASONIC CHINA. The establishment of the Grand Lodge of England (1717) marked the beginnings of modern Freemasonry here. Early symbols on eighteenth-century pottery and porcelain included the beehive (industriousness) and ladder. In addition to the square, trowel, and compass (with the motto 'Keep within compass'), there came the all-seeing eye of God, the 24in rule (a reminder that each hour of the day must be passed honourably and charitably), and Classical columns (for stability of character). One inscription reads: 'The World is in pain our secrets to gain'.

Masonic emblems can occur on a wide variety of ceramics – on Chinese imports and on late nineteenth-century Sunderland lustre jugs, etc.

MASON'S PATENT IRONSTONE CHINA (1813+). Possibly because of its inspired name, the most successful of the various types of Stone China, patented by C. J. Mason of Lane Delph (Staffordshire). Its most familiar form is the octagonal jug with snake handle and all-over japan patterns in shades of pale blue and red, as Plate 65. Great quantities of dinner and dessert services were made, durable though very heavy. After 1848 the moulds and engravings passed to other firms and eventually to Ashworths, who continued to use the name Mason's Patent Ironstone China but lightened the weight of the body.

65   *Two very characteristic Mason Ironstone jugs decorated in a typical manner. This jug form has been produced from at least the 1820s onwards and has been copied by several other makers. Blue-printed 'Mason's Patent Ironstone China' mark. 5¼ and 4½in high. c.1840.*

In 1968 the Ashworth firm was retitled Mason's Ironstone China Ltd; as such it continues to produce a range of traditional style earthenwares just across the road from the Museum and Art Gallery at Hanley.

Specialist books on these popular wares are *The Masons of Lane Delph* by R. G. Haggar (Lund Humphries, 1952), *Mason Porcelain & Ironstone 1796–1853* by R. G. Haggar and E. Adams (Faber & Faber, 1977), and *Godden's Guide to Mason's China and the Ironstone Wares* by G. A. Godden (Antique Collectors' Club, 1980).

MEIGH FAMILY (pronounced 'mee'). Staffordshire potters at Hanley, trading as Job Meigh & Son (*c*.1812–34) and then Charles Meigh (& Son) (*c*.1835–62). Charles built up a large business, mainly in blue and white, but also painted earthenware ('opaque porcelain'), Gothic-style jugs in white stoneware, parian figures, etc. He exhibited a good range of good quality and decorative earthenwares at the 1851 Exhibition but his productions are seldom marked. The City Museum at Hanley has a selection of the 1851 exhibits in the reserve collection. Much of Meigh's earthenware is of porcelain quality and would repay study and research.

The separate firms of Hicks & Meigh (*c*.1803–22) and Hicks, Meigh & Johnson (*c*.1822–35) produced at Shelton a very good range of Stone China and also fine porcelains. See Godden's *Staffordshire Porcelain* (Granada, 1983), chapter 17.

MINIATURE CHINA. Sets of porcelain or pottery table services, too large for the doll's house, made as children's toys and as cabinet pieces by many firms, some in early saltglaze, tortoiseshell, or pearlware. Leading eighteenth-century firms, such as Worcester, Bow, Caughley, and Lowestoft, made such child's sets usually decorated in underglaze blue. Many sets are true replicas of adult-sized wares, subsidiary items included. A nineteenth-century Staffordshire firm, Green & Co., specialized in them; they were also made by Coalport, Rockingham, Minton, Swansea, Ridgway, etc. and are still being made by Worcester and Copeland.

These miniature items have always been popular with collectors and the older pieces are now rare and very collectable. These scaled-down wares are not traveller's samples as suggested in the past. Mr & Mrs M. Milbourn's pleasing book *Understanding Miniature British Pottery & Porcelain* (Antique Collectors' Club, 1983) is one of several books on such pieces.

MINTON (1793–present day). A factory founded at Stoke-on-Trent, Staffordshire, by Thomas Minton, an engraver who previously worked for Turner (at Caughley) and Spode; it was greatly expanded by his son Herbert (1836–58). The range of products has been exceptionally varied and always of high quality, from the early blue-printed earthenwares (including Willow-type patterns) and bone china. Minton's contribution to the fine porcelain of the first half of the last century has, in the past, been greatly underrated. In particular, most of the best flower-encrusted 'Coalbrookdale' wares are now known to have come from Minton (1825–40); and quantities of figures, busts and groups (celebrities, fictional characters, dogs, figures designed for use as candle extinguishers, etc.), some in the biscuit, have formerly been attributed to Coalport, Derby or Rockingham but were made at Minton's (*c.*1825–50). Ground colours were very varied, the most famous being a distinctive turquoise.

From the 1840s the firm diversified into parian figures, majolica, Sèvres-styled porcelains decorated by foreign artists (Colour Plate V), and M. L. Solon's Pâte-sur-Pâte vases (1870–1904); all these were of very high quality. Minton have made a point of employing first-class artists, including the Derby artists Joseph Bancroft, Thomas Steel, and George Hancock, who arrived from Derby in the 1830s.

This factory's later wares, when marked, are more easily datable than most; pattern numbers were introduced early, reaching 9999 by October 1850. A new G Series was then commenced. For one hundred years from 1842 there was a distinguishing symbol for each year; see the companion *Handbook of British Pottery & Porcelain Marks*. The standard specialist book is Godden's *Minton Pottery & Porcelain of the First Period, 1793–1850* (Barrie & Jenkins, 1968) but more general books such as his *Encyclopaedia of British Porcelain Manufacturers* (Barrie & Jenkins, 1988) give helpful information and illustrate typical pieces. A recent book is *The Dictionary of Minton* by Paul Atterbury (Antique Collectors' Club, 1990).

66 *A tastefully decorated Minton bone china waste-bowl from a tea service, decorated with various shell groups by the bat-printing process and with gold enrichments. Painted crossed L's mark with pattern number 634. Diameter 5¾in. c.1810.*

126

67   A Sèvres-form Minton bone china jug painted with flowers, the front with long personal inscription and dated November 1843. 10in high. 1843.

68   A Sèvres-form covered Minton vase also decorated in the French manner with green ground, tooled gilding, and birds in compartment. 13¼in high. c.1845.

MOCHA WARE (*c.*1790–present day). Cheap colour-banded pottery, mostly mugs and jugs, decorated with fern-like designs (as Plate 69) resembling those in moss agate ('Mocha-stone', once shipped from Mocha on the Red Sea). Bands carrying the Mocha design were of alkaline slip on which, while wet, were put drops of acid 'tea', originally concocted from tobacco juice, urine or hops coloured with a metallic oxide; by capillary action, assisted by tilting the piece or by blowpipe, the 'tea' stains spread to form feathery designs, normally brown, sometimes blue or green. In early creamware specimens the bands were blue, yellow, white, or brown; in late Victorian times, grey and blue. Mocha ware, introduced in Staffordshire, was made all over Britain and even in France. The mugs were much used in pubs, and sometimes carry excise marks which, by the initials, can show the approximate date, i.e. a 'V R' stamp is of the Victorian period. Few examples bear a maker's mark and some present-day potters use the same technique. The standard pub mugs are still not rare or costly.

69   *A group of Mocha decorated domestic earthenwares of the type made throughout the nineteenth-century for pub, cottage or kitchen use. Such wares are seldom marked. Jugs 6¼in high. c.1850.*

MONEY-BOXES. As these were made to be broken open, preferably at Christmas, few ceramic examples survive from the eighteenth century, when the favourite forms were a hen on a nest-box or the Sussex piggy-bank; some in speckled green. A group of farmer, wife, and cows is another eighteenth-century form. Those of later date that survive were probably used, if not intended, as chimney ornaments; there are many kinds of slotted cottages, some marked 'Saving Bank', one of the commonest being flanked by a boy and girl, with faces peering from the windows. This model has been reproduced. Other types include cats and dogs, perhaps in 'Rockingham' glaze.

MONKEY BAND. A set of twenty or so monkeys playing musical instruments, first modelled by Kändler at Meissen *c*.1750; the story that they caricature the royal orchestra of Saxony is unlikely.

They were copied by Chelsea, Derby, and from *c*.1833 by Copeland & Garrett but most examples are late German hard-paste replicas made from about 1870 onwards. These unlovely novelty figures have always been popular but they are very prone to damage.

MOORCROFT (*c*.1897–present day). William Moorcroft (1872–1945) produced some Art Nouveau style, mainly floral, compositions for James Macintyre & Co. of the Washington Works at Burslem, in the 1890s after having studied at the Burslem School of Art. From March 1897, William Moorcroft's name appears on Macintyre's Art Pottery – pottery designed by him. Much of this was made for the large London store Liberty & Co. and such pieces bear their name, up to the time that Macintyre's closed this department in 1913.

William Moorcroft then established his own new factory at Cobridge and there traded under his own name, with backing from Liberty. The new works opened in August 1913 and quickly built up or upon his existing reputation. He was later joined by his son Walter and the factory continues to the present day but under new ownership.

Moorcroft pottery, especially the earlier wares, is today widely appreciated. Colour Plate VI shows a typical example. An exhibition was held at the Victoria & Albert Museum in 1972 and another in New Bond Street by the later owner of the Company, Richard Dennis. This later exhibition led to a good well-illustrated catalogue *William Moorcroft and Walter Moorcroft 1897–1973* (Richard Dennis, 1973). The standard book is *Moorcroft Pottery. A Guide to Pottery of William and Walter Moorcroft 1897–1986* by Paul Atterbury (R. Dennis & H. Edwards, 1987). Photographs of the Moorcrofts and of typical examples of their designs are included in Geoffrey Godden's comprehensive work *British Pottery. An Illustrated Guide* (Barrie & Jenkins, 1974), Plates 508–616.

Apart from Richard Dennis of 144, Kensington Church Street, London W8 another specialist firm which exhibits a large stock at various Collectors' Fairs is The Lions Den, 11 St Mary's Crescent, Leamington Spa, CV31 1JL.

MOORE BROTHERS (*c.*1870–1905). Bernard and Samuel Moore succeeded their father, at the St Mary's Works at Longton in the Staffordshire Potteries in 1870. For a relatively small concern they produced surprisingly good quality porcelains. A popular speciality was ornamental objects enriched with applied cactus or hop motifs. The porcelains normally bear a 'Moore' or 'Moore Bros' mark as reproduced in the *Handbook of British Pottery & Porcelain Marks*.

MOUSTACHE CUPS. Large-size cups fitted with a shaped china trough across the drinking side of the rim (as Plate 70) to keep the typically luxuriant moustache of a Victorian or Edwardian head of

70   *A Hammersley bone china moustache cup with the inner ledge designed to hold the moustache out of the liquid. Printed Hammersley mark. 3¼in high. c.1901.*

family out of his morning tea or other beverage. Made by many firms, sometimes with wifely inscriptions such as 'Remember Me'. They tend to be of porcelain rather than pottery but were usually inexpensive novelties.

NANTGARW-SWANSEA (1813 and c.1817–20). William Billingsley, with his son-in-law Samuel Walker set up a very small factory at Nantgarw, near Caerphilly in Wales and produced a beautiful porcelain which he hoped would rival the old eighteenth-century soft-paste Sèvres; it was exceptionally translucent and white. Unfortunately it was not an economic proposition as it was too glassy to stand up to high temperatures, and kiln losses were immense. Probably no products of his first Nantgarw period have survived.

In 1814 Dillwyn, of the Cambrian Pottery (Swansea) came to Billingsley's rescue, hoping to improve the Nantgarw paste at his larger and better equipped factory. Nantgarw was temporarily closed, and Billingsley and Walker transferred to Swansea.

Kiln losses, however, continued high, and Dillwyn abandoned the Nantgarw formula and introduced (1816–17) three new pastes. The first, known as 'duck-egg Swansea' from its green translucency, contained bone-ash; it was most attractive, with a glaze that never crazed, but 'wasters' were still too numerous. The second was tougher, containing soapstone, and very glassy. The third (called 'trident' from its mark) was also a soapstone body, but proved unreliable and had a dull and pitted glaze. Dillwyn retired temporarily, handing over to the Bevington brothers (1817–1824), and porcelain production ceased at Swansea.

Billingsley and Walker returned to Nantgarw and, financed by W. Young, resumed production, this time with an improved version of their original porcelain which had a warm white appearance and a beautiful glaze, and was even more translucent, more manageable, though still subject to uneconomic kiln losses, as indeed was the old Sèvres soft-paste porcelain which it so closely resembled. In 1820 the two partners suddenly left.

Both factories were restricted by the nature of the pastes mainly to flatware (such as plates and dishes) and the smaller items of hollowwares; figures and large jugs could not survive the heat. Tea and dessert wares were the chief products, together with such items as inkwells, candlesticks, spill-vases, and cabinet cups and saucers mostly in French Empire shapes that appealed to Regency tastes.

Whether decorated in Wales or, as so much of it was, in London, Nantgarw (and Swansea) wares are alike famous for the high quality of the painting on most of them, especially the floral designs, no doubt, inspired by the flower-painter *par excellence*, Billingsley.

Most Nangarw and much of the duck-egg Swansea were bought in the white by London dealers whose artists decorated them lavishly in the eighteenth-century Sèvres style, with exotic birds, figure groups, named landscapes, etc. For ten years or so after Billingsley disappeared 'production' continued, inasmuch as large stocks in the white, accumulated in London and at both factories, were being decorated and sold. At Nantgarw these were unglazed and included, unfortunately, 'seconds'; under Young's direction they were given an inferior glaze, decorated by Thomas Pardoe and sold locally.

Some, but by no means all, Nantgarw porcelain bears the impressed name 'NANT GARW' sometimes with C.W. below. Fakes of Nantgarw wares, however, exist. The reader is referred to E. Morton Nance's classic work *The Pottery & Porcelain of Swansea & Nantgarw* (Batsford, 1942) and to *Nantgarw Porcelain* by W. D. John (R. H. John, 1948).

71 An impressed-marked 'NANTGARW' C.W. porcelain plate, with floral centre. The moulded edging is not unique to this factory. Diameter 8¾in. c.1817–20.

NEALE. On the bankruptcy of the Hanley potter Humphrey Palmer in 1778, James Neale the London dealer took over the Church Works and continued them under his own name, with Robert Wilson in charge of the potting. The Neale earthenwares and porcelains (Plate 72) are amongst the most attractive of any made in the 1780–92 period. In April 1792 the partnership between James Neale and Robert Wilson was terminated and Wilson continued the works.

Various name-marks 'Neale', 'Neale & Co.', 'Neale & Wilson' or 'Neale & Bailey' occur (the last refers to the London retail shop) but by no means all wares were marked.

For further information the reader is referred to Diana Edwards's *Neale Pottery and Porcelain* (Barrie & Jenkins, 1987). The very rare porcelains are featured in *Staffordshire Porcelain* (Granada, 1983).

72   *A rare but typical Neale porcelain covered cup and stand of Derby type. A very well potted piece with good-quality gilding. Diameter of stand 5¾in. c.1790.*

NEW HALL (1782–1835). A Staffordshire company or partnership known as 'New Hall' (after an initial start at Tunstall *c.*1781–2), at Shelton (Hanley), which made a durable hybrid hard-paste porcelain and, from *c.*1814, bone china; tea, coffee, and dessert sets predominated.

The hard-paste was based on the patent bought from Champion of Bristol, but differed in appearance from Bristol hard-paste because it was amended and fired differently. Translucency is un-even and the body shows greyish against the light. The glaze is clear and free from crazing, but is prone to small bubbles. Some wares, especially of the first decade, are of excellent quality but there was a gradual lowering of sights to suit a middle-class market especially from about 1820. The main pieces (not cups and saucers) usually bear a boldly written pattern number, sometimes preceded by 'N' or 'No'. Decoration was drawn free-hand at first and there were many pleasingly restrained designs with high-quality gilding (a New Hall speciality); polychrome, painted, and transfer-printed blue and white decoration were all used.

'Typical' New Hall shapes were often based on silver counter-parts, e.g. the fluted polygonal teapots and helmet-shaped cream jugs; they are misleading guides to recognition, however, as similar shapes were made by Caughley, Coalport, Minton, and Chamber-lain, and there are many near copies in hard-paste by unknown fac-tories in addition to the Caughley/Coalport hard-paste.

The bone china was cheaper to make and much whiter; it was often decorated with the earlier but still popular patterns, new pat-terns being numbered from about 1050 upwards. Some bone china of the approximate period 1815–25 bears a printed circular 'New Hall' mark but the main bulk of the output is unmarked.

The term 'New Hall' is often applied incorrectly to a number of simple floral designs, in the style of the Chinese export market por-celains. These inexpensive designs were extremely popular and were made by most English factories of the 1785–1825 period. The identification of the different makes is a continuing struggle as most examples are unmarked and very similar.

For further information the reader is referred to David Holgate's two books *New Hall and its Imitators* (Faber & Faber, 1971) and *New Hall* (Faber & Faber, 1987). Godden's *Staffordshire Porcelain* (Gra-nada, 1983) and *Encyclopaedia of British Porcelain Manufacturers* (Barrie & Jenkins, 1988) are also helpful on both the true New Hall wares and on the contemporary makers of similar porcelains. Anthony de Saye Hutton's *A Guide to New Hall Porcelain Patterns* (Barrie & Jen-kins, 1990) lists all known pattern numbers with brief descriptions and frequently illustrations.

NODDERS. Porcelain (sometimes pottery) figures with detachable heads with oscillate, usually nodding but sometimes wagging side-ways. Through the neck a pin is fixed which should be of flat metal on edge (often replaced by a round pin) resting on grooves in the shoulders. The earliest (mandarins) are rare; the commonest are blue and white pairs of children dressed up as elders, with metal spectacles; there are also Buddhas, animals, clowns, and groups of figures (e.g. a tea party). The best are French but most come from the smaller German factories.

Originally most examples of this type of ceramic were inexpensive novelties purchased for the amusement of children.

NORTHERN CERAMIC SOCIETY (N.C.S.). This very active society holds various meetings and seminars and issues interesting Newsletters and Journals. Membership is by no means limited to persons living in the northern parts of the British Isles. The Membership Secretary is Anthony Thomas, Bramdean, Jackson's Lane, Hazel Grove, Cheshire.

NOTTINGHAM STONEWARE (c.1690–1850). A form of fine lightweight saltglazed stoneware with a bronze sheen (sometimes called Brownware). The rare early stonewares include pierced, double-walled teapots, puzzle-jugs, and 'decantors' (necked jugs), etc., some with incised decoration, as Plate 73.

73   A rare but very typical Nottingham stoneware handled mug. Incised 'Nott. 1703'. 4in high. 1703. **(Sotheby's).**

Much later Nottingham-type stonewares, made by various potters, bear names, inscriptions, or dates. Such features obviously add to the interest and value. The specialist books on stoneware, such as *English Brown Stoneware* by A. Oswald, R. Hildyard, and R. Hughes (Faber & Faber, 1982) and the 1985 Victoria & Albert Museum exhibition catalogue *Brown Muggs, English Brown Stoneware*, give information on the Nottingham makers and illustrate typical products.

PALISSY WARE. Minton's name for relief-decorated colour-glazed earthenwares. Some of it imitated the work of the sixteenth-century French potter Bernard Palissy, who made distinctive (but much-copied) wares decorated with lizards and other creatures or plants in high relief and harmonious coloured lead glazes. Like the rather similar majolica wares the best Palissy style earthenwares were modelled or designed by leading Victorian sculptors or designers.

PAP-BOAT. A shallow small boat-shaped vessel often with a tubular spout, for feeding infants or invalids. Most are in pottery and are of nineteenth-century date (Plate 74).

74   A simple blue printed earthenware pap-boat, designed to be held easily in the hand. 4¼in long. c.1840.

PARAGON CHINA (LTD). This Longton company produced in the 1920s and 1930s a very good range of bone china useful wares, mainly tea wares. They enjoyed the Royal Warrant and several standard printed marks incorporate the Royal Arms and By Appointment wording. The firm has changed hands several times but now continues as part of the Royal Doulton group.

PARIAN (*c.*1842 onwards). Unglazed fine-grained porcelain, introduced by Copeland & Garrett as 'Statuary porcelain' and by Minton as 'Parian', named after the famous Greek marble from the island of Paros. These two firms were the principal producers; Wedgwood's 'Carrara' was similar. Quality ranged from excellent to sickly sentimental. Some copies of sculpture were made with a device (resembling the pantograph used to copy maps on a different scale) invented by Benjamin Cheverton; these small copies often bear his name.

Thousands of figures, busts, and groups were mass-produced by various firms from the 1840s into the 1880s, after which production declined. A host of useful wares, jugs and butter-boats were also made in parian, which was sometimes decorated. The best models

75 A typical parian figure. A Minton copy of Hiram Power's 'The Greek Slave', a model introduced in 1848. Incised model number '207' with year mark for 1853. 14in high. 1853.

by the leading makers are of superb quality and are very decorative but the smaller firms tended to lower standards.

The reader is referred to *The Illustrated Guide to Victorian Parian China* by C. and D. Shinn (Barrie & Jenkins, 1971), Godden's *Victorian Porcelain* (Herbert Jenkins, 1961) and *English China* (Barrie & Jenkins, 1985), and Paul Atterbury's *The Parian Phenomenon* (Richard Dennis, 1989).

PÂTE-SUR-PÂTE (*c*.1870 onwards). A very elaborate and expensive method of relief decoration introduced at the Minton factory (from Sèvres) by M. L. Solon, who signed his work. The typical form was a classical vase with reliefs built up by thin coats of white slip laboriously applied one on top of another on an unfired but coloured parian body, to produce cameo-like designs of figures etc. against a dark background, see Colour Plate VII and Plate 76. The rough result was carefully tooled into shape, glazed, and fired. This Continental technique was imitated by Grainger's Worcester, Royal Worcester, George Jones, Moore Brothers, and others.

76 A typical Minton Pâte-sur-Pâte vase, a unique design by M. L. Solon, the white raised design worked on a slate blue ground. Gilt Minton globe mark with year mark for 1894. 22in high. 1894.

These hand-modelled designs, rather in the style of Wedgwood's white reliefs on a jasper ground (but made in a different manner) represent a great art and production was slow and costly. Solon, at Minton's, trained several apprentices to work in this style but the most commercially desirable signature is that of Solon. With a few exceptions the compositions were unique. Plaques and plates are not as valuable as vases.

For further information the reader is referred to Godden's *Victorian Porcelain* (Herbert Jenkins, 1961), *British Porcelain. An Illustrated Guide* (Barrie & Jenkins, 1974), or *English China* (Barrie & Jenkins, 1985).

PATTERN NUMBERS. The painted pattern numbers on a piece of porcelain or pottery can sometimes help to identify a piece or approximately date the introduction of that design. However, one does need to refer to a specialist book on that factory. One must be quite certain that the correct design bears the correct pattern number for that pattern. The same pattern in itself is not enough.

Basic information on the different pattern numbering systems is given in Godden's *Encyclopaedia of British Porcelain Manufacturers* (Barrie & Jenkins, 1988), pp. 35–50.

PEARLWARE. In the mid 1770s Josiah Wedgwood introduced his 'Pearl White' body as a change from the established cream-coloured Queen's Ware – which may still be preferred. The new Pearl White or Pearlware was whiter than the cream wares and to achieve this a small amount of blue was added to the glaze. It is now thought that the whiter body had been produced by various potters prior to Josiah Wedgwood's introduction of the name 'Pearl White' in about 1779. A dated (non-Wedgwood) example of 1775 may not have been the earliest example to have been made. It is thought that the eighteenth-century term 'china glaze' (q.v.) was used for what we now call Pearlware, both before and after Wedgwood introduced the term Pearl.

Most post-1790 blue-painted or blue-printed Staffordshire pottery is Pearlware or 'china glaze' ware. These terms are not, however, now in everyday use except in collecting circles. An even whiter earthenware was introduced early in the nineteenth century as Whiteware.

PINXTON (1796–1813). A Derbyshire factory near Mansfield founded by John Coke and William Billingsley of Derby. For a brief period before one of Billingsley's characteristic desertions (in 1799) the factory was able to make a good porcelain resembling Derby. The products, almost exclusively useful wares, resembled Derby in both body and decoration, the latter notable for landscape vignettes in monochrome or colours (as Plate 77), floral designs, naturally excellent under Billingsley's influence, and first-class gilding; coloured grounds were less successful and tended to be pale.

Pinxton is rather scarce and very rarely marked although some pieces have a pattern number prefaced by a cursive capital P.

The standard reference book is C. L. Exley's slim work *The Pinxton China Factory* (privately published by Mr & Mrs R. Coke-Steel, 1963), but most modern reference books, such as Godden's *Encyclopaedia of British Porcelain Manufacturers* (Barrie & Jenkins, 1988) illustrate typical examples.

77   A typical Pinxton scenic panelled bowl from a tea service. Painted pattern number P.108, note the prefix 'P'. Diameter 6¾in. c.1796–1800. **(Beaverbrook Art Gallery, Fredericton, Canada).**

PLYMOUTH (*c.*1768–70). The earliest English true or hard-paste porcelain factory, founded by William Cookworthy who had been trying since the 1740s to discover the right materials to imitate Chinese porcelain. Finding them at last in Cornwall, he took out a Patent which gave him the monopoly of their exploitation and he set up a factory in Plymouth. This proved too remote and he moved to Bristol, but handed over to Richard Champion *c.*1773. It is more useful to classify their products as Cookworthy's (1768–73) and Champion's (1773–81), since those made under Cookworthy's management at Bristol are indistinguishable from Plymouth.

Cookworthy's paste was not a commercial success. It had to be fired at a higher temperature than other English porcelain. It tended to be discoloured by the smoke from fuel, and was prone to warping in the kiln, bubbled and flecked surfaces, firecracks, etc. Most products were painted in an inky underglaze blue with floral or Chinese themes, or enamelled with flowers, exotic birds in landscapes, *etc.* The enamels often flaked and colours were sometimes spoilt by overfiring. Straight-sided and also bell-shape mugs were very popular; also sauce-boats. Perhaps the most successful pieces were the large and well-decorated hexagonal vases. A few figures (Seasons, Continents, etc.), some copying Longton Hall models, were made, with rococo bases. Animal and bird figures were also made.

The mark is the sign for tin ♃. Not all pieces were marked but the quite common reproductions do tend to bear a faked mark.

The reader is referred to F. Severne MacKenna's now scarce book *Cookworthy's Plymouth and Bristol Porcelain* (F. Lewis, 1946) or general books such as Godden's *Encyclopaedia of British Porcelain Manufacturers* (Barrie & Jenkins, 1988).

78 A Plymouth hard-paste porcelain white figure on a characteristic raised scroll base. Coloured examples were also made. 5⁷⁄₈in high. c.1768–70. **(Victoria & Albert Museum).**

POOLE POTTERY. The various present-century earthenwares produced by Carter, Stabler & Adams Ltd from 1921 at Poole in Dorset and generally known as Poole Pottery are today collectable, decorative and interesting. They have a rather formal 'house-style' of their own (Plate 79) and the majority of pieces bear a clear Poole trade-mark. The present works, now Poole Pottery Ltd, are open to visitors and there is a display of past and present products.

The standard book is Jennifer Hawkins's *The Poole Potteries* (Barrie & Jenkins, 1980).

79   A selection of 'Poole Pottery' of the 1930s showing typical clean-cut shapes and the broad style of hand-decoration. Impressed Poole name-mark, with various painters' marks. Diameter of shallow bowl 8¾in. c.1930–9.

POSSET POTS AND CAUDLE CUPS. Two-handled lidded pots for hot drinks. The posset pots date from at least the seventeenth century and contained hot spiced milk curdled with ale or wine, apparently a kill-or-cure for colds.

Caudle cups replaced them in favour in about 1750, and differed from them in being smaller and having a saucer but no spout. They were made in elaborately decorated porcelain, specially for presents to women who had just had a baby. Caudle (contracted from the Latin *calidum*, 'hot drink', was a thin hot gruel, sweetened, spiced, and laced with wine or even spirits, a pick-me-up for nursing mothers and invalids.

After *c*.1820 they continued to be made as cabinet pieces. Some chocolate cups were decorated in the same rich styles.

POT-LIDS. Small circular earthenware lids often decorated with underglaze multicolour transfer prints, made in Staffordshire, mostly by F. & R. Pratt of Fenton but also by Mayer and related firms at Dale Hall (Longport) and some other firms. They covered shallow pots (Plate 80) of bear's grease (hair pomade), fish or meat pastes, face cream, etc.

The original copper plates of many Pratt designs were skilfully engraved by Jesse Austin, whose name or initials appear on some lids. He used one engraved plate for the outline and others for each of the colours (yellow, blue, red), accuracy of registration being ensured by small circles which may be seen on either side of the finished product.

There were about 600 designs, including bear motifs, scenes at Pegwell Bay (Kentish fishing and shrimping centre), the Great Exhibition, portraits, Old England, sports and pastimes, animals, flowers, and landscapes. Some subjects are very rare, others are quite common. Many have been produced down to quite recent times and are classed as reissues.

80   A typical Bears Grease pot and its decorative multicolour printed cover. Made by F. & R. Pratt of Fenton. This example is rare as the pot still bears the remains of the original paper sealing-strip showing the name of the supplier, 'S Cleaver' and the contents, in this case Bears Grease used as a hair dressing. Diameter 3in. c.1850–60.

The best lids and those with the richest colours are of the approximate period 1850–70. On the other hand some are present-century examples made purely for the collectors, without the bases which accompanied the original lids.

These essays in marketing a product on its decorative ceramic packaging are extremely collectable and the rarer subjects when in good condition can be costly. The same printed subjects can also occur on other objects such as mugs and jugs or plates.

Not all pot-lids bear multicolour printed pretty pictures, some being in one colour only with wording mainly or wholly for advertising purposes. In recent years these too have become sought after but in a low price bracket.

Recommended books on the colour-printed pot-lids and the related other objects include *Staffordshire Pot Lids and their Potters* by C. Williams-Wood (Faber & Faber, 1972) and A. Ball's *The Price Guide to Pot Lids* (Antique Collectors' Club, 2nd edition 1980). The standard (now rather outdated) work is the late H. G. Clarke's *The Pictorial Pot Lid Book* (Courier Press, 1970).

The plainer advertising lids are covered in *Collecting Pot Lids* by E. Fletcher (Pitman, 1975) and R. Dale's *Price Guide to Black & White Pot Lids* (Antique Collectors' Club, 1977).

THE POTTERIES. The six Staffordshire towns (Arnold Bennett's 'Five Towns'), joined since 1910, comprise the borough of Stoke-on-Trent, adjacent to and east of the M6. From north to south they are: Tunstall, Burslem (with Cobridge), Hanley (with Shelton), Stoke, Fenton and Longton (with Lane End and Lane Delph).

For interesting details of these districts in the nineteenth century the reader should consult Godden's *Staffordshire Porcelain* (Granada, 1983), Appendix I.

The initials of these towns are sometimes added to initial marks – as R. & S.L. (Robinson & Son, Longton) – a feature that helps to pin-point the correct manufacturer when several used the same initials. The town of Longton was the centre of the middle range of porcelain manufacturers, although some top-rate firms were also located there.

PRATTWARE, EARLY (*c.*1780–1835). A generic term for earthenware decorated in a distinctive range of underglaze colours, with ochre, blue, and green predominant; the other colours are yellow, purple-brown, grey-brown, and black. These had to withstand high temperatures as they were painted or sponged on to the body, which was then fired, finished with lead glaze, and refired. Often the colours were applied over relief-moulding, to accentuate the design.

Prattware, a collectors' term only, is named after, and was possibly first produced by, William Pratt (1753–99) of Lane Delph (Staffordshire), grandfather of the Felix Pratt who made pot-lids (Plate 80). Pratt-type wares were also, however, made by many other potters not only in Staffordshire but in Yorkshire, Sunderland, and Scotland. The wares most often seen are jugs and plaques. The jugs bear moulded designs, the commonest being celebrities (e.g. Nelson), groups such as 'The Leek Loyal Volunteers', grotesque caricatures of bewigged men, hunting scenes, etc. There were also single figures and groups, some very crudely modelled and decorated with haphazard spots of colour, Toby jugs, cow-cream-ers, watchstands, and teapots also decorated in the so-called Pratt-ware range of colours.

The standard modern work is *Pratt Ware* by John & Griselda Lewis (Antique Collectors' Club, 1984).

PRATTWARE, LATE (*c.*1847–88). The generic term for wares, espe-cially dessert and tea services and jugs, made by F. & R. Pratt of Fen-ton (Staffordshire), a firm founded by Felix (1780–1859), and carried on by his son, Felix Edwards Pratt (1813–94). These tablewares were decorated by the same process as the pot-lids (q.v.) and some rich examples have mock malachite printed borders. Another favourite border had an intricate oak-leaf design.

F. & R. Pratt showed a good range of such wares at the 1851 Ex-hibition, including superb framed plaques. The Pratt wares con-tinued in production to the present century but some very similar pieces were made by T. J. & J. Mayer and succeeding firms at the Dale Hall Works at Longport. The standard modern work on the multicolour printed Pratt wares is A. Ball's *The Price Guide to Pot Lids* (Antique Collectors' Club, 1980).

PRICE GUIDES. In recent years many price guides have been published and are readily available. These appear to sell in large numbers but in our opinion these are often more misleading than helpful. Several are based on auction prices, but there are good and very bad buys at any auction sales. Some examples are 'knocked down' for under their average shop price, other pieces (for various reasons) command an inflated price.

If a reader takes undue notice of a guide price, say £200 for a Wor-cester teapot he or she may well miss buying some wonderful examples that might be modestly priced at £250 or £350. These could well have been a better buy than an average example purchased at £150 – only because by reference to the price guide this was under the so-called market price.

It is as well also to bear in mind that no price guide is up to date – it is out of date the day it is published but the market price can decrease as well as increase. No price guide can be comprehensive and such title description as 'Official' is meaningless!

In general terms it is better to buy one good, better than average, perfect example of any type than a dozen inexpensive average or in-ferior pieces. Buy what you like – not necessarily what is fashionable – but never spend more than you can reasonably afford from surplus funds.

PUBLISHED BY . . . Various British ceramics (and objects made from other materials) can bear standard wording commencing with 'Published by' and followed by the name and date of first publica-tion of a design. Such form of copyright protection arises from the Sculpture Copyright Act of 1797 and its 1814 amendment.

As with other copyright or registration wording or devices it must be remembered that the object is likely to have been mass-produced and that the date given is only the very earliest date of protection. The object cannot be earlier but it could well have been produced several years later. However, the inclusion of the name of the manufacturer is most helpful.

This system was largely superseded by the 1842 Designs Copyright Act and its diamond-shaped registration device, see under Registration Marks and Numbers below, p. 149.

PUNCH-BOWL. A large bowl, made in most kinds of pottery and porcelain, often transfer-printed in black with hunting, shipping, or political themes. Punch was originally an Indian drink of five (Hindi *punch*) ingredients, including arrack (fermented coconut milk, etc.) and tea. Punch was transformed in England into a spiced and sweetened mixture of brandy, rum, or wine with fruit juices, usually served hot.

Many eighteenth-century porcelain punch-bowls, especially the larger sizes, are of Chinese porcelain although they may be decorated with European subjects – a fox hunt or English shipping subjects. The English makers experienced difficulty in producing or successfully firing bowls over about 16in diameter.

PUZZLE JUG. Jug, usually pierced, from which it is impossible to drink successfully unless one knows the trick. Typically there is a hollow handle (sometimes with a hole in it) leading to a tube round the rim connecting three or more spouts (Plate 81); drink can be

81 *An English (Liverpool) delftware puzzle jug decorated in blue and with typical teasing rhyme. 7¼in high. c.1760.* **(Sotheby's).**

sucked through one of these if all other apertures are stopped. Such jugs were made from early times until the early 1800s, in delftware, brown saltglaze, creamware, and even in porcelain. Some kinds, to make things more difficult, had openwork decoration round the jug below the spouts. All are amusing novelties and some rare examples have a rhyme or verse.

QUEEN'S WARE (*c*.1765). The name given by Josiah Wedgwood to his improved creamware after Queen Charlotte had been presented with some; it captured the market, at home and overseas. The name was taken up by many other Staffordshire potters, and was even used as part of the mark by some firms such as W. Smith (& Co.) of Stockton-on-Tees.

For further information see under Creamware and Donald Towner's standard book *Creamware* (Faber & Faber, 1978).

RAILWAY THEMES. The sudden transition to mechanical transport is vividly commemorated by a Minton moulded jug (1847) contrasting stage-coach and rail travel. Other pottery jugs, mugs, and plates depict such scenes as the inauguration of the Liverpool–Manchester line (1830), one showing the Duke of Wellington in the front seat of a carriage, doubtless deafened by a band in the adjacent truck, George Stephenson driving one of his locomotives (1832), the 'Rocket', viaducts, railway stations, etc. all transfer-printed.

These Railway ceramics in both pottery and porcelain are popular but some mugs, jugs, and bowls bearing a 'Railway' mark with the maker's initials are relatively plentiful. That shown in Plate 82 is, however, of a rare, two-handled form.

REDWARE. Eighteenth-century red stoneware, usually unglazed and often decorated with applied motifs in relief. The term includes Elers Ware and similar products; the harder, polished 'red china' patented (1729) by Samuel Bell of Newcastle; and the more attractively coloured 'rosso antico' of Wedgwood (1760s).

These trimly-potted Elers-type redwares are very collectable and costly but of course reddish clay bodies were made throughout the nineteenth century: 'copper lustre' is on such a body. These later wares should not be associated with the earlier essays.

REFERENCE BOOKS. Good, authoritative, and well-illustrated standard books represent very good investments for the collector, dealer, or auctioneer. Indeed, in the case of the last two groups such 'tools of the Trade' are a tax-deductible expense.

Standard reference books tend to be expensive. The second-hand price of works out of print can be spectacular, if the book is well illustrated and has a helpful text or represents the only source of information on that subject. However, as a general rule a seemingly expensive serious book represents better value than a shelf full of cheap works written by persons who are not masters of their

82   A printed earthenware two-handled large mug bearing a typical early Railway design. Printed mark 'Railway J & RG' (for J. & R. Godwin of Cobridge). 6¼in high. c.1845–55.

subject. A book that attempts to cover an over-large subject (such as world-ceramics) in a couple of hundred pages obviously cannot offer the depth of a specialist volume. A list of recommended reference books is given at the end of this book and various titles are mentioned in relevant places in the text.

The reader may find difficulty in tracing old titles. Most can be found in the larger Reference Libraries, but if you wish to purchase your own copies there are various firms or individuals who should be able to supply copies of both current ('in print') and the older ('out of print') works. The following British sources have proved most helpful to the writer:

Barry Lamb, Reference Works (Publishing & Distribution) Ltd, 12 Commercial Road, Swanage, Dorset, BH19 1DF.

Terence A. Lockett, 6 Tideswell Road, Hazel Grove, Stockport, SK7 6JG.

Potterton Books, The Old Rectory, Sessay, Nr Thirsk, North Yorkshire, YO7 3LZ.

City of Stoke-on-Trent Museum & Art Gallery, Book Dept, Bethesda Street, Hanley, Stoke-on-Trent, ST1 3DE.

Most of these and other major suppliers publish lists or catalogues of available books. Modern 'in print' books should be available at your local book shop or at least you should be able to order them.

REGISTRATION MARKS AND NUMBERS. The Designs Copyright Act of 1842 (5 & 6 Victoria, c. 100) introduced a system of design or shape protection valid for three years. The designs so registered were marked with a diamond-shaped device with numbers and letters in the four inner corners, each design having a unique combination which linked with the Designs Office files.

From the year and month letters and the day number one can discover the date on which the entry was made in the records. This in effect gives the earliest possible date of the object – not the actual date of manufacture, although this was normally within three years of the initial date. The key for decoding the date is here given. The basic arrangement was changed in 1868 when the year letter was moved from the upper angle to the right-hand one.

The Act covered all types of material, which were divided into classes. Class IV relates to Ceramics. The 'parcel number' links with the official entry number in the official record, for many were received each day. In the first example here given parcel number 8 would have been the eighth entry entered on the first of January 1842.

As a general rule impressed or relief-moulded marks relate to a registered shape, the printed diamond-shaped marks usually relate to the added pattern.

Several illustrations in this book are of registered shapes. A good range of such forms and added patterns will be found featured in *Staffordshire Porcelain* edited by Geoffrey Godden (Granada, 1983). That work also lists the manufacturers of those designs that were registered by Staffordshire firms and which were produced in porcelain. The original files are preserved at the Public Record Office at Kew but some volumes are not available due to their poor condition.

From January 1884 a new system of marking registered designs with a simple number was introduced. Usually the number was preceeded by $R^D N^O$ for Registered Number. The following list shows the number reached at the opening of each year, so giving a very good guide to the date of introduction of each shape or design bearing such a number.

TABLE OF REGISTRATION MARKS
1843–83

Above are the two patterns of Design Registration Marks that were in current use between the years 1842 and 1883. Keys to 'year' and 'month' code-letters are given below.

The left-hand diamond was used during the years 1842 to 1867. A change was made in 1868, when the right-hand arrangement was adopted.

INDEX TO YEAR AND MONTH LETTERS

YEARS

		1842–67						1868–83			
		Year Letter at Top						*Year Letter at Right*			
A	=	1845	N	=	1864	A	=	1871	L	=	1882
B	=	1858	O	=	1862	C	=	1870	P	=	1877
C	=	1844	P	=	1851	D	=	1878	S	=	1875
D	=	1852	Q	=	1866	E	=	1881	U	=	1874
E	=	1855	R	=	1861	F	=	1873	V	=	1876
F	=	1847	S	=	1849	H	=	1869	W	=	(Mar 1–6)
G	=	1863	T	=	1867	I	=	1872			1878
H	=	1843	U	=	1848	J	=	1880	X	=	1868
I	=	1846	V	=	1850	K	=	1883	Y	=	1879
J	=	1854	W	=	1865						
K	=	1857	X	=	1842						
L	=	1856	Y	=	1853						
M	=	1859	Z	=	1860						

MONTHS (BOTH PERIODS)

A	=	December	G	=	February	M	=	June
B	=	October	H	=	April	R	=	August (and
C or O	=	January	I	=	July			September 1–19
D	=	September	K	=	November (and			1857)
E	=	May			December 1860)	W	=	March

TABLE OF REGISTRATION NUMBERS 1884-1987

1	=	1884	471860	=	1906	734370	=	1928
19754	=	1885	493900	=	1907	742725	=	1929
40480	=	1886	518640	=	1908	751160	=	1930
64520	=	1887	535170	=	1909	760583	=	1931
90483	=	1888	552000	=	1910	769670	=	1932
116648	=	1889	574817	=	1911	779292	=	1933
141273	=	1890	594195	=	1912	789019	=	1934
163767	=	1891	612431	=	1913	799097	=	1935
185713	=	1892	630190	=	1914	808794	=	1936
205240	=	1893	644935	=	1915	817293	=	1937
224720	=	1894	653521	=	1916	825231	=	1938
246975	=	1895	658988	=	1917	832610	=	1939
268392	=	1896	662872	=	1918	837520	=	1940
291241	=	1897	666126	=	1919	838590	=	1941
311658	=	1898	673750	=	1920	839230	=	1942
331707	=	1899	680147	=	1921	839980	=	1943
351202	=	1900	687144	=	1922	841040	=	1944
368154	=	1901	694999	=	1923	842670	=	1945
385180	=	1902	702671	=	1924	845550	=	1946
403200	=	1903	710165	=	1925	849730	=	1947
424400	=	1904	718057	=	1926	853260	=	1948
447800	=	1905	726330	=	1927	856999	=	1949

860854	=	1950	909364	=	1963	973838	=	1976
863970	=	1951	914536	=	1964	978426	=	1977
866280	=	1952	919607	=	1965	982815	=	1978
869300	=	1953	924510	=	1966	987910	=	1979
872531	=	1954	929335	=	1967	993012	=	1980
876067	=	1955	934515	=	1968	998302	=	1981
879282	=	1956	939875	=	1969	1004456	=	1982
882949	=	1957	944932	=	1970	1010583	=	1983
887079	=	1958	950046	=	1971	1017131	=	1984
891665	=	1959	955342	=	1972	1024174	=	1985
895000	=	1960	960708	=	1973	1031358	=	1986
899914	=	1961	965185	=	1974	1039055	=	1987
904638	=	1962	969249	=	1975			

REPAIRS. We have given a personal review of the pros and cons of damage under 'Damage'. It may be thought that repaired damage is more acceptable than an untreated piece. This is not necessarily the case. With an unrepaired piece the buyer can see the extent of the fault and form his own judgement to buy or to leave. Once this piece has been repaired and the surfaces sprayed (as is the normal treatment) then there is often no clue as to the seriousness of the underlying damage. If the repair is recent the piece may well look extremely good but repair pigments have a tendency to darken and the repair may later become extremely unsightly. Remember also that repairs cost money – sometimes a great deal. This expenditure is passed on to the buyer. There is often a good case for repairing a damaged piece of pottery or porcelain but it should not then be passed off as a perfect specimen! Before and after photographs show good faith and can be helpful to the purchaser.

Repairers, as with all other trades, come in all shapes and sizes or rather some are more competent and experienced than others. Some repairs are almost too good in that even a practised eye has difficulty in detecting the repair. It is therefore a wise precaution to ask of a seller if the piece you are interested in is repaired. If the answer is no, then ask for this fact to be recorded on the invoice – 'A genuine Chelsea figure of Apollo, c.1760, in unrestored condition' or some such wording.

CHARLOTTE RHEAD. The work of this member of the talented Rhead family has recently become collectable and the subject of a serious reference book. Charlotte Rhead (1885–1947) was a ceramic designer whose work was reproduced by several pottery firms in earthenware. Her popular mass-produced and relatively inexpensive designs were normally marked with a facsimile of her signature, although she would only have produced the original design.

Charlotte Rhead started work as a tube-liner at Wardle & Co.'s Hanley pottery in 1901. She later worked as an enameller at Keeling & Co.'s Dale Hall Works at Burslem. Her own designs date from about 1914. Her main work was for Wood & Sons (also makers of

*83 A 'Crown Ducal' earthenware
vase (A. G. Richardson & Co.)
showing a typical Charlotte Rhead
floral design on a mottled grey ground.
Printed 'Crown Ducal' mark with the
signature 'C. Rhead' and design
number 129. 8½in high. c.1931–5.*

'Bursley Ware'); from *c.*1926 for Burgess & Leigh, makers of 'Bur-
leigh Ware'; for A. G. Richardson, makers of 'Crown Ducal Ware'
(see Plate 83) from *c.*1931; and in the 1940's for H. J. Wood Ltd.

Today, these pieces are still quite modestly priced but Bernard
Bumpus's book *Charlotte Rhead, Potter & Designer* (Kevin Francis
Publishing, 1987) will no doubt increase interest in these present-
century earthenwares.

RIDGWAYS. A family of Staffordshire potters chiefly associated, in
a series of partnerships, with two Shelton (Hanley) potteries: Bell
Works (1792) and Cauldon Place (1802). The brothers Job and George
were partners at the former until Job built the Cauldon Works where
he was joined by his sons John and William (who traded as John &
William Ridgway, 1814–30). Then until *c.*1855 William ran the Bell
Works and John the Cauldon Place Works, the latter passing by
stages into the ownership of Brown-Westhead, Moore & Co. (1862)
and then to Cauldon Ltd (1905).

Both potteries produced high-quality useful wares in porcelain,
earthenware, and stoneware, especially tea and dessert services.
The porcelain of the 1808–40 period was rarely marked and its technical and artistic standards (particularly the floral and landscape
painting, see Plate 85) have led to much of it being attributed to Worcester, Rockingham, or Spode, as has been shown by recent study of
pattern books and numbers. The range included splendidly
elaborate tureens, fruit baskets, and two-handled dessert dishes of
the 1810–20 period. William Ridgway after 1830 produced some very
fine moulded stonewares, jugs, teapots, candlesticks, etc. and some

delicate and well decorated porcelain-like tinted earthenware as well as stone china.

For further information the reader is referred to Godden's *Ridgway Porcelains* (Antique Collectors' Club, revised edition 1985), *Staffordshire Porcelain* (Granada, 1983), chapter 12, or *Encyclopaedia of British Porcelain Manufacturers* (Barrie & Jenkins, 1988).

84   A J. & W. Ridgway blue printed stone china covered tureen and ladle from a dinner service. Printed initial mark with 'India Temple' and 'Stone China'. 6in high. c.1820–30.

85   A good-quality Ridgway bone china dessert plate, of a unique form. Underglaze blue ground, with gilt enrichments and hand-painted landscape panels. Pattern number 1078. 9½ × 8½in. c.1820.

ROCKINGHAM. A name normally reserved for the fine and often lavishly decorated porcelain produced (*c*.1826–42) at Swinton in Yorkshire, but also applicable to pottery which was first made there in the eighteenth century. The factory was taken over by the Brameld family (1806), who began to make porcelain commercially about 1826. The site was on the Marquess of Rockingham's estate, which passed to his nephew, Earl Fitzwilliam, in 1782; the latter took great personal interest in the firm and rescued it from bankruptcy several times. The Rockingham name is taken from this association.

Rockingham's reputation was chiefly due to Thomas Brameld, a man of great taste who relied (unduly, it seems) on profits from pottery (as Plate 86) to subsidize losses on porcelain, and to his brother John, who decorated some of the products. Their market was primarily the aristocracy, particularly after the completion for William IV on his accession (1830) of a magnificent dessert service, still used at Buckingham Palace.

86   A large 'Brameld & Co', Rockingham earthenware transfer-printed tureen and cover from a dinner service. 15in long. c.1830–5.

In potting, glaze, and decoration Rockingham was very good and the Rockingham name is internationally famous. The griffin mark (from the Fitzwilliam crest) was at first printed in red and after 1830 in puce. The red-griffin porcelain was finer, shapes and decoration simpler; the outstanding feature was the fine coloured ground in

87 *A blue ground Rockingham porcelain spill vase, with hand-painted floral panel. Printed Griffin mark, with 'Manufacturers to the King'. Also painted mark 'cl 3'. 4½in high. c.1835.*

88 *An important Rockingham pot-pourri vase and cover, with fruit painting in the manner of Thomas Steel. Printed Griffin mark, with 'Manufacturers to the King'. 10¼in high. c.1835.* **(Sotheby's).**

shades of blue, green, or red, often with reserved panels painted with romantic scenes and surrounded by elaborate gilding. The puce-griffin porcelain followed the revived vogue for rococo; shapes were more elaborate, grounds were less colourful – grey or green surrounded by distinctive gilt lacework scrolls; great use was made of small applied flowers, as Plate 88.

Tea and dessert services were the chief ware throughout; spill-vases (Plate 87) and large hexagonal vases were also made. Figures were probably made only in the earlier period, some biscuit, some coloured, modelled in clear detail and standing on plinths. Human figures included theatrical, rural and child subjects and a series of named 'foreign peasants'; poodles and sheep have smooth coats. These are usually marked; there is no evidence that the traditional 'Rockingham' animals with rough coats of shredded china come from Rockingham, and the same applies to 'Rockingham' flower-encrusted cottages.

Contrary to tradition, true Rockingham porcelain is relatively scarce and most of it is unmarked. In services the griffin appears, in general, only on plates and saucers, but painted pattern numbers on the unmarked pieces assist identification, and shapes are often distinctive, as is a fine, barely visible, crazing. Cabinet pieces often bear a class reference mark, such as 'Cl. 1.' Much so-called 'Rockingham' is now known to be Coalport (especially wares encrusted with larger flowers than Rockingham used), Bloor Derby, Davenport, Copeland, etc. Excessively rococo designs are unlikely to be Rockingham but may be Coalport, Grainger's Worcester, or Samuel Alcock.

As to pottery, little is known of the coarse brown earthenware made at Swinton in the eighteenth century. A thick manganese brown 'Rockingham glaze' was used on earthenware Cadogan teapots, Toby jugs, coffee-pots, etc. Not all 'Rockingham glaze' wares however were made at this factory. Swinton was once (1787–1806) controlled by Leeds and made creamware. Transfer-printed wares in blue or other colours and earthenware hand-painted with naturalistic flowers are marked 'Brameld', later 'Rockingham'.

Several good books have added to our knowledge of true Rockingham. These include D. G. Rice's two works, *Rockingham Ornamental Porcelain* (Adam Publishing Co., 1965) and *The Illustrated Guide to Rockingham Pottery & Porcelain* (Barrie & Jenkins, 1971), T. A. Lockett and A. E. Eaglestone's *The Rockingham Pottery* (David & Charles, 1973), and A. and A. Cox's *Rockingham Pottery & Porcelain 1745–1842* (Faber & Faber, 1983).

Do note that your 'Rockingham tea service' is probably not, and that some good fakes occur bearing mock Rockingham marks.

ROGERS FAMILY. Staffordshire potters at Longport from *c*.1784. John Rogers & Son (1815–36) were prolific producers of blue and white wares, mostly marked, decorated with series of oriental and classical themes, 'The Drama' (scenes from popular plays and operas with details on the back), and many other designs.

The earthenwares often bear the impressed name-mark 'Rogers' and the quality of such pieces is extremely good.

ROYAL ALBERT. This trade-name appears on a good range of present-century bone china produced by T. C. Wild & Sons (Ltd) of the Royal Albert Crown China Works, Longton, in the 1894–1970 period. Royal Albert Ltd have continued to the present time.

Most examples bear the Royal Albert name or the initials T.C.W. Examples are tasteful and of good quality but not expensive.

ROYAL WORCESTER PORCELAIN CO. (1862–present day). Founded by R. W. Binns, this factory was first notable for ivory-tinted porcelain decorated in popular Japanese styles, including

89   Royal Worcester 'Norman Conquest' ewer and stand, painted in slightly tinted white enamel on a deep blue ground in the Limoges Enamel style by Thomas Bott. Printed Royal Worcester mark. Ewer 11½in high. c.1870. **(Worcester Works Museum Collection).**

90   A large Royal Worcester covered vase (shape 1428), the Highland cattle scene painted by J. Stinton in his characteristic style. Printed Royal Worcester mark, year code for 1918. 12in high (this shape was made in three different sizes). 1918. **(Sotheby's).**

vases modelled by James Hadley (see Colour Plate VIII). This versatile artist also modelled a series of Kate Greenaway children. He set up on his own in 1875 but the Royal Worcester Company bought all his work until 1896, when he and his sons began making 'Hadley ware', vases with coloured clay embellishments and floral designs, a line which continued after his death in 1903. Many figures were made with painted details; others tinted in cream shading into dark brown. There was also a delightful series nicknamed 'Down-and-outs' – men in battered headgear intended for use as menu-holders.

The other main product was expensive tableware, etc. decorated with tinted gold and other metallic colours. From just before the turn of the century the firm employed many notable artists, e.g. Harry Davis (landscapes and sheep), C. H. C. Baldwyn (birds, swans, etc.), and John Stinton (landscapes, cattle, sheep, as Plate 90); the last had previously worked for Grainger, before the Royal Worcester management took over this firm.

The Royal Worcester firm has produced thousands of fine models and shapes which have been decorated in a bewildering range of patterns. All products are of a very high standard. The Works at Worcester include a magnificent museum displaying a range of the company's products.

For further information the reader is referred to Henry Sandon's standard work *Royal Worcester Porcelain from 1862 to the Present Day* (Barrie & Jenkins, 1973) or to *The Sandon Guide to Royal Worcester Figures 1900–1970* (Alderman Press, 1987).

SALTGLAZE (*c.*1720–80). Staffordshire white stoneware glazed by throwing rock-salt into the kiln at its peak temperature; the volatilized salt combined with the silicon and aluminium oxides in the clay to form a pitted 'orange-peel' surface. The white body was developed from earlier brown stoneware (also saltglazed) by using Devon pipeclay mixed with calcined flint; it appears to have been introduced *c.*1671 by John Dwight of Fulham and adopted in Staffordshire (and other centres) shortly afterwards.

Among the wares so made were loving-cups, mugs, bowls, plates, numerous teapots (some shaped as houses, see Plate 91), animals, jugs in the shape of an owl or of a bear hugging a terrier (the heads being detachable as cups), etc. There was a wide range of decoration – moulded, applied relief, incised (including Scratch Blue, see Plate 93), agate ware, and eventually overglaze enamels, but many pieces were left undecorated.

Most interesting was the quaintly amusing series of small hand-modelled figures and groups attributed to Astbury, Aaron Wood (1717–85), and others, especially the oddly named pew-groups (1730–40). In these, two or three pop-eyed persons sit stiffly on a high-backed bench engaged in flirtation or playing improbable musical instruments; details are picked out in dark brown clay. In similar style are the 'arbour groups' (lovers seated under a crudely-modelled tree), horsemen holding charmingly rigid postures as if struck by lightning, a bell shaped like a woman, an Adam and Eve group, birds, dogs, cats, etc.

These saltglaze stoneware figures have a family resemblance to the earthenware figures made contemporaneously (and sometimes by the same potters). Both kinds command very high prices and are not often seen outside museums; there have, however, been fakes. Those 1730s and 1740s unsophisticated products of Staffordshire humour ante-date even the earliest English porcelain figures.

The standard reference book is Arnold Mountford's *The Illustrated Guide to Staffordshire Saltglaze Stoneware* (Barrie & Jenkins, 1971).

91 A moulded Staffordshire saltglaze stoneware house teapot – an amusing and saleable eighteenth-century gimmick. 5¾in high. c.1750. (Auckland Institute & Museum).

SAMSON. This name is associated with French reproductions of English (and other) porcelains. However, not all such pieces originated from Samson of Paris. This is only the best known and the finest of the many firms engaged in this trade. Samson figures and groups (as Plate 92) sometimes have numbers impressed into the base, a feature not found on the original pieces.

In recent years it has been appreciated that the Samson reproductions are collectable in their own right and they are certainly as decorative as the original, costly pieces. If only Samson, like Wedgwood, Spode, Dresden, etc. had used his own name or mark there would be superb collections of his porcelains. Even so don't purchase Samson as an original Chelsea, Bow, or Derby specimen!

92   *Good-quality nineteenth-century Samson (hard-paste) porcelain copies of Bow (soft-paste) eighteenth-century originals. Impressed Samson model numbers. 5½ and 9in high. c.1860–70.* **(Christie's).**

SCENT OR SMELLING BOTTLES. The magnificent 'Chelsea toys' have been mentioned under Chelsea and Girl-in-a-Swing factory. Other eighteenth-century bottles were made at Chamberlain's Worcester and at Derby. Wedgwood later made them in jasper. The early examples were used more as 'smelling bottles', i.e. vinaigrettes with an ornamental grille holding in a sponge steeped in aromatic vinegar ('smelling salts'), important amid the stenches of that epoch and also as a cure for 'the vapours', common when women had 14in waists. There were flower-encrusted examples and some double-ended Victorian types in porcelain (as well as in glass), handkerchief scent at one end, smelling salts at the other.

Godden's *Chamberlain-Worcester Porcelain, 1788–1852* (Barrie & Jenkins, 1982) features some of that factory's smelling bottles (Plates 367–8) and quotes the original prices.

SCRATCH BLUE. A form of sgraffito ware (q.v.) in which the incisions are filled in with cobalt blue pigment to accentuate the incised lines, as Plate 93. This decoration is found on early saltglaze, especially on dated and named loving-cups, and was revived in the 1870s by Doultons, where, for example, Hannah Barlow (q.v.) was famous for her animal studies incised on jugs and vases, etc., as Plate 7.

*93 A very rare saltglaze stoneware jug decorated in the scratch blue technique. The design was incised into the unfired clay and blue pigment was then applied to accentuate the pattern. 9in high. c.1750–60. **(Sotheby's).***

SEMINARS. Collectors' seminars or meetings give a wonderful opportunity to expand one's knowledge, to hear specialist speakers, and to meet fellow collectors. Whilst they are not aimed at the complete novice, every effort is made to make all collectors feel at home and at ease. The speakers are normally happy to answer questions and to clarify any troublesome points.

A list of the main Seminars is given below, but the reader should remember that these events are very popular and there is a real need to book your place well in advance. Information on these gatherings can be obtained by writing to the following:

Antique Collectors' Club – weekend meeting, July or August. The Secretary, Antique Collectors' Club, 5 Church Street, Woodbridge, Suffolk.

Coalport Conference – Ironbridge Gorge Museum, October. Dr Michael Stratton, Ironbridge Gorge Museum, Ironbridge, Telford, Shropshire TF8 7AW.

Godden Weekend Meeting – July or August. Geoffrey Godden, 19A Crescent Road, Worthing, West Sussex BN11 1RL.

International Ceramics Fair & Seminar – June. Secretary, J. Thomas, 3B Burlington Gardens, Old Bond Street, London W1X 1LE.

Keele University Summer School – August. Terence A. Lockett, 6 Tideswell Road, Hazel Grove, Stockport SK7 6JG.

Morley College Weekend Seminar – November. The Secretary, Morley College Ceramic Circle, Morley College, 61 Westminster Bridge Road, London SE1.

SÈVRES-STYLE. The French National factory at Sèvres (and formerly at Vincennes) was a market leader. Leading factories such as Chelsea and Worcester sought to reproduce Sèvres-style designs. Occasionally the Sèvres factory mark was also copied.

In the 1850–70 period our leading porcelain manufacturers, particularly Minton's, produced really magnificent copies of Sèvres shapes and styles, see Colour Plate IX and Plate 94.

On a general point do note that Sèvres styles and marks have been very widely copied, particularly on the Continent.

94 *A mid-Victorian Minton vase (one of a pair) made to emulate in both shape and the added decoration an eighteenth-century Sèvres original. This is not a fake as it bears only the Minton trade mark, but such high quality copies were extremely fashionable and suitable for French taste furniture and interiors. 8¾in high. c.1860–70.*

SGRAFFITO WARE. A form of Slipware (also called sgraffiato or scratch ware) in which the surface coating of slip is scratched away to produce patterns in the contrasting colour of the underlying body; the scratching is done before glazing. Sgraffito has a long history but in England is chiefly associated with eighteenth-century Staffordshire mugs and jugs decorated with animals, birds, fish, etc., and with a revival at art potteries more recently, especially in the West Country. The jug shown in Colour Plate X is a particularly fine and rare dated example.

SHAVING MUG. A lipped mug partly covered with a perforated soap-dish; the brush was wetted in the hot water through the remaining aperture and the soap lathered with it *in situ*. Made from the 1840s, they were sometimes quite decorative but were mainly produced to a low price by the smaller firms. Many were imported from the Continent.

These are rather similar to the more highly decorated Moustache cup (Plate 70) in which the platform served to keep the moustache away from the tea.

SHELLEY. Some of the most attractive present-century English bone china was produced under the brand name 'Shelley'. This name was used by Wileman & Co. of the Foley Works at Fenton in the 1872–1925 period and subsequently by Messrs Shelleys (*c*.1925–9), Shelley Potteries Ltd (1929–65), and then Shelley China Ltd. These porcelains bear clear marks comprising or incorporating the name 'Shelley'.

For further information the reader is referred to *Shelley Potteries, the History and Productions of a Staffordshire Family of Potters* by C. Watkins, W. Harvey, and R. Senft (Barrie & Jenkins, 1980).

OBADIAH SHERRATT (worked *c*.1830–41). A Burslem (Staffordshire) potter whose crude figure groups usually differed sharply in theme and appearance from other Staffordshire types. The best-known Sherratt-type group is of a man urging on his dog to bait a bull; like most of his work it is illiterately captioned – 'Bull-beating. Now Captain lad'. 'Death of Monrow' celebrates the killing of a Lt. Monroe in a Bengal tiger-hunt; the vast animal biting off the head of the toy-like officer (in full dress uniform) is no less realistic than that labelled 'Roran [roaring] lion'. A more ambitious group is 'Polito's Menagerie'. Isaac's near-sacrifice is labelled 'Abram stop', *tout court*. Domesticities are dealt with in two 'Ale-bench' groups in which a wife forcibly converts her husband to teetotalism, and in 'Who shall ware the Breches'. Most of these groups are on rickety-looking four or six-legged bases.

Hamlet Sherratt followed Obadiah at the Waterloo Road Pottery, Burslem, to about 1854.

SLIPWARE. Earthenware decorated with white or coloured slip, i.e. clay mixed with water to a creamy consistency. The slip was used in various ways: as an overall coating or trailed over the pottery much as cakes are iced, as Plate 95. Slipware was usually given a yellowish lead glaze.

There are examples from many previous cultures. The art was revived early in the seventeenth century at Wrotham, Kent (pronounced rootem), where they made ornate tygs (mugs with more than one handle, for passing round at convivial gatherings) and lidded Posset Pots. Similar wares were made in Staffordshire and the West Country.

95   A Staffordshire slip-decorated posset cup, inscribed 'Robert Pool mad this cup and with a guid poset fil'. Such inscribed or dated pieces are extremely rare. 8in high. c.1690. **(Victoria & Albert Museum).**

Best known are dishes (*c.*1670–85) with Thomas Toft's name prominently trailed in slip on the rim; these bore extraordinary childlike and attractive designs such as Charles II conspicuously hiding in his oak-tree, the heraldic pelican 'in her piety', a mermaid, or Adam and Eve (a theme taken from delftware). Various forms of slipware were still being made by country potters in the nineteenth century, notably the striped 'welsh ware' meat dishes with zigzag patterns. Some modern Studio Potters still use these traditional techniques.

The technique is well explained and illustrated in a book by a potter who still specializes in this ancient style of decoration, *Mary Wondrausch on Slipware* (A. & C. Black, 1986).

SPODE (1770–present day). A Staffordshire firm established at Stoke-on-Trent by the Spode family and continued from 1833 by the Copeland family in whose hands it remained until recently, famous for bone china and blue and white printed earthenwares of very good quality. Josiah Spode I, who had been apprenticed to Whieldon, ran the firm until his death (1797), making fine stoneware, creamware, black basalt (Plate 8), and other types of pottery, introducing to Staffordshire transfer-printing in underglaze blue (*c*.1781). The invention of bone china is traditionally attributed to his son and successor, Josiah II.

Josiah II (1797–1827) also introduced 'New Stone China' (*c*.1805), probably the best of its kind. This was intended for the cheaper market; for the gentry 'Felspar porcelain' was made (*c*.1815–33).

In the early years most of the bone china products were tablewares, especially tea-sets, but also dinner and dessert services. Painted decoration varied in quality but was often very good, flowers, birds, and landscapes being the chief themes. Since the blue and white was intended to compete with Chinese imports, Chinese-inspired designs predominated in the earliest printed wares and have remained favourites ever since. But from *c*.1805 many series of designs were taken from recently published books of prints, e.g. the 'Caramanian' (scenes from Turkish Levant), Indian hunting scenes, romantic Italian ruins, and English rural subjects. Spode was one of the first to develop Imari and other Japan patterns, see Colour Plate IV.

From 1833 to 1847 the firm traded as Copeland & Garrett, and towards the end of this period introduced its 'Statuary Porcelain' or parian ware. W. T. Copeland then became sole proprietor. An increasing output of elaborately decorated cabinet pieces reflected contemporary taste, which sometimes ran to extremes in such matters as gilding and colour grounds; but all products were of high technical quality and often in good taste. The flower paintings (1859–97) of the German painter C. F. Hürten are particularly praised.

Pottery usually bore a 'SPODE' name-mark from 1790 as did most of the later bone china, though unmarked pieces can often be identified by pattern numbers.

The Spode wares are of a uniformly high quality and are very collectable. In 1970 the Copeland firm reverted to the name Spode Ltd.

For further information the reader is referred to *Spode* by L. Whiter (Barrie & Jenkins, revised edition 1989) or to Robert Copeland's chapter 8 in *Staffordshire Porcelain*. Mr Copeland is Historical Consultant to Spode Ltd at Stoke-on-Trent. The Works have a private museum and there is a Spode Society. In addition an excellent collection is housed at Trelissick House, near Truro in Cornwall and a well-illustrated booklet is available entitled *The Copeland China Collection* by Vega Wilkinson, published by Mr R. Spencer C. Copeland at Trelissick.

STAFFORDSHIRE DOGS. No book dealing with inexpensive ceramics could be complete without mention of Staffordshire spaniel-type earthenware dogs (Plate 96). These have been produced in hundreds of thousands over more than a hundred years. They are still being produced today and they seem to have an ageless charm.

They are normally unmarked and were made by very many firms large and small. Sampson Smith of Longton advertised '. . . dogs, white and gold, black and gold, red and white and black and white'. Kent & Parr of Burslem advertised in the 1890s 'Dogs, white and gold, black and white, red and white. Hounds . . . Poodle Dogs, all in several sizes'. William Machin of Hanley was also a leading maker of such inexpensive ornaments.

Charming and traditional as these may be the standard models are not of great value but on the other hand unusual models, porcelain examples, or those having rare features are very collectable and may command prices many times that of a regular model.

96   Two typical late Victorian Staffordshire dogs. Such examples were produced in extremely large numbers from simple two-piece moulds and were quite inexpensive. Their enduring popularity is evidenced by the fact that similar dogs are still in production. 7in high (also made in other sizes). c.1880.

STAFFORDSHIRE EARTHENWARE FIGURES. The making of clay 'images' or 'toys', as they were called, to ornament farmhouse and cottage chimney-pieces flourished throughout most of the eighteenth century.

The earliest saltglaze (stoneware) figures and those in earthenware are often classified as Astbury, Astbury-Whieldon and Whieldon wares (1720–80) and most ante-date the first English porcelain figures. The transition from folk-art to more sophisticated themes and techniques is spanned by the numerous Wood family, who worked in Burslem c.1754–1846; first they developed the use of coloured glazes, a form of decoration they learnt from Astbury and Whieldon, and then, c.1790, turned to painting in overglaze enamels. To the rustic and biblical themes and mild satires on the village parson which seem more appropriate to their market, they began to add Olympic gods and similar signs of the Neo-Classical times, mistakenly (as some think) trying to imitate Derby and other porcelain models in an unsuitable pottery medium.

More successful in this trend was a London dealer, James Neale, who in effect took over Palmer's factory at Hanley (c.1776–92) and produced dainty porcelain-type figures, e.g. a set of Seasons, Minerva, Diana, and even a 'Sorrows of Goethe' – which could not have had much local appeal.

Rustic trends were better represented by the Toby jug and the ochre-and-blue dominated Prattware, and particularly by the figures emanating from the Walton School (c.1806–46), with their distinctive green bocages and typically high roundish bases contrasting with the square bases (Plate 97) hitherto in favour.

97   *A typical early nineteenth-century Staffordshire earthenware figure, on simple square base and with slight bocage. Such religious figures were popular, rather more so than now! 11in high. c.1810–20.*

It is, however, surprising that so much sweetness and light should have emerged from the insanitary shacks in which so many of these figures were made. With drunkenness and absenteeism rife, much of the work must have fallen to the children; as recently as 1842 an official report recorded the case of a boy of 9 producing 40 dozen small figures each day of a 6-day week – at 4d. a day.

Except in a few cases these earthenware figures are unmarked and many were produced by small, little-known firms. The names which collectors ascribe to so many examples are generic rather than exact.

Victorian examples. Three years after coming to the throne in 1837 Queen Victoria married Prince Albert. This event coincided with an outburst of activity in the making of figures in a new tradition, most of them portrait figures and commemorating current events, in the fields of war, sport, crime, entertainment, and religion; but first came the Royal Family. In addition vast quantities of 'china' dogs were made, the most familiar being the soulful-looking spaniel which gazes out of most antique-shop windows and which, after the first shock, tends to grow on one.

These figures were no longer hand-modelled but moulded on bold simplified lines in white earthenware; skilful design cut costs by reducing the number of mould-sections to two or three (Plate 98). Decoration was characterized for the first twenty years by a brilliant underglaze blue (especially handy for uniforms), to which was added further embellishment in bright overglaze enamels and gilt.

98   A selection of inexpensive Staffordshire 'flat-back' earthenware figures, of the type that do not bear a maker's mark. Cottage art but charming and dateless. Large group 10½in high. c.1850–70.

As the years went by decoration was simplified until by the late 1860s it was usually a matter of black and white with a touch of gilt. Realizing that these figures would grace not the dining-table but the mantelpiece, and would thus be viewed from the front only, the potters gradually stopped colouring or moulding the back, thus producing the familiar Victorian so-called 'flatback'.

Mounted figures were vastly popular (Plate 99). The diminutive horses look as if they were sired by rocking-horses or circus ponies;

99   *A rare and good-quality Staffordshire named figure – a portrait figure. In 1861 Victor Emmanuel II was declared the first King of Italy. 14¾in high. c.1856–61.*

their uniformed riders gaze stiffly sideways at the onlooker as if defying impudent criticism, and in the end the critical may well succumb to their primitive charm, the effect having been likened to that of the works of Le Douanier Rousseau.

The portrait figures were often named on the base, but as likenesses were usually perfunctory, it was simple to switch titles. Queen Victoria suffered this indignity at the commencement of her reign; overwhelmed by public demand the potters took the figure of an actress, stuck a crown on her head, and labelled it 'Her Majesty Queen Victoria'.

In the first few years of the 1840s there were already, in addition to Royalties, figures commemorating personalities in cricket, crime, the circus; Grace Darling, the lighthouse-keeper's daughter who helped rescue passengers from a wreck; and Afghan war heroes. Authorities have noted the radical and nonconformist bias of the potters, allied to intense patriotism and loyalty to the throne. Tories are virtually ignored in favour of Peel and Cobden (repeal of the Corn Laws, 1846), Gladstone, etc.; Wesley, Sankey, and Moody are commemorated and 'No Popery' themes of 1851, but no archbishops; Napoleon III is welcomed as an ally in the Crimean War (1854). Wars, in particular, stimulated production, whether the Indian Mutiny (Colin Campbell, Highland Jessie), Crimean War (Florence Nightingale), American Civil War (John Brown, Uncle Tom, Lincoln), or the Franco-Prussian War (1870), in which Staffordshire sympathies swung from Germany to France. Byron, Scott, Burns (with or without Highland Mary) are among those representing literature, and Sir John Franklin the explorer.

Two interesting series of figures have been distinguished, well moulded and decorated all round. The factories that made them are unknown, but they are so well done that until recently they were often called 'Rockingham', although not porcelain. One, given the name 'Alpha factory', in the period c.1845–51 produced figures with titles usually in impressed capitals. The other was called the Tallis factory (c.1849–67) because the figures first noticed were copied from engravings in Tallis's Shakespeare Gallery. They differ from the Alpha figures in being very heavy, having no underglaze blue, and sometimes in having transfer-printed titles. The Tallis and many other early Victorian moulds came into the hands of William Kent (1885 onwards) and eventually William Kent (Porcelains) Ltd, who used them until 1962. It has been suggested that they may have been made by Thomas Parr of Burslem (worked 1852–70) and then passed to Kent & Parr (1880–94).

The many reproductions of Victorian figures are usually referred to as 'Kent copies'; colouring, in which iron-red predominates, is crudely done and the indented titles clumsily filled in with black. Many of the flatbacks, which flourished particularly in the 1850s, were made by Sampson Smith of Longton (c.1846–78); his name and moulds were used by successor firms until at least the 1960s. Some flatbacks were made elsewhere in Staffordshire, and in Scotland

(Portobello, Prestonpans) or at other ceramic centres. Some Victorian Staffordshire-type figures, dogs and other animal models are now being made by Rushton Ceramics Ltd, The Mill Pottery, Tynwold, St Johns, Isle of Man. In 1989 this firm, owned by Mr & Mrs J. Liddle, advertised themselves as 'Makers of Fine Reproduction Figures, including dogs, flatbacks, cottages etc. Made from original moulds – with crazed glaze . . .'

Books on Staffordshire figures include *Staffordshire Chimney Ornaments* by R. G. Haggar (Phoenix House, 1955), *Staffordshire Portrait Figures* by P. D. G. Pugh (Antique Collectors' Club, 1987), *The Victorian Staffordshire Figure* by A. Oliver (Heinemann, 1971), and *Staffordshire Pottery* by A. Oliver (Heinemann, 1981). Most general books such as Godden's *British Pottery. An Illustrated Guide* (Barrie & Jenkins, 1974) illustrate typical examples and types.

THOMAS STEEL (1771–1850). This entry features one of our most celebrated fruit and flower painters on porcelain. It also serves to illustrate how talented ceramic painters were inclined to move from one factory to another as fortunes changed or as they were offered higher wages. Thomas Steel (the older books use the spelling Steele) was trained at the Derby factory, although he had been born in the Staffordshire Potteries. He left for the Rockingham Works probably in the mid or late 1820s. The Rockingham tray shown here (Plate 100) represents one of the few fully-signed examples of his work.

100   A rare early Rockingham porcelain tray, the centre painted by Thomas Steel and signed 'T. Steel Pinx'. Rockingham Griffin mark printed in red. 10½ × 9in. c.1826–30. **(Rotherham Museum).**

He then moved back to Staffordshire and his name appears in the Minton wage records from 17 March 1832. He worked for Minton's until his death in 1850 and examples of his work for this firm are shown in Geoffrey Godden's *Minton Pottery & Porcelain of the First Period 1793–1850* (Barrie & Jenkins, 1968). Thomas Steel's two sons Thomas (b.1836) and Edwin (b.1839) followed their father's calling. The work of all the Steel family is of high quality and is commercially very desirable.

STIRRUP-CUP. As this was handed to people in the saddle, to fortify them at meets, it did not have to stand up and could take any fanciful shape, usually an animal's head – fox, deer, hare, fish, many kinds of dog. It was an ancient Greek idea, and their name for it, rhyton, is sometimes used in learned catalogues. Stirrup-cups, especially those of the 1800–20 period, are very collectable.

STONE CHINA. A form of heavy compact earthenware made with felspar, resembling porcelain in outward appearance and 'ring', but cheaper to make. The type was first patented (1800) by the Turner brothers of Lane End, Staffordshire. Josiah Spode II reputedly bought the rights and made a very dense and durable variety, marked 'Stone China' or 'New Stone'. Mason's Patent Ironstone

101   A durable yet decorative 'Stone China' meat dish from a large Maddock dinner service. Well-printed in underglaze blue with a fashionable mock Anglo-Oriental landscape design. Printed elaborate 'Fairy Villas. Stone China' mark. 21¾ × 17½in. c.1842–5.

China (1813) is similar. Eventually most other potters made 'Stone China', 'ironstone', or 'granite' dinner services, often decorated with Japan patterns or blue and white transfer-prints as the Maddock example shown in Plate 101.

It should be noted that such durable bodies were not true china and that the term 'Stone' or 'Stone China' was sometimes used in the eighteenth century to describe the imported Chinese dinner wares.

For information on the many makers of this type of ware the reader is referred to *Godden's Guide to Mason's China and the Ironstone Wares* (Antique Collectors' Club, 1980).

STONEWARE. Earthenware relatively rich in vitreous material and fired at so high a temperature (about 1300°C) that it becomes as hard as stone and non-porous; one kind has long been familiar in the form of drainpipes. At Fulham John Dwight produced Brownware and Redware before he developed white saltglaze stoneware; brown saltglaze was also made at Nottingham. From the late 1600s Lambeth and Fulham produced characteristic saltglaze jugs in two colours, dark brown band at the top, buff below; also buff and brown spirit flasks shaped as figures (contemporary celebrities, Mrs Caudle, etc.). 'Reform' flasks, made by Bourne of Denby among others, celebrated the Reform Bill (1832).

There is really no hard and fast dating for stoneware. Doultons of Lambeth produced both decorative and utilitarian wares up to recent times and very many modern potters produced decorative and useful stonewares. The pre-1860 examples tend not to bear a maker's mark.

STUDIO POTTERY. Stoneware or earthenware individually designed and made by one potter or a small team. The Studio Pottery movement gathered strength in the twentieth century and is still flourishing. Its origins may be traced back in England to the Martin Brothers, the Barlows' work at Doultons, Castle Hedingham, Della Robbia Ware, etc. The best-known of the moderns has been Bernard Leach who, after studying pottery in Japan, set up his studio in St Ives, Cornwall (1920), continuing here to train a succession of like-minded potters until his death in 1979.

There are today hundreds if not thousands of so-called Studio Potters practising their craft in this country and using their individual taste and skill to produce a vast mass of contemporary ceramics. Not all work in earthenware or stoneware – those that use porcelain are listed in Godden's *Encyclopaedia of British Porcelain Manufacturers* (Barrie & Jenkins, 1988), see pp. 26–8 as well as the main listing. There are many good books on Studio Pottery, including Paul Rice and Christopher Gowing's well-illustrated *British Studio Ceramics in the 20th Century* (Barrie & Jenkins, 1989). The Craftsmen Potters Association issues a magazine *Ceramic Review*

102   An imposing Studio Pottery type stoneware vase hand-made by Derek Emms of Longton. Impressed D E seal mark. 15in high. 1962.

and a list of members entitled *Potters* (8th edition, 1989). The association's shop can supply details of these and standard books: write to Contemporary Ceramics, The Craftsmen Potters Shop and Gallery, 21 Carnaby Street, London W1V 1PH.

SUNDERLAND. There have been many potteries in the neighbourhood of this Durham town, some going back to the early eighteenth century. Most of them made lustreware, especially of the splashed-pink type.

Other common features were transfer-prints in black, often on seafaring themes, or of the Wearmouth bridge, the longest single-span cast-iron bridge when built in 1796, commemorative wares, including named and dated christening mugs and frog-mugs, usually in creamware, and wall plaques. Many pieces have verses or other inscriptions in black.

The best-known is the Garrison Pottery (1803–65), associated with the names of Dixon and Austin. The engraved copper plates passed to the Ball Brothers (of Deptford, Sunderland, 1865–1918) but they used them for coloured, not black, transfers, and their lustre was an orange tint. The Southwick pottery (1788–1897) is associated with the Scott family but not, apparently, with the Portobello Scotts.

The Sunderland Museum & Art Gallery has an interesting collection of local wares and has published a guide entitled *The Potteries of Sunderland and District*.

SWANSEA. This South Wales city was one of the leading centres of the ceramic industry. A good range of earthenwares was made here from the mid 1760s onwards but Swansea is perhaps best known for its fine porcelains, which were produced for a brief period from *c*.1814 when William Billingsley was associated with the venture. Several different types of body were produced, not all of which have the good translucency which is traditionally associated with Swansea porcelain, but always the decoration is of high quality. The 'Swansea' name-mark was sometimes used but fakes or redecorated specimens can also be so marked.

For further information the reader is referred to E. Morton Nance's specialist work, *The Pottery and Porcelain of Swansea & Nantgarw* (Batsford, 1942), *Swansea Porcelain* by W. D. John (Ceramic Book Company, 1958), and *Swansea Porcelain, Shapes and Decoration* by A. E. Jones and Sir Leslie Joseph (D. Brown & Sons, 1988).

TEA AND COFFEE SETS. In the eighteenth-century the two sets were integrated, the same saucers serving teacups (or tea bowls) and coffee cups. Coffee cans (which were straight-sided as Plate 28) were made, mainly for sets of the period *c*.1800–20. Apart from the teapot and its stand, there would normally be a covered sugar bowl (sometimes called a sucrier), a cream or milk-jug (often, but not always, with a cover), a slop or waste-bowl, a spoon-tray, and two bread-and-butter or cake plates. In some services there was also a tea canister or tea vase and cover. Early teapots were small, tea being expensive (even when smuggled, as it often was), so that in some quarters the used tea-leaves were spread on bread and butter, sugared, and eaten! There was a magic about tea which, Pepys was told, was good for the defluxions.

Handleless tea-bowls in the Chinese style were used at first (New Hall and some other firms went on making them after the turn of the century for their less expensive sets). The aged and ague-stricken might drink safely from a two-handled trembleuse cup which fitted into a gallery or depression in the saucer. Tea for one or up to four people might be served on a cabaret (French for, *inter alia*, a tea-tray or tea service) special shapes were sometimes used and the teapot, etc. was of a small size.

Afternoon tea did not become fashionable until near 1800; the main tea-drinking occasion was immediately after dinner.

Tea-wares formed the staple product of all the English porcelain factories, with the possible exception of the up-market Chelsea manufactory. Consequently parts of tea services are the most commonly found eighteenth-century ceramic articles and any book on an individual factory will feature a good range of their tea-wares.

There are several specialist books on teapots and the reader will find the following two books helpful in gauging the changing styles and basic shapes: *An Anthology of British Cups* by Michael Berthoud (Micawber, 1982) and *An Anthology of British Teapots* by Philip Miller and Michael Berthoud (Micawber, 1985).

'TEBO'. An elusive figure who drifts through the history of eighteenth-century English porcelain, sometimes leaving his mark

('T' or 'To') on figures and other assembled or modelled pieces made at Bow (*c*.1750–60), Worcester (*c*.1760–9), Plymouth (*c*.1769–70), Bristol (*c*.1770–5), Caughley (*c*.1775–85), and slightly later at Chamberlain's Worcester.

Research on the archives of this later factory suggests that these often relief-moulded or impressed initial marks relate to John Toulouse, rather than to the mysterious 'Mr. Tebo', as stated in earlier books. For further information the reader is referred to Godden's *Chamberlain-Worcester Porcelain, 1788–1852* (Barrie & Jenkins, 1982).

TERRACOTTA. Josiah Wedgwood revived the name, particularly associated with ancient Greek pottery (including the fourth-century BC Tanagra statuettes) and imperial Roman 'samian' ware, for the unglazed porous earthenwares, usually red, in which he made classical-shaped vases. Later, terracotta wares were made by Minton, Copeland, F. & R. Pratt, and many others. Good figures, groups, and busts were made with local Devon clay at Watcombe (Torquay)

103   A Bishops Waltham terracotta vase and a jug decorated with printed classical figure designs. Printed Bishops Waltham mark. Jug 6¾in high. c.1867.

from 1867 and the Doulton factory made figures, large and small, of celebrities and Royalties in the 1880s.

The unglazed terracotta wares are usually trimly potted and can be very attractive (see Plate 103).

THIMBLES. There is a great range of gaily-decorated porcelain thimbles, those made by e.g. Chelsea or Derby being very rare and costly.

In the nineteenth century some extremely well-decorated examples were made, but except for the Royal Worcester examples the thimbles were usually unmarked and difficult to attribute. Being thin many were broken so that antique examples are very rare.

As they take up little display space these dainty objects are now very collectable and very many modern examples are made for the thimble collector – some seemingly in limited editions, rather than for use. They are fun to collect and can mark an occasion or visit to a special place, but the modern examples should not be regarded as a short-term investment.

TILES. Walls have been decorated with tiles for some 3000 years, originally to keep rooms cool in Middle Eastern countries, as they do today in the dairies and larders of northern climes. Moors brought them to Spain and the Dutch brought them to England in the sixteenth-century. Dutch tiles were of tin-glazed Delftware, hand-painted with all kinds of design from geometrical to ships and Aesop's Fables. One attractive use was to decorate the central stove which dominates many Continental living-rooms.

In England Dutch styles were copied at first, especially at Lambeth and Bristol. Creamware and other forms of pottery eventually replaced this delftware. Sadler & Green (of Liverpool) specialized in transfer-printed designs mainly on creamware tiles. In the eighteenth-century it became fashionable for the drawing-room to have tiled dados, fireplaces, etc.

Interest in tiles revived in the 1850s and they were used extensively in Victorian churches, shops, pubs, banks, etc. There was a wide range of themes, e.g. Japanese, Burne-Jones, floral, geometrical; sets representing arts and crafts, or Seasons (Minton), months of the year (Wedgwood and Copeland); scenes from Dickens, Scott, and Shakespeare. William De Morgan also made artistic tiles for William Morris. Several firms and potters still produce tiles, some in old styles.

There must be tens of thousands of different decorative tile designs – mostly Victorian – and they can be very interesting and decorative if you have room to mount them or display them.

Books devoted to tiles include *English Delftware Tiles* by A. Ray (Faber & Faber, 1973), *Collecting Victorian Tiles* by T. A. Lockett (Antique Collectors' Club, 1979), *William De Morgan Tiles* by J. Catleugh (Trefoil Books, 1984), *Decorative Tiles Throughout the Ages* by H. van Lemmen (Bracken Books, 1988), and *English Tinglazed Tiles* by J. Horne (J. Horne, 1989).

There is also a 'Tiles and Architectural Ceramics Society' which publishes a newsletter and a journal. The Membership Secretary is Miss K. Huggins, Reabrook Lodge, 8 Sutton Road, Shrewsbury, Shropshire, SY2 6DD.

TOBY JUG. Generic name for a series of jugs representing a seated figure usually holding a foaming mug of ale and wearing a three-cornered cocked hat (as Plate 104), the crown of which (now often missing) is detachable for use as a cup. The original and most familiar Toby Philpot was supposed to be a Yorkshire toper of fabulous capacity, but many similar jugs represent e.g. Bluff King Hal, Admiral Howe, Martha Gunn (who traditionally gave the future Prince Regent his first dip in the sea at Brighton), and a standing 'Hearty Good Fellow'. They first appeared in the 1760s, possibly originated by Aaron Wood but copied by very many others, in-

104   *A rare marked Neale & Co. earthenware Toby jug decorated with attractive semi-translucent glazes. Later examples have opaque enamel colours added over the glaze. 9¾in high. c.1785–90.*

cluding early versions in Prattware colouring. In the early versions the face is full of character, and the richness of the semi-translucent coloured glazes in the Ralph Wood models is outstanding; late nineteenth-century copies are poor relations of the originals.

However, in recent years several firms have produced Toby-type jugs depicting modern characters and these have merit, as long as they are not looked upon as a reliable short-term investment.

Vic Schuler's little book *British Toby Jugs* (K. Francis Publishing, 1986) is a good, inexpensive introduction to a large subject.

TORQUAY. The town and district of Torquay in Devon has, from the nineteenth century, supported several potteries which have mainly produced art-type pottery or motto-wares for local markets.

The best known of these potteries was that of the Watcombe Terra Cotta Clay Company founded in 1869. The wares were at first of unglazed terracotta, quality clay being available locally. The Watcombe firm under various owners continued to the 1960s. The Watcombe (Plate 105) and other South Devon wares are now very collectable. For further information and details of the many marks used the

105   *A very good quality Watcombe terracotta vase with charming decoration and gilt enrichments. 10¾in high. c.1875–85.*

reader is referred to *The Old Torquay Potteries* by D. and E. Lloyd Thomas (A. H. Stockwell Ltd & Guildart, 1978). There is also a 'Torquay Pottery Collectors' Society' which issues a helpful magazine. The Membership Secretary is Mrs Shirley Everett, 23 Holland Avenue, Cheam, Surrey. This society has published a booklet, *Torquay Motto Wares*, edited by Virginia Brisco (1989).

TORQUAY FAKES. This description is not generally applied to possible reproductions of Torquay or other West Country tourist-type earthenwares but rather to very good-quality essays in re-producing collectable eighteenth-century ceramics such as Bow, Chelsea, Derby, or Longton Hall porcelains. The list may well be extended for we do not know the extent of these essays.

These porcelains (and perhaps some earthenwares) are believed to have been made in the South Devon town of Torquay, in the 1950s and 1960s. These clever copies of original eighteenth-century models do not bear a mark and have, on occasions, been sold and accepted as originals.

For further information the reader is referred to Geoffrey Godden's *Encyclopaedia of British Porcelain Manufacturers* (Barrie & Jenkins, 1988), p. 267, Creative Studios (Torquay) Ltd.

TRANSFER-PRINTING. The decoration of ceramics with printed designs transferred to them by specially prepared paper from engraved and etched copper plates; a large number of identical copies could be taken from one engraving, thus greatly reducing the cost of decoration, although this hot technique (the coppers had to be heated) was quite time-consuming and required a team of two or three persons.

Nevertheless, the essential point is mass-production whereby a large number of articles can be relatively speedily decorated in an identical manner, a process so suitable for long runs of plates, tiles, or suchlike. As early as July 1756 John Sadler and Guy Green of Liverpool certified that they 'did within the space of six hours . . . print upwards of twelve hundred earthenware tiles of different patterns . . . more in number and better and neater than one hundred skilful pot-painters could have painted in the like space of time . . .'

We cannot now be certain what type of printing was involved, perhaps the cold 'bat-printing' method rather than the more troublesome 'hot method' used with conventional underglaze blue printing, but the basic advantages are the same. Soon the surface printing of enamels was widely practised as was the printing of porcelains at Bow, Liverpool, Worcester, and Vauxhall.

At first the transfers were applied over the glaze. The 'ink', a mixture of enamel colour and oils, was usually grey-black, red, or lilac. Sadler & Green, of Liverpool, were so decorating Longton Hall porcelain c.1760 and Wedgwood creamware soon afterwards on a contract basis.

The commonest form of transfer-printing, however, is underglaze printing, at first in cobalt blue; this was introduced at Worcester c.1759, probably by Robert Hancock. This design was applied to the biscuit porcelain, fired (to burn off the oil) and then glazed and refired. The practice spread to other porcelain factories, e.g. Caughley, Lowestoft, Liverpool, and Bristol, and became the mainstay of the pottery industry after Spode and others introduced it to Staffordshire. Smudgy outlines were an early defect, but in 1806 the invention of a better transfer paper permitted the addition of stipple to line engraving, and increased clarity and finer gradations of tone. Underglaze pink, brown, and green colours were used from *c*.1828, and three or four-colour prints from the 1840s; but blue continued to predominate.

In overglaze printing greater clarity was achieved by bat-printing, in which a flexible 'bat' (pad) of glue and treacle was substituted for transfer paper. This was a cold process not as troublesome as the hot transfer system, but only small areas could reliably be treated. The bat-printing process was used from the earliest days of printing on ceramics, but in the 1790–1825 period it reached perfection and some wonderfully delicate engravings (as Plate 9) were used on both porcelain and pottery. In this technique the lightly engraved (and etched) copper plate was charged with oil, not pigment. The oil was then transferred onto the ceramic via the glue bat and pigment then dusted on to the oil. A final firing blended the colour with the glaze. See also under 'Bat-Printing'.

Books on individual factories will give information on their printed wares. Specialist works on printing are *English Transfer Printed Pottery & Porcelain* by C. Williams-Wood (Faber & Faber, 1981) and *Spode Printed Ware* by D. Drakard and P. Holdway (Longman, 1983).

Collectors of eighteenth-century printed wares will find the following books helpful: *The Life and Work of Robert Hancock* by C. Cook (Chapman & Hall, 1948, supplement 1955) and *English Blue & White Porcelain of the 18th Century* by B. Watney (Faber & Faber, 1973). Collectors of blue printed earthenwares will find A. W. Coysh and R. K. Henrywood's *The Dictionary of Blue & White Printed Pottery 1780–1880* (Antique Collectors' Club, 1982, vol. II, 1989) particularly helpful.

TRIO. The name given to a set of one saucer, a teacup, and a coffee cup. These pieces originally were part of a complete service which included twelve saucers, twelve teacups, and twelve coffee cups. It is advantageous to have all three units rather than just one cup and saucer.

The teacups are normally wider and shallower than the taller rather narrow coffee cups or the straight-sided coffee can. A typical trio of the 1820s is here shown in Plate 106. Specialist books on any factory will include illustrations of typical cup shapes. There is also Michael Berthoud's *An Anthology of British Cups* (Micawber, 1982).

TURNER (1756–1803). Staffordshire potters practising their craft at Lane End. John I from 1756 made fine stoneware jugs and vases, often with applied ornament. His sons John and William produced a good range of earthenwares (including dry-bodies, jasper, etc.) as well as some porcelains. In 1800 John and William Turner patented two new bodies (one for earthenware, one porcelain): examples are sometimes marked 'Turner's Patent'. These were perhaps the forerunners of a host of later durable earthenwares of Ironstone or Stone

China (q.v.) type. The Staffordshire Turners should not be confused with Thomas Turner of the Caughley factory in Shropshire.

The standard book on these uniformly well-potted Staffordshire wares is Bevis Hillier's *The Turners of Lane End* (Cory, Adams & Mackay, 1965). For the Turner porcelains the reader is referred to *Staffordshire Porcelain* (Granada, 1983), chapter 6 or to G. A. Godden's *Encyclopaedia of British Porcelain Manufacturers* (Barrie & Jenkins, 1988).

106   A Coalport porcelain 'trio' of saucer plus the tall coffee cup and the wider shallow teacup. Diameter of saucer 5¾in. c.1820–5.

VAUXHALL. The attractive mid eighteenth-century porcelains formerly attributed to William Ball of Liverpool are now believed to have been produced at John Sanders's pottery at Vauxhall (or Lambeth) on the south bank of the Thames, near the present Waterloo Station, with Nicholas Crisp(e) a wealthy jeweller and merchant acting as a backer and having retail premises in Bow Church Yard.

The *Public Advertiser* of 21 May, 1753, contains an advertisement concerning the new 'Porcelaine Ware' then available at 'Mr. Sanders' near the Plate Glass house [factory], Vauxhall . . .' But Sanders and Crisp(e) had obviously hoped to produce porcelain before this, for they took out a license to mine Cornish Soaprock in June 1751. However, in the 1760s Crisp(e) was in financial difficulties and he was bankrupt in November 1763. By at least 1767 he was carrying out trials for further porcelain manufacture at Bovey Tracey. The Vauxhall porcelain manufactory probably closed in about 1764, but in some ten years this little-known works produced some neatly-potted delightful porcelains, which on chemical analysis contain soaprock (magnesium silicate). Underglaze painted patterns in the

107   A rare Vauxhall (London) porcelain teapot and cover decorated with printed designs coloured-over by hand. 4¼in high. c.1755–60. **(Private collection).**

108   A Vauxhall porcelain tea-bowl and saucer decorated in underglaze blue and overglaze enamels. Part of an initialled and dated tea-set formerly attributed to Liverpool. Diameter of saucer 4in. 1764

oriental style predominated but no blue printing is known. Attractive on-glaze printing in multicolour outlines was produced and figures were also made. No mark is known or recorded.

For information on John Sanders and on Nicholas Crisp(e) see Godden's *Encyclopaedia of British Porcelain Manufacturers* (Barrie & Jenkins, 1988). The story of the trial excavations and a good history of the concern with numerous illustrations of porcelains now attributed to the Vauxhall factory is given in Dr Bernard Watney's pioneer Paper 'The Vauxhall China Works, 1751–1764', *Transactions of the English Ceramic Circle,* vol. 13, part 3, 1989.

CHARLES VYSE (1882–1971). In the 1890s Charles Vyse was apprenticed to Doultons, for whom he later produced many models, including the very popular 'Darling'. However, in the 1920s and 1930s he produced under his own name in his London studio a series of finely modelled and neatly decorated earthenware figures (Plate 109) and groups. These are usually signed or initialled and dated.

He was in later life more interested in his stonewares and oriental-style glaze-effect, one-off vases, bowls, etc. which also bear his name, initials (or monogram) often with the date added (Plate 110).

109   A Charles Vyse earthenware figure 'A Bit of Old Chelsea' (model 38), introduced in 1934, marked 'Charles Vyse. Chelsea'. 10½in high. c.1935.

Although the Vyse wares have risen in price in recent years, they are still probably undervalued. Richard Dennis of 144 Kensington Church Street, London W8, held an exhibition of Vyse wares in 1974 and then published a well-illustrated catalogue. Paul Rice and Christopher Gowing's book *British Studio Ceramics in the 20th Century* (Barrie & Jenkins, 1989) includes illustrations of Vyse's work and a supporting text.

110   A selection of Charles Vyse signed stonewares showing oriental-style glaze effects on simple shapes. Larger vase 7in high. c.1932–5.

WALL PLAQUES. A ceramic substitute for pictures. Oval or rectangular, sometimes moulded in low relief and occasionally with an elaborately moulded 'frame', they were made in every sort of material – delftware, creamware, and other kinds of pottery or porcelain. They might depict domestic animals, flowers, kings and queens, biblical or historical themes, etc. The most familiar are the forbidding Sunderland lustre texts, such as 'Prepare to meet thy God'. 'The Sailor's Farewell', with doggerel verse, and transferprints of Sunderland's Wearmouth iron bridge (built 1796) were also favourites over a long period.

There were also many other types of wall plaque. Some were merely porcelain slabs, painted as a canvas would have been and likewise framed for hanging on a wall.

In the Victorian period many potters produced large circular wall plaques for the large number of amateur (and professional) ceramic artists to decorate. Painted plaques vary greatly in quality but signed examples by well-known painters can be very fine – and they can also be very costly!

WALTON SCHOOL (*c*.1818–60) A name given to Staffordshire figure-makers who worked in the tradition of John, and later James, Walton of Burslem and Hanley. John may be said to have brought to the cottage mantelpiece pottery versions of the Derby porcelain groups, adapting their bocages in a characteristic highly stylized form. Against these stood figures or groups, not only versions taken from Derby and other porcelain factories but from earlier potters (e.g. the Wood family); most of these became standard themes for later potters, e.g. the Shepherd and Shepherdess, Gardener and Mate, Huntsman and Mate, the Tithe Pig, Elijah, the Flight from Egypt, and many animals. These often bear titles on the front of the base and, except for early examples, the name 'Walton' on a scroll at the back. They were gaily painted in green, blue, yellow, brown, etc., often with dappling on the base. Some later reproductions occur with the 'Walton' scroll device.

The best of his followers was Ralph Salt of Hanley (worked *c*.1820–46), who sometimes added his surname on the back. His bocages were less symmetrical, the spelling of titles can be bizarre (Shepherdiss, Archar, Sport Man) and he displayed more humour and less sentiment than Walton. The typical base was high, waisted, and sometimes had an oak-leaf on the front. One of the large Tittensor family, possibly Charles (working *c*.1815–25), also made bocage figures; the bocages were smaller and carelessly modelled but the colouring was attractive.

111 A typical Walton earthenware group 'Tenderness' decorated with overglaze enamel colours. Raised 'Walton' name-scroll on back. 8½in high. c.1820–30.

These Staffordshire figure makers are known because they some-times used name-marks. It should be remembered, however, that there were very many more who did not use a mark and therefore we cannot now attribute their work. We should not relate all such figures of the 1820–40 period to John Walton just because some marked specimens are recorded. We should also remember that the mark comprises only the surname, so examples could relate to James, John, Joshua, or William Walton. The term Walton School is a convenient general description for Staffordshire earthenware figures of the type shown in Plate 111. Helpful reference books are listed in Appendix C under the sub-heading Figures and Groups.

WASHSTAND OR TOILET SETS. Sets consisted of ewer and basin, soap-dish, sponge-dish, toothbrush-tray, slop-pail, and chamber-pot. Colourful sets were made in the nineteenth century by Minton, Wedgwood, and many other firms, large and small. They were the staple diet of the earthenware trade, especially in the 1860–1910 period when every bedroom had a washstand and its earthenware (or china) fittings.

These sets can still be seen in the bedrooms of stately homes open to the public. Rather special sets are in the Royal residences such as Osborne House on the Isle of Wight.

These Victorian or Edwardian toilet sets are still in demand as they add a period flavour and some individual pieces can be adapted to a more modern use, the large ewers and basins to hold or display flowers or fruit, for example. Note that reproductions are still being made.

WATCH-STANDS. Ceramic ornaments have been designed to hold a watch at night-time from at least the eighteenth century, but most examples found today will be Victorian.

The design incorporated a circular aperture about two inches in diameter with a curved half shelf at the back. Into this the old large watch could be placed to form a handy and ornamental mantel or bedside clock. These should not be confused with the larger clock cases which were intended to contain a permanent clock.

WATERING-CANS. Charming early nineteenth-century ceramic, usually porcelain, miniature versions, were about three inches high and were used to sprinkle lavender water, etc. on porcelain or wax flowers, or to water real flowers growing indoors. However, some seem to be merely decorative toys. There is a wide variety, made e.g. by Spode, many of them most attractive and collectable but difficult to find.

WEDGWOOD (1759–present day). A Staffordshire firm famous for many innovations in pottery manufacture, founded at Burslem by Josiah Wedgwood. From 1754 he had with Thomas Whieldon de-veloped and perfected agate, marbled, and tortoiseshell wares and a fine deep green glaze particularly associated with the table-ware moulded in cauliflower, melon, or pineapple patterns which he later made at his own pottery.

At first Wedgwood made mainly useful wares at Burslem, but in 1769 he entered into partnership with Thomas Bentley and opened a new, model factory named Etruria because the classical Greek and Roman pottery recently excavated at Pompeii and Herculaneum was at that time thought to be Etruscan. The Etruria output comprised ornamental wares in the Neo-Classical taste derived from those finds, and here Wedgwood perfected his famous Black Basalt (c.1767) and blue Jasper Ware (1774). Ornamental wares marked 'Wedgwood and Bentley' (1769–80) are of the highest quality (Plate 112). The manufacture of domestic wares continued at Burslem under Wedgwood's name.

From the beginning Wedgwood also made creamware; this was called Queen's Ware when he was appointed Potter to Queen Charlotte (1765). Creamware table services, with printed patterns or painted borders, were exported in vast quantities to the Continent, where they superseded delft and faience; creamware is still one of the firm's staple products. Some Victorian examples, painted in a free style by Émile Lessore (1858–67) and signed, are much in demand.

112 A typically graceful 'Wedgwood & Bentley' earthenware vase on a black basalt plinth. Moulded circular name-mark. 18½in high. c.1770–80. **(Christie's).**

113   A group of Wedgwood jasper small plaques decorated in a typical manner with sprigged relief patterns, produced in separate moulds. Impressed 'Wedgwood' name-marks. Central plaque of George III. 2½in high. c.1790–1830. **(Sotheby's).**

Other innovations were buff creamware with 'Rosso Antico' (i.e. red) reliefs, 'variegated lustre' (pink, with marbled effects in other colours), 'Carrara' (i.e. parian) figures (1848), and green-glazed Majolica. Bone china was introduced in 1812 but was discontinued *c.*1829, to be revived from 1878. Wedgwoods, now at Barlaston, south of the main Potteries district, still make jasper and basalt wares in addition to bone china and creamware. In the 1920s a series of lustre-ware bowls, etc. was introduced decorated with 'Fairyland

114   A Wedgwood coffee can and saucer with two-coloured jasper and white relief design – the so-called three-colour jasper. Diameter of saucer 4¼in. c.1820.

115   A selection of late Victorian Wedgwood wares produced in a dark blue jasper body. The popular biscuit barrels and the cheese dishes are forms not produced before about 1880. Candlestick 9in high. c.1890–1900.

lustre' (elves and pixies in dreamlands, mixed up with gondolas and Chinese figures), Dragon, Fruit, and Butterfly lustres, the names indicating the dominant themes. Almost all Wedgwood products

190

made after 1770 are clearly marked. However, several other potters in England and abroad sometimes used marks that could be taken for Wedgwood. Do note that there should not be a middle 'e' and that only the surname was used not '& Co.' In addition the correct rendering 'Wedgwood' has been faked.

There are many specialist books on Wedgwood, ranging from Robin Reilly's two volume work *Wedgwood* (MacMillan, 1989) priced at £500 to inexpensive little handbooks. For the later wares the reader will find Maureen Batkin's *Wedgwood Ceramics 1846–1959* (Richard Dennis, 1982) very helpful. There is even a specialist book on the pre-war 'Fairyland' designs, Una des Fontaines's *Wedgwood Fairyland Lustre* (Sotheby Parke Bernet, 1975). There is a Wedgwood Society which holds lecture meetings and publishes newsletters, etc. (For details contact Mr J. K. des Fontaines, Flat 3, 75 Anson Road, London, N7 0AS). There is also an excellent and extensive Works Museum at the Wedgwood factory, Barlaston, Staffordshire.

WEMYSS WARE (1880–1930). A very decorative pottery made at the Fife Pottery (established 1817) near Kircaldy, by the Heron family assisted by a Czech named Carl Nekola. Vases, mugs, tea-sets, bowls, candlesticks, bedroom sets, etc. were made, typically painted underglaze with naturalistic fruit or flowers (especially a

116   Two characteristic Scottish 'Wemyss' earthenware pigs with typical bold painted decoration. Printed Heron 'Wemyss' mark. Larger pig 10in high. **(Laurence Fine Art of Crewkerne).**

large pink rose) or a cock-and-hen design in black. Characteristics include fine crazing and a blue-green rim. Most pieces were marked 'Wemyss'; the name of the London retailer 'T. Goode & Co.' can also occur or the name or initials of Robert Heron & Son. Wemyss ware (named after nearby Wemyss Castle, pronounced weemz) was only a small part of the pottery's output. The production of Wemyss was continued by Nekola's son Joe at Bovey Tracey, Devon (1930–57) by the Bovey Tracey Pottery Co.

In recent years the Wemyss wares have become very collectable and some examples (the rarer forms, animals, etc., and patterns) have commanded very high prices.

WEST PANS. West Pans is near Musselburgh, not far from Edinburgh. Here in the approximate period 1764–77 William Littler (formerly of Longton Hall in Staffordshire) operated a small pottery where at least some porcelain was produced. It is also very possible that some Longton Hall porcelain (of the 1750–60 period as Plate 117) was decorated at West Pans.

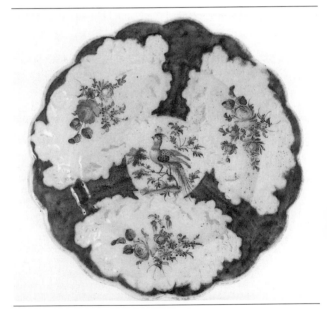

117   A late Longton Hall or a West Pans porcelain plate with uneven blue ground and hand-painted decoration. Diameter 6¼in. c.1765–70. **(Sotheby's).**

For further information see Bernard Watney's *English Blue & White Porcelain of the 18th Century* (Faber & Faber, revised edition 1973), Geoffrey Godden's *Staffordshire Porcelain* (Granada, 1983), and his *Encyclopaedia of British Porcelain Manufacturers* (Barrie & Jenkins, 1988), where references to papers on West Pans published in the *Transactions of the English Ceramic Circle* are also given.

WHIELDON WARE (*c.*1740–80). A convenient label for Staffordshire lead-glazed earthenwares distinguished from Astbury ware in three respects: greater reliance for decoration on a wider range of more brilliantly coloured glazes (yellow, blue, green, brown, etc.); the use of an improved cream-coloured body and greater sophistication. Brilliant mottled and tortoiseshell effects were produced by dissolving the metal oxides in the liquid lead glaze or by dabbing on the coloured glaze with sponges. The term is usually used in a generic manner, not as a firm attribution of the piece to Thomas Whieldon (1719–95).

Table-ware included tortoiseshell-like mottled plates (relatively common), teapots with crabstock handles and spouts in a paler shade of clay matching the relief decoration but contrasting with the pot itself, jugs, tureens, etc.

Figures of the earlier types were made, but also others inspired by Chinese or classical originals, portrait busts of celebrities or fictional characters, early examples of later favourites such as the Lost Sheep, Shepherd and Shepherdess, etc.

They were made by many Staffordshire potters (e.g. the Wood family) but are associated with a leading innovator in this field, Thomas Whieldon (1719–95), who worked at Little Fenton (1740–80) and took on Josiah Wedgwood as his partner (1754–9). The classification (like the other two mentioned) is arbitrary, inadequately defined and subject to erosion as research into this obscure period advances. For example, Whieldon also made agate and Jackfield ware, and saltglaze figures, not only the lead-glazed types normally associated with his name. The eighteenth-century Whieldon wares do not bear a maker's mark. The products are very varied and can be most attractive and costly!

Information on Thomas Whieldon is contained in Donald Towner's standard book *Creamware* (Faber & Faber, 1978) and in Arnold Mountford's *The Illustrated Guide to Staffordshire Saltglazed Stoneware* (Barrie & Jenkins, 1971).

WILLOW PATTERN. A term best reserved for only one type of mock-Chinese blue and white transfer-printed pattern found on English pottery and very rarely on porcelain – that for which the tale was invented of a girl who eloped with her mandarin father's secretary on the day she should have wedded a rich old merchant. The mandarin chased them across a bridge but they escaped by boat to the young man's island home; later they were arrested, threatened with death but, changed by the gods into turtledoves, flew away.

All this is nonsense invented to give a story to a stock printed design made in the basic style of Chinese export market dinner wares.

The design usually shows two fleeing figures on a bridge and usually a third in pursuit; a pagoda, boat, two doves, and top left the island home; prominent in the foreground are a willow and an 'apple' tree. Very many variations occur – for example, in the pull from a copper plate shown in Plate 118 the couple are advancing towards the pagoda, not fleeing from it. The true Willow pattern seems to have been introduced in about 1800. It is not found on earlier Worcester, Caughley, or Coalport porcelains. Indeed it is almost entirely restricted to earthenwares.

The Willow pattern has proved immensely popular from the early 1800s, being allegedly copied by two hundred or more potters by the 1860s. There are many variants, but the number of people on the bridge or of 'apples' on the tree are uncertain guides to date or factory. There are also many 'willow-type' patterns of similar style but they lack some essential features. The Willow pattern is still in production and can look very appropriate in a cottage-style setting. However, odd plates or even dishes are not valuable unless by a rare and collectable maker. The design (in complete dinner services) was made by so many potters over such a long period that most examples are quite common and have a decorative value only.

118   A pull from an engraved copper plate from which hundreds of Willow pattern dishes would have been printed in underglaze blue. Most potteries have produced versions of this popular inexpensive design from about 1810 onwards. Unmarked useful wares have no great value or rarity.

Nevertheless the pattern continues to give pleasure to tens of thousands and there is a Willow (Collectors) Society centred in Canada, but catering for all North American collectors. Contact address: 39 Medhurst Road, Toronto, Ontario, M4B 1B2.

WOOD FAMILY (worked *c*.1754–1846). A family of Staffordshire potters at Burslem, famous for earthenware figures and groups. Ralph Wood senior (1715–72) worked for John Astbury and Thomas Whieldon probably only as a modeller. Ralph Wood II (1748–95) probably produced the figures and groups formerly attributed to his father. His products may be distinguished by their excellent modelling and the use of beautifully lustrous coloured glazes painted on with the brush instead of being dabbed on almost at random in the Astbury-Whieldon tradition.

Some authorities think that Ralph I's figures were modelled by his brother Aaron, who had learnt his craft from Thomas Wedgwood and from Whieldon. Another modeller who worked (*c*.1770–90) for one or both of the Ralphs was the maverick Jean Voyez. To him are attributed rather sentimental figures, e.g. the Lost Sheep – a biblical theme much copied in later years. He also originated the 'Fair Hebe' jug (on which a youth offers a girl a nest of eggs).

Recent research carried out on the Wood sales ledger and crate book by Mrs Pat Halfpenny (Keeper of Ceramics, City Museum & Art Gallery, Stoke-on-Trent) has suggested that our old idea of Ralph Wood I and II's figure products are incorrect as has been our dating of these models which, seemingly, were produced in the approximate period 1789–1801. It should be borne in mind that the little-known John Wood (1778–1848) produced figures and like wares and that some examples previously attributed to one of the three Ralph Woods may well have been made by John. Mrs Halfpenny is preparing for publication a book on Staffordshire figure-makers, a work which promises to contain much new information on the Wood family and others.

WORCESTER (First Period, 1751–83). The porcelain factory founded by Dr Wall, William Davis, and others has continued at Worcester, under various names, down to today. Its most prized products belong to the first period, divisible into the Dr Wall period to 1774, when he retired, and the Davis period to 1783.

Early Worcester porcelain was the finest in England, denser, more thinly and evenly potted and generally better finished than Bow or Chelsea; unlike most soft-pastes, it did not crack under boiling hot tea. The soapstone body, made to a formula bought from Lund's Bristol factory (q.v.), shows green against the light (but it is not unique in this regard); the glaze, like Caughley's, never crazed. The absence of glaze round the foot-rim of bases, once used in identification, is not peculiar to Worcester or due to 'glaze shrinkage'; the glaze was cut or wiped away round the inner side of the foot to stop it flowing over when fired.

119   An early Worcester part tea service painted (or 'pencilled') in black, emulating a class of Chinese export market porcelain. Teapot 7in high. c.1755–60.

The principal wares were tea and coffee sets, moulded tureens, sauce-boats, bowls, and jugs, pierced openwork 'chestnut' baskets, small leaf-shaped pickle dishes, etc. Complete dinner services are uncommon, as the soapstone body was unsuitable for large plates: figures also are very rare. At first most pieces were painted in under-glaze blue, with Chinese-styled designs. Transfer-printing was introduced by Robert Hancock in about 1756, at first overglaze, mostly in black, with Hancock's designs (see Plate 120) of classical ruins, landscapes, celebrities (e.g. Frederick the Great), etc. Underglaze blue and white printed wares soon followed, mostly with landscape or floral designs, and were later produced in vast quantity; the tone varied from sapphire at first to violet-blue after Wall's retirement. Some designs were outlined in black print and coloured-in with enamels; others were 'pencilled' (painted with very fine brushwork).

From the 1760s there was much overglaze polychrome (often in the *Famille Verte* style) painting of oriental themes, Meissen flowers, or European landscapes. Worcester is famous for its ground colours, emulating Sèvres and Chelsea; by 1769 there was a wide range, including powder-blue (powdered pigment dusted on), mazarine, turquoise, claret, a rare yellow, 'apple' (actually, pea) green. These grounds have often been added to genuine Worcester by fakers. Blue grounds were frequently lightened by wiping out the colour in fish-scale patterns, to form the much prized scale-blue (Plate 121). Reserves (i.e. shaped patches of white) were also left in the ground colour and decorated, notably by the Chelsea artists who arrived *c.*1768, possibly working free-lance; they traditionally include O'Neale (Aesop's fables) and Donaldson (copies of Boucher subjects). Many such wares were also decorated at the Giles studio in

120 *A Worcester porcelain tankard transfer-printed on the glaze. The central design includes Robert Hancock monogram, as the engraver, the place-name Worcester, and the anchor device – a rebus on the surname Holdship. 3¼in high. c.1757–62.*

121 *A typical Worcester bowl decorated with 'scale blue' ground and panels of colour-ful exotic birds', butterflies, and insects. Note the blue 'square' or 'seal' mark. Later copies abound! Diameter 6¾in. c.1760–5.*

London. Kakiemon and, later, Imari designs were also borrowed and turned into rich new forms called 'Worcester japans', many with radiating whorled panels.

In the Davis period (1774–83), although the old lines were con-tinued, there was a switch to emphasis on lower-priced blue and white ware with cheaper materials, to meet competition from Caughley and Liverpool. The body became heavier and greyish, translucency straw-coloured, glaze blued, bubbled, and speckled. Much of this is marked with 'Chinese' disguised numerals.

In 1783 Davis died and Thomas Flight bought the Worcester factory, leaving its management to his sons. When one of them died, Martin Barr was taken on as partner (see under Flight & Barr).

There are several good books on early Worcester porcelain. The blue and white pieces are covered in B. Watney's *English Blue & White Porcelain of the 18th Century* (Faber & Faber, revised edition 1973) and in *Worcester Blue & White Porcelain 1751–1790* by L. Branyan, N. French, and J. Sandon (Barrie & Jenkins, revised edition 1989). Henry Sandon's *Worcester Porcelain 1751–1793* (Barrie & Jenkins, revised edition 1980) is a helpful general guide to the Worcester porcelains of the first period. The Dyson Perrins Museum, at the Worcester factory in Severn Street, contains a very fine collection of these attractive and highly collectable procelains.

Typical marks are included in the companion *Handbook of British Pottery & Porcelain Marks* and in Geoffrey Godden's *Encyclopaedia of British Porcelain Manufacturers* (Barrie & Jenkins, 1988) but very many examples are unmarked.

The later periods of Worcester porcelain are discussed here under Flight & Barr, Kerr & Binns, and Royal Worcester Porcelain Co.

There were also other firms producing fine quality porcelains within the City of Worcester, for which see above under Chamberlain's Worcester, Doe & Rogers, Grainger's Worcester, and James Hadley.

X CLASS. The name given to a class of unmarked English porcelain produced (probably in Staffordshire) within the approximate period 1785–1815.

In a general way much of the porcelains, which almost exclusively comprise tea-wares (Plates 122–3), are decorated with simple floral designs (Plate 124) in the so-called New Hall style. Indeed much 'X class' porcelain has in the past been attributed to this well-known company.

122   An early 'Factory X' globular teapot painted with a mock-oriental figures pattern that also occurs on New Hall porcelains. 6½in high. c.1790–5. *(Neal French collection).*

For further information on the subject of 'X class' porcelain wares, the reader is referred to David Holgate's book *New Hall and Its Imitators* (Faber & Faber, 1971), to *Staffordshire Porcelain*, edited by Geoffrey Godden (Granada Publishing, 1983), or to Godden's *Encyclopaedia of British Porcelain Manufacturers* (Barrie & Jenkins, 1988), pp. 805 and 450–1.

123   An oval, spiral-fluted 'Factory X' teapot decorated with underglaze blue bands and gilt. Pattern number 167 written in blue. 6¾in high. c.1805–10.

124   A 'Factory X' bone china teapot of a characteristic shape, painted in red with simple 'cottagey' floral design. Painted pattern number 351. 6¾in high. c.1810–15.

Y CLASS. Like the 'X class' and 'Z class', a group of unmarked porcelains usually following in general style the popular New Hall porcelains. The rather rare 'Y class' tea-wares seem to have been produced in the 1795–1810 period and many specimens have been attributed in error to New Hall.

For further information the reader is referred to David Holgate's *New Hall and Its Imitators* (Faber & Faber, 1971).

YATES. John Yates's compact and very well decorated porcelains of the 1820–35 period represent one of the newly rediscovered Staffordshire classes of quality, unmarked, china. The Shelton (Hanley) pottery was continued by the Yates & May partnership in the 1835–43 period.

John Yates and the later partnership also made earthenwares but, as yet, only the porcelains have been identified (Plate 125). There were also early firms of Yates & Shelleys (c.1800–2) and Yates & Shelley (c.1803–8). The Yates porcelains are of good quality and several of the tea-ware and dessert service shapes seem unique. For further information see *Staffordshire Porcelain* (Granada, 1983), chapter 20 or Godden's *Encyclopaedia of British Porcelain Manufacturers* (Barrie & Jenkins, 1988).

125   A very good quality Yates porcelain dish of characteristic shape from a dessert service. Note the moulded-edge design which seems unique to this firm. Painted number 1191. 9¾ × 8½in. c.1820–30.

Z CLASS. The name given to an unmarked class of English (probably Staffordshire) porcelain produced in the approximate period 1800 (or earlier) to 1820.

The porcelains, which appear to be predominantly tea and coffee wares, are usually well potted and neatly decorated (Plate 126). Some well-engraved bat-printed designs occur and the gilding is trim. The 'Z class' porcelains are most attractive and interesting. The maker was obviously a competent potter, catering for a large, above average market and a potter happy to go his own way and not always slavishly copy others' shapes or designs. On the post-1805 wares silver (platinum) lustre was sometimes used to good effect. Several researchers have been studying this class for years, endeavouring to identify the maker, but truly the 'Z class' porcelains hardly need a name, they are beautiful and collectable for their visual appeal alone.

For further information see David Holgate's *New Hall and Its Imitators* (Faber & Faber, 1971), *Staffordshire Porcelain,* edited by Geoffrey Godden (Granada, 1983), and Godden's *Encyclopaedia of British Porcelain Manufacturers* (Barrie & Jenkins, 1988).

126   A rare 'Factory Z' bone china coffee-pot and a matching teapot painted in red-brown with gilt borders. Coffee pot 9¼in high. c.1805–10.

APPENDIX A
Useful Dates from 1720

Many of these dates are approximate as rarely do we now have documentary proof of the date of opening or closure of a factory, or of the introduction of a new body or technique. Nevertheless, even approximate dates can be helpful – for example, a lustre jug cannot be eighteenth-century as it must have been made after 1804 or 1805. In most instances further information on the wares mentioned below is given in the main section of this Handbook.

1720+	Cream-coloured earthenware introduced
1720+	White saltglaze and Astbury figures first appeared
1727	Accession of King George II
1740–80	Astbury-Whieldon type earthenwares
1740–80	Jackfield-type ware
1745+	Rococo reaches England
1745–70	Chelsea porcelains
1746–76	Bow porcelains
1746+	So-called Pomona wares
1749–51	Lund's Bristol – soapstone porcelain
1749–60	Longton Hall porcelains
1750–1848	Derby porcelains – 1st period
1751–4	Girl-in-a-swing factory
1751–74	Worcester, Dr Wall or 1st period
1752–8	Chelsea Red Anchor period
1752	Gregorian calendar introduced to Britain
1753–64	Vauxhall porcelains
1754–99	Liverpool porcelains
1756	Transfer-printing (overglaze) introduced on Bow and Worcester porcelains
1756	Commencement of Seven Years War
1757–99	Lowestoft porcelains
1759–69	Chelsea Gold Anchor period
1759–61	Reid & Baddeley's Shelton porcelains
1759+	Wedgwood's superb wares
1759	Underglaze blue printing introduced
1760	Accession of King George III
1763	Wedgwood introduces engine-turning for ceramics
1764–77	West Pans Scottish porcelains
1765+	Refined creamware introduced by Wedgwood as Queen's ware
1768+	Wedgwood's Black basalt introduced and much copied
1768–70	Plymouth hard-paste porcelains
1770–84	Chelsea-Derby period
1770–81	Bristol hard-paste porcelains
1770+	Josiah Spode I's wares
1774–83	Davis period of Worcester porcelain

1775	Start of American War of Independence
1775–99	Caughley porcelains
1775+	Josiah Wedgwood introduced coloured Jasper
1775–1800	Neo-Classical styles in favour
1777	Trent & Mersey Canal links Staffordshire with port of Liverpool
1779	Pearlware introduced by Wedgwood
1781–1815	New Hall (hard-paste) porcelains
1783–92	Flight period of Worcester porcelain
1788–1852	Chamberlain-Worcester porcelains
1791	English East India Company ceases bulk imports of Chinese porcelain
1792–1804	Flight & Barr period of Worcester porcelain
1793–1887	Davenport wares
1793+	Minton wares
1796+	Pinxton porcelains
1796+	Coalport porcelains
1796+	Herculaneum (Liverpool) wares
1800+	Spode introduces refined 'bone china'
1804+	Miles Mason's Staffordshire wares
1805	Lustre decoration introduced
1806–89	Grainger-Worcester porcelains
1808+	Ridgway porcelains
1810	Warburton's Patent for printing in gold
1811–48	Bloor period of Derby porcelain
1812+	'London'-shape teawares in fashion
1812–29	Wedgwood's bone china, 1st period
1813	Introduction of Mason's Patent Ironstone china
1814+	Swansea porcelains
1817–20	Nantgarw porcelains
1820	Felspar glaze and body introduced
1820	Death of King George III
1821	Coronation of King George IV
1822	H. Daniel separated from Spode
1826–42	Rockingham Works porcelain period
1830	Accession of King William IV on death of King George IV
1830	Opening of Liverpool–Manchester railway
1833	English East India Company's trading monopoly to and from China ended.
1833–47	Copeland & Garrett period, succeeding Spode
1837	Queen Victoria succeeded King William IV
1840	Marriage of Queen Victoria and Prince Albert
1842	Introduction of the parian body
1842	Introduction of Registered Design system
1847	W. T. Copeland succeeded Copeland & Garrett
1847+	Multicolour printed pot-lids and related wares
1848	Closure of main, old, Derby factory
1848	French Art Director, L. Arnoux, taken on at Minton
1851	The Great Exhibition (The Crystal Palace) in Hyde Park

1852–62	Kerr & Binns succeeded Chamberlain at Worcester
1858+	Goss wares
1861	Death of Prince Albert
1862	Worcester Royal Porcelain Company established (Royal Worcester), continues to present day
1862	Brown-Westhead, Moore & Co. succeeded J. Ridgway
1863	Acid gilding introduced
1870+	Pâte-sur-Pâte technique introduced into England
1871	W. Brownfield & Son introduced their porcelains
1873–1915	Martinware made by the Martin brothers
1876	New Derby Crown Porcelain Company established. Royal Crown Derby from 1890
1878	Wedgwood reintroduces bone china
1882	Doulton's took over Staffordshire factory
1884	Registered number system introduced
1893–1910	Influence of Continental Art Nouveau style
1901	Death of Queen Victoria, accession of King Edward VII
1910	Death of King Edward VII, accession of King George V
1910	Federation of the Pottery towns – Burslem, Fenton, Hanley, Longton, Stoke, and Tunstall – to form County Borough of Stoke-on-Trent
1914–18	The Great War
1920s	The Jazz Age
1929	The Wall Street crash
1930s	Art Deco designs in favour, Clarice Cliff, etc.
1936	Death of King George V, accession of King Edward VIII
1936	Abdication of King Edward VIII
1936	Accession of King George VI
1939–45	World War II
1951	Festival of Britain
1952	Death of King George VI, accession of Queen Elizabeth II
1971	Introduction of decimal currency in Great Britain
1973	United Kingdom joins the European Community

APPENDIX B
NOTABLE MUSEUM COLLECTIONS

Alton, Hampshire. Curtis Museum
Bedford. Cecil Higgins Art Gallery
Birkenhead. Williamson Art Gallery and Museum
Birmingham. City Museum and Art Gallery
Bootle, Lancs. Museum and Art Gallery
Brighton. Art Gallery and Museum
Bristol. City Art Gallery
Cambridge. Fitzwilliam Museum
Cardiff. National Museum of Wales
Castle Howard, near Malton, Yorks.

Cheltenham. Art Gallery and Museum
Coalport, Shropshire. Ironbridge Gorge Museum
Derby. Museum and Art Gallery, Wardwick
Derby. Royal Crown Derby Company Works Museum
Edinburgh. Lady Stair's House
Harrogate. Royal Pump Room Museum
Hastings. Public Museum and Art Gallery
Hove. Museum and Art Gallery
Leeds. City Art Gallery
Lincoln. Usher Art Gallery
Llandudno. Rapallo House Museum
London. British Museum
   Fenton House, Hampstead
   Victoria and Albert Museum
Luton Hoo, Beds. Wernher Collection
Manchester. Fletcher Moss Museum;
   Heaton Hall;
   Wythenshawe Hall
Melton Mowbray. Stapleford Park
Norwich. Castle Museum
Oxford. Ashmolean Museum
Paisley. Museum and Art Gallery
Plymouth. City Museum and Art Gallery
Port Sunlight, Cheshire. Lady Lever Art Gallery
Preston. Harris Museum and Art Gallery
Rotherham, Yorks. Museum and Art Gallery
Shrewsbury. Clive House Museum
Stoke-on-Trent. City Museum and Art Gallery, Hanley
   Minton Museum
   Spode Copeland Museum
   Wedgwood Museum, Barlaston
Sunderland. Museum and Art Gallery
Swansea. Glynn Vivian Art Gallery
Warrington. Municipal Museum
Wolverhampton. Municipal Art Gallery and Museum
   Bantock House
Worcester. City Museum
   Dyson Perrins Museum, Royal Worcester Porcelain Co.

Some Museums have only displays of specialized types, especially those within factories, e.g. Minton, Spode, Wedgwood, or Worcester. Times or days of opening should be checked before making a special journey. Few Museums are open on Sundays, while some galleries may be closed for rearranging, etc.

  The reader should bear in mind that many Stately Houses or National Trust properties open to the public contain good collections of ceramics. It would also be as well to remember that in some collections the captions and descriptions may not necessarily reflect the latest research or knowledge.

Useful Books, Magazines, and Societies

Useful Books

This list includes those standard British reference books which the author finds most useful and turns to frequently, arranged in the sequence Mark Books, General Works, then individual factories or ceramic types. Not all are in print and readily available in bookshops but the more elderly works can usually be obtained from specialist suppliers (see Reference Books in main text) or borrowed from Public Libraries. We are unable to denote which works are in print as this can vary from year to year or even from month to month. However, most larger bookshops can inform you which titles are available provided you are able to quote accurately the title, the author's name and initials, and the publisher of the required book. With very few exceptions, books published before 1970 are not still in print.

For individual factories or ceramic types, several very collectable wares have attracted a multitude of books and Price Guides – Doulton and Goss are examples of this. The reader need only consult the latest example to find a full list of books on that one subject.

Good, up-to-date general reference books such as *Staffordshire Porcelain* (1983), *Eighteenth-century English Porcelain* (1985) or the *Encyclopaedia of British Porcelain Manufacturers* (1988) will be found to contain very useful chapters or entries on the main manufacturers and their marks together with details of relevant recommended reference books, magazines, articles, etc. Much very helpful information and up-dating is published in learned Journals or in collectors' magazines, see p. 213 below.

The following books are arranged in order of first publication date: the later works should contain the most up-to-date information. Do remember that we have a really excellent Library Service in the British Isles. Most of the books below should be available from at least the larger libraries but, if not, they can be obtained for you. If you feel so inclined ask the Chief Librarian to stock a book you think is particularly helpful. You pay for the service by way of your taxes!

Mark Books

Handbook of Pottery & Porcelain Marks. J. P. Cushion and W. B. Honey (Faber & Faber, 1956 and revised editions).

Pocket Book of British Ceramic Marks. J. P. Cushion (Faber & Faber, 1959 and revised editions).

Encyclopaedia of British Pottery & Porcelain Marks. G. A. Godden (Barrie & Jenkins, 1964).

Handbook of British Pottery & Porcelain Marks. G. A. Godden (Barrie & Jenkins, 1968 and later revisions).

Encyclopaedia of British Porcelain Manufacturers. G. A. Godden (Barrie & Jenkins, 1988).

GENERAL WORKS

The Ceramic Art of Great Britain. L. Jewitt (Virtue & Co., 1878, revised edition 1883).

Staffordshire Pots and Potters. G. W. and F. A. Rhead (Hutchinson, 1906).

Old English Porcelain. W. B. Honey (Faber & Faber, 1928 and revised editions).

English Pottery & Porcelain. W. B. Honey (Faber & Faber, 1933 and revised editions).

Staffordshire Chimney Ornaments. R. G. Haggar (Phoenix, 1955).

The Concise Encyclopaedia of English Pottery & Porcelain. R. G. Haggar and W. Mankowitz (Deutsch, 1957).

Victorian Porcelain. G. A. Godden (H. Jenkins, 1961).

Victorian Pottery. H. Wakefield (H. Jenkins, 1962).

English Blue & White Porcelain of the 18th Century. B. Watney (Faber & Faber, 1963, revised edition 1973).

English Porcelain. Edited by R. J. Charleston (Benn, 1965).

Antique China & Glass under £5. G. A. Godden (A. Barker, 1966).

An Illustrated Encyclopaedia of British Pottery & Porcelain. G. A. Godden (Barrie & Jenkins, 1966).

A Collector's History of English Pottery. G. Lewis (Studio Vista, 1969, revised edition 1986).

Staffordshire Salt-glazed Stoneware. A. Mountford (Barrie & Jenkins, 1971).

Commemorative Pottery 1780–1900. J. and J. May (Heinemann, 1972).

An Illustrated Dictionary of Ceramics. G. Savage and H. Newman (Thames & Hudson, 1974).

British Porcelain. An Illustrated Guide. G. A. Godden (Barrie & Jenkins, 1974).

British Pottery. An Illustrated Guide. G. A. Godden (Barrie & Jenkins, 1974).

Godden's Guide to English Porcelain. G. A. Godden (Granada, 1978).

Collecting Victorian Tiles. T. A. Lockett (Antique Collectors' Club, 1979).

18th Century English Porcelain Figures 1745–1795. P. Bradshaw (Antique Collectors' Club, 1981).

English Transfer-Printed Pottery and Porcelains. C. Williams-Wood (Faber & Faber, 1981).

English Brown Stoneware 1670–1900. A. Oswald, R. Hildyard and R. Hughes (Faber & Faber, 1982).

The History of Porcelain. Edited by P. Atterbury (Orbis, 1982).

English Delftware in the Bristol Collection. F. Britton (Sotheby, 1982).

An Anthology of British Cups. M. Berthoud (Micawber, 1982).

Blue & White Transfer Printed Pottery. R. Copeland (Shire, 1982).

Dictionary of Blue & White Printed Pottery 1780–1880. A. Coysh and R. Henrywood (Antique Collectors' Club, 1982, vol. II, 1989).

Staffordshire Porcelain. Edited by G. A. Godden (Granada, 1983).

Studio Ceramics. P. Lane (Collins, 1983).

An Anthology of British Teapots. P. Miller and M. Berthoud (Micawber, 1985).

English China. G. A. Godden (Barrie & Jenkins, 1985).

Eighteenth-century English Porcelain (A Selection from the Godden Reference Collection). G. A. Godden (Granada, 1985).

Encyclopaedia of Pottery & Porcelain. The 19th & 20th Centuries. E. Cameron (Faber & Faber, 1986).

London Delftware. F. Britton (J. Horne, 1987).
Art Deco Tableware. J. Spours (Ward Lock, 1988).
Decorative Tiles Throughout the Ages. H. Van Lemmen (Bracken Books, 1988).
Encyclopaedia of British Porcelain Manufacturers. G. A. Godden (Barrie & Jenkins, 1988).
British Studio Ceramics in the 20th Century. P. Rice and C. Gowing (Barrie & Jenkins, 1989).

BLUE-PRINTED EARTHENWARES

Staffordshire Blue. W. L. Little (Batsford, 1969).
Blue & White Ware. A. Coysh (David & Charles, 1970).
Spode's Willow Pattern. R. Copeland (Studio Vista, 1980).
Dictionary of Blue & White Printed Pottery 1780–1880. A. Coysh and R. Henry-wood (Antique Collectors' Club, 1982, vol. II, 1989).
Spode Printed Ware. D. Drakard and P. Holloway (Longman, 1983).

BOW

Bow Porcelain. E. Adams and R. Redstone (Faber & Faber, 1981).
Bow Porcelain – the collection formed by Geoffrey Freeman. A. Gabszewicz and G. Freeman (Lund Humphries, 1982).
See also Dr Watney's general book on blue and white (1963 and 1973) and Peter Bradshaw's book on porcelain figures (1981)

BRISTOL (HARD-PASTE)

Cookworthy's Plymouth & Bristol Porcelain. F. Severne MacKenna (F. Lewis, 1946).
Champion's Bristol Porcelain. F. Severne MacKenna (F. Lewis, 1947).

CAUGHLEY

Caughley & Worcester Porcelains 1775–1800. G. A. Godden (Antique Collectors' Club, 1981).
Chamberlain-Worcester Porcelain, 1788–1852. G. A. Godden (Barrie & Jenkins, 1982).

CHAMBERLAIN-WORCESTER

Chamberlain-Worcester Porcelain, 1788–1852. G. A. Godden (Barrie & Jenkins, 1982).

CHELSEA

Chelsea Porcelain at Williamsburg. J. C. Austin (Colonial Williamsburg Foundation, USA, 1977).
18th Century English Porcelain Figures 1745–1795. P. Bradshaw (Antique Collectors' Club, 1981).
Chelsea Porcelain. E. Adams (Barrie & Jenkins, 1987).

APPENDIX C

COALPORT

Coalport & Coalbrookdale Porcelains. G. A. Godden (Antique Collectors' Club, 1981).

CREAMWARE

Creamware. D. Towner (Faber & Faber, 1978).

Creamware & Pearlware. 1986 Stoke Exhibition Catalogue. T. A. Lockett and P. A. Halfpenny (Stoke-on-Trent City Museum & Art Gallery, 1986).

DANIEL

H. & R. Daniel 1822–1846. M. Berthoud (Micawber, 1980).

The Daniel Tableware Patterns (Supplement to above book). M. Berthoud (Micawber, 1982).

DAVENPORT

Davenport China, Earthenware and Glass. T. A. Lockett and G. A. Godden (Barrie & Jenkins, 1989).

DERBY

Ceramics of Derbyshire 1750–1975. Edited by G. Bradley (Privately published, 1978).

Derby Porcelain. J. Twitchett (Barrie & Jenkins, 1980).

Derby Porcelain. The Golden Years 1750–1770. D. G. Rice (David & Charles, 1983).

Painters and the Derby China Works. J. Murdoch and J. Twitchett (Trefoil Publications, 1987).

Royal Crown Derby. J. Twitchett and B. Bailey (Antique Collectors' Club, 1988).

Derby Porcelain Figures 1750–1848. P. Bradshaw (Faber & Faber, 1990).

DOULTON

Royal Doulton 1815–1965. D. Eyles (Hutchinson, 1965).

The Doulton Lambeth Wares. D. Eyles (Hutchinson, n.d. 1975?).

Doulton Burslem Wares. D. Eyles (Barrie & Jenkins, 1980).

The Lyle Price Guide to Doulton. M. Yewman (Lyle Publications, 1986).

Royal Doulton Figures. D. Eyles, R. Dennis and L. Irvine (Royal Doulton Ltd and R. Dennis, 1987).

FIGURES AND GROUPS

Staffordshire Chimney Ornaments. R. G. Haggar (Phoenix House, 1955).

English Porcelain Figures of the Eighteenth Century. A. Lane, (Faber & Faber, 1961).

The Illustrated Guide to Staffordshire Salt-glazed Stoneware. A. R. Mountford (Barrie & Jenkins, 1971).

Staffordshire Pottery. The Tribal Art of England. A. Oliver (Heinemann, 1981).

18th Century English Porcelain Figures 1745–1795. Peter Bradshaw (Antique Collectors' Club, 1981).

Staffordshire Portrait Figures of the Victorian Era. P. D. Gordon Pugh (Antique Collectors' Club, revised edition 1987).

GOSS WARES

Crested China. The History of Heraldic Souvenir Ware. S. Andrews (Springwood Books, 1980).
The Price Guide to Goss China. N. Pine (Milestone, 1984 and later editions).
Goss and other Crested China. N. Pine (Shire, 1984).
William Henry Goss. L. and N. Pine (Milestone, 1987).

LEEDS (TYPE) WARES

The Leeds Pottery. D. Towner (Cory, Adams & Mackay, 1963).
Yorkshire Pots & Potteries. H. Lawrence (David & Charles, 1974).
Creamware. D. Towner (Faber & Faber, 1978).

LIVERPOOL (HERCULANEUM)

The Illustrated Guide to Liverpool Herculaneum Pottery. A. Smith (Barrie & Jenkins, 1970).
The Liverpool Porcelains. M. Hillis (Northern Ceramic Society Occasional Paper, 1985).
The reader is also referred to such general works as B. Watney's *English Blue & White Porcelain of the 18th Century* (Faber & Faber, 1973) and G. Godden's *Encyclopaedia of British Porcelain Manufacturers* (Barrie & Jenkins, 1988).

LOWESTOFT

Lowestoft Porcelain in Norwich Castle Museum. Vol. I: *Blue & White.* S. Smith (Norfolk Museum Service, 1975).
Early Lowestoft. C. Spencer (Ainsworth & Nelson, 1981).
Lowestoft Porcelain in Norwich Castle Museum. Vol. II: *Polychrome Wares.* S. Smith (Norfolk Museum Service, 1985).
Lowestoft Porcelains. G. A. Godden (Antique Collectors' Club, 1985).

MAJOLICA

Majolica. Victoria Bergesen (Barrie & Jenkins, 1989).

MASON WARES

The Masons of Lane Delph. R. G. Haggar (Lund Humphries, 1952).
Mason Porcelain & Ironstone 1796–1853. E. Adams and R. G. Haggar (Faber & Faber, 1977).
Godden's Guide to Mason's China and the Ironstone Wares. G. A. Godden (Antique Collectors' Club, revised edition 1980).

MINTON

Minton 1798–1910. Victoria & Albert Museum Exhibition Catalogue, by E. Aslin and P. Atterbury (Victoria & Albert Museum, 1976).
Minton Pottery & Porcelain of the First Period 1793–1850. G. A. Godden (Barrie & Jenkins, revised edition 1978).
The Dictionary of Minton. P. Atterbury (Antique Collectors' Club, 1990).
The reader is also referred to Chapter 9 of *Staffordshire Porcelain.*

Nantgarw

The Pottery & Porcelain of Swansea & Nantgarw. E. Morton Nance (Batsford, 1942).
Nantgarw Porcelain. W. D. John (R. H. John, 1948).

Neale Wares

Neale Pottery & Porcelain. D. Edwards (Barrie & Jenkins, 1987).
The reader is also referred to Chapter 4 of *Staffordshire Porcelain*.

New Hall

New Hall and Its Imitators. D. Holgate (Faber & Faber, 1971).
New Hall. D. Holgate (Faber & Faber, 1987).
A Guide to New Hall Porcelain Patterns. A. de Saye Hutton (Barrie & Jenkins, 1990).

Parian

The Illustrated Guide to Victorian Parian China. C. and D. Shinn (Barrie & Jenkins, 1971).
English China (Chapter 13). G. A. Godden (Barrie & Jenkins, 1985).
Parian Ware. D. Barker (Shire, 1985).
The Parian Phenomenon. P. Atterbury ed. (Richard Dennis, 1989).

Pot-lids and other colour printed wares

The Price Guide to Pot Lids. A. Ball (Antique Collectors' Club, revised edition 1980).

Pratt-type Wares

Pratt Ware. J. and G. Lewis (Antique Collectors' Club, 1984).

Ridgway

Ridgway Porcelain. G. A. Godden (Antique Collectors' Club, 1985).
The reader is also referred to Chapter 12 of *Staffordshire Porcelain*.

Rockingham

Rockingham Ornamental Porcelain. D. G. Rice (Adam Publishing, 1965).
The Illustrated Guide to Rockingham Pottery & Porcelain. D. G. Rice (Barrie & Jenkins, 1971).
The Rockingham Pottery. A. E. Eaglestone and T. A. Lockett, (David & Charles, revised edition 1973).
Rockingham Pottery & Porcelain 1745–1842. A. and A. Cox (Faber & Faber, 1983).

Spode

Spode. L. Whiter (Barrie & Jenkins, revised edition 1989).
The reader is also referred to Chapter 9 of *Staffordshire Porcelain*.

Swansea

The Pottery & Porcelain of Swansea & Nantgarw. E. Morton Nance (Batsford, 1942).

Swansea Porcelain, Shapes & Decoration. A. E. Jones and Sir L. Joseph (D. Brown & Sons, 1988).

Tin-glazed Wares

English Delftware. F. H. Garner (Faber & Faber, 1948, enlarged by M. Archer, 1972).

English Delftware Pottery. A. Ray (Faber & Faber, 1968).

English Delftware in the Bristol Collection. F. Britton (Sotheby, 1982).

Dated English Delftware. L. Lipski and M. Archer (Sotheby, 1984).

London Delftware. F. Britton (Jonathan Horne, 1987).

Turner Wares

The Turners of Lane End. B. Hillier (Cory, Adams & Mackay, 1965).

The reader is also referred to Chapter 6 of *Staffordshire Porcelain.*

Wedgwood

Wedgwood Ware. W. B. Honey (Faber & Faber, 1948).

Wedgwood Jasper. R. Reilly (Letts, 1972).

Wedgwood Portrait Medallions. R. Reilly (Barrie & Jenkins, 1973).

The Story of Wedgwood. A. Kelly (Faber & Faber, 1975).

The Dictionary of Wedgwood. R. Reilly and G. Savage (Antique Collectors' Club, 1980).

Wedgwood Ceramics 1846–1959. M. Batkin (R. Dennis, 1982).

Wedgwood. R. Reilly (Macmillan, 1989).

The reader is also referred to good general reference books such as *British Pottery. An Illustrated Guide* (Barrie & Jenkins, 1974) which show a good selection of typical Wedgwood wares.

Worcester

English Blue & White Porcelains of the 18th Century. B. Watney (Faber & Faber, revised edition 1973).

Royal Worcester Porcelain from 1862 to the Present Day. H. Sandon (Barrie & Jenkins, 1973).

Worcester Porcelain 1751–1793. H. Sandon (Barrie & Jenkins, third edition 1980).

Chamberlain-Worcester Porcelain 1788–1852. G. A. Godden (Barrie & Jenkins, 1982).

Worcester Porcelain. The Klepser Collection. S. Spero (The Minneapolis Institute of Arts, 1984).

The Sandon Guide to Royal Worcester Figures 1900–1970. H. and J. Sandon (Alderman Press, 1987).

Worcester Blue & White Porcelain 1751–1790. L. Branyan, N. French, and J. Sandon (Barrie & Jenkins, revised edition 1989).

MAGAZINES

In addition to the reference books just listed much new information is contained in the several magazines which cater for the collector. Further information, sometimes on wares or potters which do not warrant an expensive book, are printed in the Transactions or Journals of such bodies as the English Ceramic Circle or the Northern Ceramic Society. Several such articles, papers, or contributions are quoted in the main section of this book. The British collectors' magazines relating in some degree to ceramics are:

Antique Collecting. Antique Collectors' Club, 5 Church Street, Woodbridge, Suffolk.

Antique Collector. National Magazine House, 72 Broadwick Street, London W1V 2BP.

Apollo. Apollo Magazines Ltd, 22 Davies Street, London W1Y 1LH.

Collectors Guide. IPC Magazines Ltd, King's Reach Tower, Stamford Street, London SE1 9LS.

Copies of these monthly magazines are normally stocked by the main newsagents or are available in the larger Reference Libraries, although the publishers will obviously prefer you to take out an annual subscription.

SOCIETIES

The two leading general English Ceramic Societies, which publish from time to time reports of meetings, learned papers, or general contributions in the form of Transactions, Journals, or newsletters are:

The English Ceramic Circle. Hon. Editor, John Howell, Esq., Marstons, Harleston, Norfolk, 1P20 0NJ.

The Northern Ceramic Society. Hon. Treasurer, Anthony Thomas, Esq., Bramdean, Jacksons Lane, Hazel Grove, Cheshire, SK7 5JW.

Other more specialized Clubs and Societies include:

The Derby Porcelain International Society. Hon. Secretary, Malcolm Savage, 31 Beaumont Street, Oxford, OX1 2NZ.

The Friends of Blue (Blue-decorated earthenwares). Hon. Secretary, Ron Govier, Esq., 10 Sea View Road, Herne Bay, Kent, CT6 6JQ.

The Royal Doulton International Collectors Club. 5, Egmont House, 116 Shaftesbury Avenue, London, W1V 7DJ.

The Spode Society. Hon. Editor, Bill Coles, Arley House, Bishopstone, Salisbury, Wiltshire, SP5 4BW.

The Wedgwood Society. J. K. des Fontaines, Esq., Flat 3, 75 Anson Road, London, N7 0AS.

See also Seminars in the main text. Since Society officers are liable to change, in the event of any difficulty the publisher, Barrie & Jenkins Ltd, will be pleased to respond to readers' inquiries.

APPENDIX D
GENERAL GUIDES TO DATING

The main text includes references to various marks as used by the larger manufacturers but it must be remembered that the present work is not a reference book of ceramic marks. Indeed the companion book *The Handbook of British Pottery & Porcelain Marks* is devoted to this subject. The much larger *Encyclopaedia of British Pottery & Porcelain Marks* includes many more marks and includes details of many firms not included in the condensed *Handbook*. A third book the *Encyclopaedia of British Porcelain Manufacturers* contains a wealth of information on some 2000 British porcelain manufacturers and includes details of typical pattern number systems. These three books by Geoffrey Godden are published by Barrie & Jenkins and should be readily available.

It is, however, relevant here to give some general information on methods of approximately dating an example of British pottery or porcelain, for many owners are anxious to discover how old a piece may be. But do remember that age in itself is not necessarily a virtue. A fine quality and attractive recent product may well be superior and more desirable than a poor 'antique' article which may be damaged or a faulty 'second' or even a 'third'. These terms denote that the piece was originally sold at a reduced price because it was badly decorated, or was faulty. Some manufacturers even seem to have especially catered for the large market for cheap defective examples!

The least reliable way to discover the age of a piece is to relate this to the various owners. So many folk state, for example, that the piece must be over a hundred years old because 'It belonged to my grandmother and she was eighty-eight, my mother is sixty and I am well over twenty-one so it must be very old'! In these cases the, seemingly, sensible owners add all the ages together forgetting the overlap of generations and further assume that Granny bought the piece at birth! In fact dear Granny could have purchased it new at sixty or seventy, a relatively few years previously. If we have three generations sitting around a television set and if the eldest purchased the set, these folk could prove (to themselves) that that television set was 'antique'!

The following Godden rules will prove more reliable and are based on fact. We must, however, assume that the piece under discussion is marked. If it is not – and this is a regular occurrence – do not assume that it must be old because it is unmarked. I am sure that you can easily find modern, current productions on sale without a maker's mark.

One basic rule of dating is to consider the latest feature, not the earliest. Many marks, for example, incorporate the claimed date of establishment of the company, such as 1750 for Coalport, or 1751 for Royal Worcester. These dates do not directly relate to the present firms and certainly not to the wares on which they may appear.

Pattern numbers will not occur on British ceramics before about 1790. Fractional numbers post-date 1820. Marks incorporating the Royal Arms will post-date 1795 and most are post-1830. Several manufacturers used representations of the Royal Arms in their marks. These Arms were changed at various times, the main point being that the inescutcheon (the central shield within a shield) was discontinued in June 1837. Some potters were, however, slow to amend their existing marks, so that the pre-June 1837 Royal Arms can occur on some wares sold in the 1840s. However, Victorian versions of the Royal Arms with the simple quartered shield must have been introduced in or after June 1837.

Many marks incorporate or comprise the name of a pattern – 'Willow', 'India Tree', for example. Such marks will not pre-date 1810 and most are very much later. Some pattern names were generally extremely popular so that several manufacturers will have used that pattern name. Few makers can be identified by reference only to the pattern name used.

The inclusion of the diamond-shape registration device in a mark, or alone, indicates that the particular shape or pattern was introduced after 1842 (see Registration Marks and Numbers).

Marks including trade names with the addition 'Limited' or its abbreviations such as 'Ltd' or 'Ld' postdate 1861.

Marks incorporating the term 'Trade Mark' are subsequent to the 1862 Trade Mark Act. Descriptions such as 'Registered Trade Mark' or 'Registered Trade Name' are of a twentieth-century date.

Trade marks or names incorporating the word 'Royal' are subsequent to 1850 and most are modern.

Inclusion of the word 'England' in a mark or otherwise appearing on a specimen will indicate a date after about 1880 and usually after the 1891 American Tariff Act. However, such 'country of origin' marks were only needed on articles intended to be exported, so even by 1900 some pieces not made for export did not include the country of origin; typical examples are the Goss local souvenirs, or the products of smaller art-type potteries.

The full statement 'Made in England' indicates a present-century dating, normally post-1920. But again the reader is reminded, as with the single word 'England', that these country of origin marks were required only on goods imported into foreign countries, so that this wording may not appear on home market objects. The wording 'Made in England' therefore indicates a post-1920 period, a piece without it was not necessarily made at an earlier period.

Marks including a registered number, usually prefixed 'R^{D}N^O', will post-date 1883, this system having superseded the old diamond-shape device in January 1884.

Printed marks which include the description 'Bone China', 'English Bone China', or similar wording are twentieth-century.

Many recent post-1955 marks incorporate a small ®, this device denoting that the trade name or the mark was registered. Similarly the word 'Copyright' indicates a present-century date, normally

1950 or later.

Name-marks including the new abbreviation 'plc' or 'PLC' (Public Limited Company) were introduced in recent times, after 1975.

Other later printed marks should be self-explanatory. Marks that refer to detergents or to dish-washers are obviously not antique, and mostly occur on objects or patterns introduced in or after the 1950s.

Printed marks incorporating the claim 'Hand Painted' are of a twentieth-century date and in most cases are post-1950. It should be noted that usually such objects have a mass-produced printed out-line and are merely coloured-in by hand.

Marks which note that the object is part of a 'Limited Edition' are likewise not antique and can be quite modern.

Some specimens that appear at first sight to be unmarked may bear impressed marks into which glaze has run. On porcelains, such marks can normally be seen and read if the piece is held with its face to a strong light. Some impressed marks will be found to be potters' (plate- or dish-makers') personal tally-marks or initials. Impressed numbers – especially on plates, dishes, or jugs – often indicate the size of the piece.

Other impressed marks can indicate the date of potting, either by numbers or by secret devices. The numbers can take the form 1.01 or $\frac{1}{01}$ for January 1901, or in some cases the month was indicated by a letter. Other factories used various devices to denote a year and the keys to these date codes are given in the large Godden *Encyclopaedia of British Pottery and Porcelain Marks* and in the *Encyclopaedia of British Porcelain Manufacturers,* both published by Barrie & Jenkins.

In general the many marks which feature only a trade name, not a family name, present great difficulties. The leading firms certainly registered their trade names, but many other names were not regis-tered and in numerous cases new names were introduced for special (perhaps overseas) customers, or slightly faulty or inexpensive lines were sold under a trade name completely different from that normally used by the firm for its more costly products. The popular inexpensive local souvenir wares of the 1900–30 period, for example, bear a host of different trade-names, although only a relatively small number of firms produced the models.

Many printed or painted marks relate not to the manufacturer but to the retailer. Such retailers' marks are unhelpful in attributing the manufacturer of the piece but local research may enable the approxi-mate period to be gauged. Printed marks on porcelains and most non-local earthenware bodies incorporating a town name outside the Staffordshire Potteries, Worcester or Derby, are unlikely to be makers' marks. Addresses in Brighton, Birmingham, or Blackpool, for example, obviously relate to the retailer.

The author regrets that he is unable to identify, date, or value articles from correspondence. A knowledgeable specialist has to see and handle the piece and take into account all pointers, not merely the few suggested by the owner.

Index